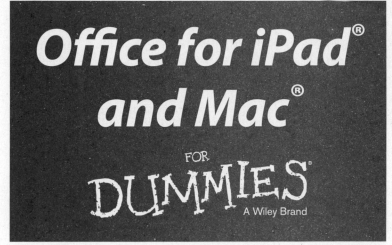

Office for iPad® and Mac® FOR DUMMIES®
A Wiley Brand

by Peter Weverka

FOR DUMMIES®
A Wiley Brand

Office for iPad® and Mac® For Dummies®

Published by: **John Wiley & Sons, Inc.,** 111 River Street, Hoboken, NJ 07030-5774, www.wiley.com

Copyright © 2015 by John Wiley & Sons, Inc., Hoboken, New Jersey

Media and software compilation copyright © 2015 by John Wiley & Sons, Inc. All rights reserved.

Published simultaneously in Canada

No part of this publication may be reproduced, stored in a retrieval system or transmitted in any form or by any means, electronic, mechanical, photocopying, recording, scanning or otherwise, except as permitted under Sections 107 or 108 of the 1976 United States Copyright Act, without the prior written permission of the Publisher. Requests to the Publisher for permission should be addressed to the Permissions Department, John Wiley & Sons, Inc., 111 River Street, Hoboken, NJ 07030, (201) 748-6011, fax (201) 748-6008, or online at http://www.wiley.com/go/permissions.

Trademarks: Wiley, For Dummies, the Dummies Man logo, Dummies.com, Making Everything Easier, and related trade dress are trademarks or registered trademarks of John Wiley & Sons, Inc. and may not be used without written permission. iPad and Mac are registered trademarks of Apple, Inc. All other trademarks are the property of their respective owners. *Office for iPad® and Mac® For Dummies®* is an independent publication and has not been authorized, sponsored, or otherwise approved by Apple, Inc.

For general information on our other products and services, please contact our Customer Care Department within the U.S. at 877-762-2974, outside the U.S. at 317-572-3993, or fax 317-572-4002. For technical support, please visit www.wiley.com/techsupport.

Wiley publishes in a variety of print and electronic formats and by print-on-demand. Some material included with standard print versions of this book may not be included in e-books or in print-on-demand. If this book refers to media such as a CD or DVD that is not included in the version you purchased, you may download this material at http://booksupport.wiley.com. For more information about Wiley products, visit www.wiley.com.

Library of Congress Control Number: 2014955783

ISBN: 978-1-119-01017-3; ISBN 978-1-119-01020-3 (ebk); ISBN ePDF 978-1-119-01018-0 (ebk)

Manufactured in the United States of America

10 9 8 7 6 5 4 3 2 1

Contents at a Glance

Table of Contents

Introduction

*T*his book is your guide to making the most of Office for the iPad and Office 2011 for the Mac. Its 21 chapters are jam-packed with how-to's, advice, shortcuts, and tips. This book is for users of Office for the iPad and Office 2011 for the Macintosh who want to get to the heart of these applications without wasting time. Don't look in this book to find out how the applications work. Look in this book to find out how *you* can get *your* work done better and faster with these applications.

I show you everything you need to make the most of Word, Excel, and PowerPoint for the iPad; and Word 2011, Excel 2011, and PowerPoint 2011 for the Mac. This book also explains the basics of using the iPad. On the way, you have a laugh or two. No matter how much or how little skill you bring to the table, this book will make you a better, more proficient, more confident user of the iPad and Office.

About This Book

Besides the fact that this book is easy to read, it's different from other books about the iPad and Office:

- **Easy-to-find information:** I have taken great pains to make sure that the material in this book is well organized and easy to find. The descriptive headings help you find information quickly. The bulleted and numbered lists make following instructions simpler. The tables make options easier to understand and compare.

- **A task-oriented approach:** Most computer books describe what the software is, but this book explains how to complete tasks with the software. I assume that you came to this book because you want to know how to *do* something — create a table, create a chart, or give a PowerPoint presentation. You came to the right place. This book describes how to get tasks done.

✔ **Meaningful screen shots:** The screen shots in this book show only the part of the screen that illustrates what is being explained in the text. When instructions refer to one part of the screen, only that part of the screen is shown. I took great care to make sure that the screen shots in this book serve to help you understand the Office programs and how they work. Compare this book to the next one on the bookstore shelf. Do you see how clean the screen shots in this book are?

I want you to understand all the instructions in this book, and in that spirit, I've adopted a few conventions.

Where you see boldface letters or numbers in this book, it means to type the letters or numbers. For example, "Enter **25** in the Percentage text box" means to do exactly that: Enter the number 25.

To show you how to step through command sequences, I use the ⇨ symbol. For example, in Word 2011, you can save a file to OneDrive by opening the File menu, choosing Share, and choosing Save to OneDrive on the submenu. Rather than go to all the trouble to describe that, this book tells you to choose File⇨Share⇨Save to OneDrive. The ⇨ symbol is a shorthand method of describing menu choices.

To give most commands, you can press combinations of keys. For example, pressing Command+S saves the file you're working on in the Office 2011 applications. In other words, you can hold down the Command key and press the S key to save a file. Where you see Command+, Control+, Option+, or Shift+ and a key name or key names, press the keys simultaneously.

I use the term *dialog box* to refer to the same element that Mac users may be accustomed to knowing as a *dialog*.

Foolish Assumptions

Please forgive me, but I made one or two foolish assumptions about you, the reader of this book. I assumed that:

✔ You own an iPad.

✔ Either Office for the iPad is installed on your iPad or you want to install it (Chapter 1 explains how to install Office for the iPad).

✔ Office 2011 for the Macintosh is installed on your desktop or laptop computer.

✔ You are kind to foreign tourists and small animals.

Icons Used in This Book

To help you get the most out of this book, I've placed icons here and there. Here's what the icons mean:

Next to the Tip icon, you can find shortcuts and tricks of the trade to make your visit to Officeland more enjoyable.

Where you see the Warning icon, tread softly and carefully. It means that you are about to do something that you may regret later.

When I explain a juicy little fact that bears remembering, I mark it with a Remember icon. When you see this icon, prick up your ears. You will discover something that you need to remember throughout your adventures with Word, Excel, PowerPoint, or the iPad itself.

When I am forced to describe high-tech stuff, a Technical Stuff icon appears in the margin. You don't have to read what's beside the Technical Stuff icons if you don't want to, although these technical descriptions often help you understand how a software feature works.

Beyond the Book

In addition to the information you find in the book, I have included these online bonuses:

✓ **Online articles covering additional topics at**

www.dummies.com/extras/officeipadmac

Here you'll see how to place watermarks in Word documents, how to use the Goal Seek command in Excel for help with financial analyses, how to add a logo or another image to a corner of all your PowerPoint slides, and how to upload and store files on OneDrive. You'll also discover ten ways you benefit by subscribing to Office 365.

✓ **The Cheat Sheet for this book is at**

(www.dummies.com/cheatsheet/officeipadmac)

Here you'll find some handy keyboard shortcuts for Office 2011 for the Mac, tips for adding visual elements to Office 2011 files, and how to customize the Standard toolbar in Office to best suit your needs.

> ✔ **Updates:** Occasionally, we have updates to our technology books. If this book does have technical updates, they will be posted at dummies.com/go/officeipadmac.

Where to Go from Here

You are invited to read this book from start to finish or to go where you need instructions for completing a task. This book's index and table of contents will help you find the information you need.

If you came to this book to become a more capable user of the iPad, look to Chapter 1, which explains iPad basics, and Chapter 2, which tells you how to customize your iPad and make it work your way. If I were you, I would also look into Chapter 21, which explains ten things all iPad users should know.

Four chapters in this book are devoted to people who use Office for the iPad applications. Chapter 3 explains basic tasks such as saving and creating files that are common to all the Office for the iPad applications. Turn to Chapter 4 to explore Word for the iPad, Chapter 9 to investigate Excel for the iPad, or Chapter 13 to master PowerPoint for the iPad.

Do you need to know about Word 2011 for the Mac? Look to Chapters 5 through 8.

Are you having trouble wrestling with the numbers in your Excel 2011 for the Mac worksheet? Fear not. You can turn to Chapters 10 through 12 and Chapter 19 to make Excel do your bidding.

Chapters 14 through 16 and Chapter 20 explain the ins and outs of working with PowerPoint 2011 for the Mac.

If you came to this book to find out how to share files and collaborate with others on OneDrive, you're in luck. This book covers those topics in Chapter 17 and 18.

Part I
Getting Started with Office for iPad and Mac

In this part . . .

✔ Find out what Office for the iPad, Office 2011 for the Mac, and Office 365 are all about, and the basics of using the iPad.

✔ Discover essential iPad tasks: working with apps, making the Home screen work your way, and managing passcodes.

✔ Master tasks that you perform in all Office for the iPad apps — creating and opening files, using the interface, handling text, making lists, and finding and replacing text.

Chapter 1

iPad for Beginners

*I*n this chapter, you waddle to the shore of the pond, put your toes in the water, and contemplate jumping in. Don't worry, I won't push you from behind.

This chapter is for people who are new to the iPad and want to get going quickly. It explains how to install Office software on an iPad and directs you over the three or four hurdles you must overtake to get going. You discover the buttons and doodads on the iPad, find your way around the Home screen, and see how to gesture at your iPad. This chapter takes you through opening and closing apps, using the volume controls, and connecting your iPad to the Internet.

What Is Office for the iPad?

Office for the iPad is an abridged version of three popular Office applications: Word, Excel, and PowerPoint. Respectively, the applications are called Word for the iPad, Excel for the iPad, and PowerPoint for the iPad.

Office for the iPad software is made for the smaller iPad screen. It is "touch friendly" in that it was designed with the understanding that you give commands on an iPad by touching the screen, not by clicking a mouse.

Figure 1-1 shows Word for the iPad in action. Like its sister applications Excel for the iPad and PowerPoint for the iPad, it doesn't offer as many commands and features as the version that is installed on laptop and desktop computers. Still, it's mighty convenient. For touching up, reviewing, and co-editing files with others, Office for the iPad software is very nice indeed.

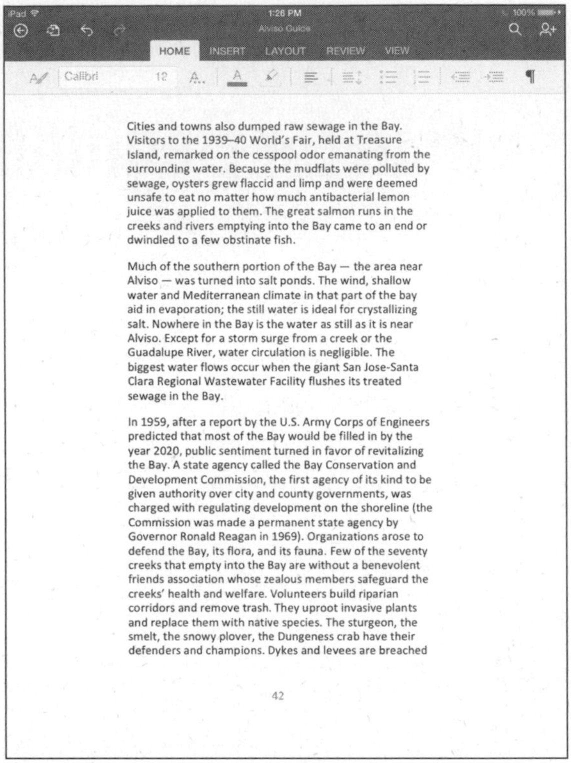

iPad 1:28 PM 100%
Alviso Guide
HOME INSERT LAYOUT REVIEW VIEW
Calibri 12

Cities and towns also dumped raw sewage in the Bay. Visitors to the 1939–40 World's Fair, held at Treasure Island, remarked on the cesspool odor emanating from the surrounding water. Because the mudflats were polluted by sewage, oysters grew flaccid and limp and were deemed unsafe to eat no matter how much antibacterial lemon juice was applied to them. The great salmon runs in the creeks and rivers emptying into the Bay came to an end or dwindled to a few obstinate fish.

Much of the southern portion of the Bay — the area near Alviso — was turned into salt ponds. The wind, shallow water and Mediterranean climate in that part of the bay aid in evaporation; the still water is ideal for crystallizing salt. Nowhere in the Bay is the water as still as it is near Alviso. Except for a storm surge from a creek or the Guadalupe River, water circulation is negligible. The biggest water flows occur when the giant San Jose-Santa Clara Regional Wastewater Facility flushes its treated sewage in the Bay.

In 1959, after a report by the U.S. Army Corps of Engineers predicted that most of the Bay would be filled in by the year 2020, public sentiment turned in favor of revitalizing the Bay. A state agency called the Bay Conservation and Development Commission, the first agency of its kind to be given authority over city and county governments, was charged with regulating development on the shoreline (the Commission was made a permanent state agency by Governor Ronald Reagan in 1969). Organizations arose to defend the Bay, its flora, and its fauna. Few of the seventy creeks that empty into the Bay are without a benevolent friends association whose zealous members safeguard the creeks' health and welfare. Volunteers build riparian corridors and remove trash. They uproot invasive plants and replace them with native species. The sturgeon, the smelt, the snowy plover, the Dungeness crab have their defenders and champions. Dykes and levees are breached

42

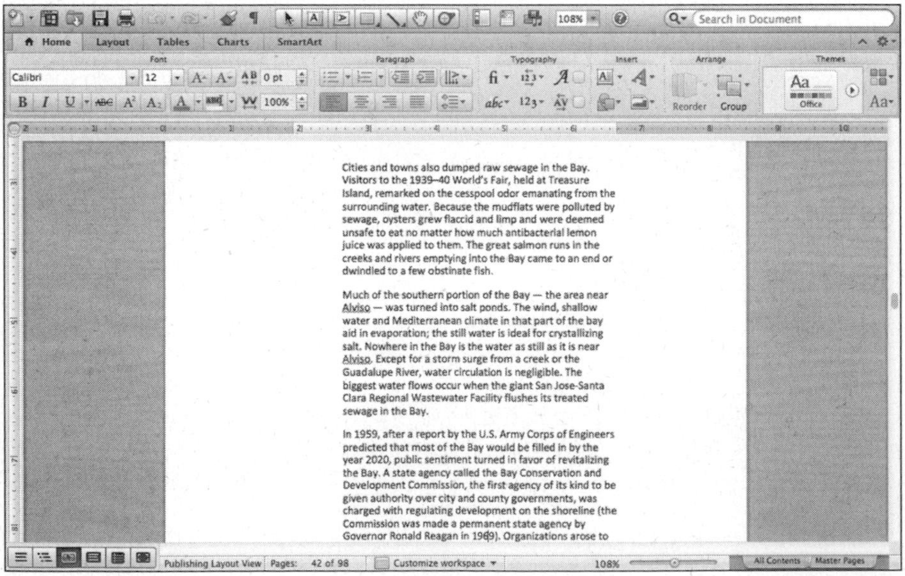

Home Layout Tables Charts SmartArt
Font Paragraph Typography Insert Arrange Themes
Calibri 12 0 pt
B I U 100% Reorder Group Office

Cities and towns also dumped raw sewage in the Bay. Visitors to the 1939–40 World's Fair, held at Treasure Island, remarked on the cesspool odor emanating from the surrounding water. Because the mudflats were polluted by sewage, oysters grew flaccid and limp and were deemed unsafe to eat no matter how much antibacterial lemon juice was applied to them. The great salmon runs in the creeks and rivers emptying into the Bay came to an end or dwindled to a few obstinate fish.

Much of the southern portion of the Bay — the area near Alviso — was turned into salt ponds. The wind, shallow water and Mediterranean climate in that part of the bay aid in evaporation; the still water is ideal for crystallizing salt. Nowhere in the Bay is the water as still as it is near Alviso. Except for a storm surge from a creek or the Guadalupe River, water circulation is negligible. The biggest water flows occur when the giant San Jose-Santa Clara Regional Wastewater Facility flushes its treated sewage in the Bay.

In 1959, after a report by the U.S. Army Corps of Engineers predicted that most of the Bay would be filled in by the year 2020, public sentiment turned in favor of revitalizing the Bay. A state agency called the Bay Conservation and Development Commission, the first agency of its kind to be given authority over city and county governments, was charged with regulating development on the shoreline (the Commission was made a permanent state agency by Governor Ronald Reagan in 1969). Organizations arose to

Publishing Layout View Pages: 42 of 98 Customize workspace 108% All Contents Master Pages

Figure 1-1:
Word for the iPad (top) and Word 2011 for Mac (bottom).

Anyone with an iPad can download and install Office for the iPad software from the App Store for free. To edit files, however, you must be a paid Office 365 subscriber. People who install the software but don't pay to subscribe to Office 365 can view files on their iPads but not edit them. (Later in this chapter, "What Is Office 365?" looks at this topic in more detail.)

What Is Office 2011 for Mac?

Office 2011 for Mac is the latest version of Office software for Macintosh computers. It includes these applications: Word, Excel, PowerPoint, and, in some versions of the software, Outlook and OneNote. Figure 1-1 shows what Word 2011 for Mac looks like.

You can purchase Office 2011 for Mac at the Office 365 website or the online Apple Store (`store.apple.com`). This website explains all a body needs to know about Office 2011 for Mac:

```
www.microsoft.com/mac
```

What Is Office 365?

Office 365 is the name of Microsoft's online services division. Anyone with an iPad can install Office for the iPad, but to edit Office files, you must be a paid subscriber to Office 365. Nonsubscribers can view the files but not edit them.

As of this writing, a subscription to the Home edition of Office 365 costs $99.99 per year or $9.99 per month (Microsoft also offers a Business edition and University edition). An Office 365 subscription entitles you to these goodies:

- The opportunity to install Word, Excel, and PowerPoint on five iPads and/or Windows tablets.
- The opportunity to install Office desktop software on five Windows computers and/or Macintosh computers.
- Automatic updates to the Office software on your iPad, tablet, Mac, or Windows computer. As long as your subscription is paid up, Microsoft updates the Office software automatically.
- The opportunity to store files on OneDrive, Microsoft's cloud service. In computer jargon, *the cloud* is the name for servers on the Internet where individuals can store files. Rather than keep files on your iPad or desktop computer, you can keep them on the Internet so that you can

open them wherever your travels take you. Subscribers to Office 365 get an unlimited amount of storage space on OneDrive. (Part V of this book explains how to store and share files with OneDrive.)

✔ Free use of Skype, the video-chatting software, for 60 minutes each month.

✔ The opportunity to use *Office Online,* the online versions of Word, Excel, PowerPoint, OneNote, and Outlook. To use an Office Online program, you open it in a browser and give commands through the browser window. Office Online software is useful for co-editing and sharing files.

To find out all there is to know about Office 365, visit this website:

```
http://office.microsoft.com/en-us/office365home
```

Subscribing to Office 365

To subscribe to Office 365, you need a credit card and a Microsoft account. If you don't already have a Microsoft account, don't fret. You can create an account when you subscribe to Office 365.

Get out your credit card and follow these basic steps to subscribe to Office 365:

1. **Open a browser in the iPad or your desktop computer.**

2. **Go to this web address:**

```
http://office.microsoft.com/en-us/office365home
```

3. **Tap or click a Buy Now button (the $9.99 per month or $99.99 per year button).**

4. **Tap or click the Checkout button.**

   You come to the Checkout page.

5. **Enter your user name and password, or if you don't yet have a Microsoft account, click the Sign Up Now link.**

   Follow the onscreen instructions. When the ordeal is finished, Microsoft sends you an email confirming that you subscribed to Office 365.

Installing Office for iPad

After you subscribe to Office 365 and log in to your Office 365 account, follow these steps to download and install the Office for iPad applications — Word for iPad, Excel for iPad, and PowerPoint for iPad — on your iPad device:

1. **On the Home screen of your iPad, tap the App Store icon.**

   The App Store opens.

2. **Tap the Search box (located in the upper-right corner of the screen), type office for ipad on the keyboard, and tap Search.**

   You see the Office for iPad applications, as shown in Figure 1-2. If you haven't yet downloaded these applications, the Get button appears beside their names (the Open button or Update button appears if you've downloaded the applications). Why does the Get button appear? Because, as I mentioned earlier, you can get Office for iPad applications without subscribing to Office 365, but unless you subscribe, you can't edit files; you can only view files.

Figure 1-2: Office for iPad applications at the App Store.

3. **Tap the Get button next to the application you want to install.**

   That's all there is to it. When the application is finished installing, the Open button appears where the Free button used to be.

4. **Repeat steps 1 through 3 to download the other Office for iPad applications.**

You can open an application by tapping its Open button in the App Store or by tapping its icon on the Home screen.

iPad — the Basics

The following pages are dedicated to people who have never used an iPad before. These pages explain how to turn the thing on and off, what the controls on the device do, how to handle the Home screen, and what changing the screen orientation is all about.

Turning your iPad on and off

Feel along the top of the iPad and you will find, on the right side, a button called *Sleep/Wake*, as shown in Figure 1-3. This button is for turning the device on and off and for making the iPad hibernate. Press and hold the Sleep/Wake button to do these tasks:

- **Turn the iPad on:** Press and hold down the button. The Apple logo appears and, a moment later, you see the Lock screen. Use your finger to slide the Slide to Unlock notice to the right side of the Lock screen. You see the keypad. Enter your passcode and tap Done. (Chapter 2 explains passcodes and how to change them.)

- **Turn the iPad off:** Press and hold down the button until you see Slide to Power Off on the screen. Then slide these words to the right side of the screen with your finger.

- **Put the iPad to sleep (to save power):** Quickly press the button.

- **Awaken the iPad from Sleep mode:** Quickly press the button. You see the Lock screen. Slide the Slide to Unlock notice to the right side of the Lock screen, enter your passcode on the keypad, and tap Done.

To save power, the iPad goes into Sleep mode after a certain amount of time has elapsed. To tell the iPad when to go into Sleep mode, tap Settings on the Home screen to open the Settings window. Then choose General ⇨ Auto-Lock and choose an Auto-Lock option.

Figure 1-3:
The front
(left) and
back (right)
of the iPad.

Front camera

Sleep/Wake

Back camera

Home button

Side switch

Volume control

Getting the lay of the land

All around the iPad are doodads that you need to know about. Glance at Figure 1-3 to see precisely where these doodads are:

- **Front camera:** For taking self-portraits and chatting by video.

- **Home button:** For returning to the *Home screen,* the screen with icons showing the applications you installed. See "Getting to know the Home screen," later in this chapter, for details.

- **Sleep/Wake button:** For turning the iPad on and off. See "Turning your iPad on and off," the previous topic in this chapter, for details.

- **Side switch:** For locking the screen rotation or muting sound. How you want to use the Side switch is up to you. See the sidebar "Deciding what to do with the Side switch."

- **Volume control:** For turning the volume up or down. Press the top of the control to turn the volume up; press the bottom to turn the volume down.

- **Back camera:** For taking photos and videos with the Camera app.

Deciding what to do with the Side switch

The Side switch is located on the right side of the iPad, above the Volume control (see Figure 1-3). The makers of the iPad give you the choice of how to use this switch. You can use it to lock the screen rotation or mute the sound.

✔ **Lock rotation**: The iPad is made so that when you turn it in your hands, the screen rotates along with the device. You can view a wide screen or a narrow screen, whatever is best for the task at hand. But if for some reason you want to keep the screen from rotating, you can do it.

✔ **Mute sound**: You can mute sound effects, alerts, notifications, and audio from games but not sounds played by multimedia apps (videos, TV, podcasts, and the like). Being able to mute the sound with the Side switch is convenient. All you have to do is flick the Side switch.

Follow these steps to tell the iPad how you want the Side switch to operate:

1. **On the Home screen, tap Settings.**

2. **On the Settings screen, tap General.**

3. **Under Use Side Switch To, select Lock Rotation or Mute.**

USE SIDE SWITCH TO:

Lock Rotation

Mute   ✓

Rotation Lock is available in Control Center.

Whatever choice you made for the Side switch, you can still lock the screen rotation or mute the sound by going to the Control Center. To make the Control Center appear, swipe from the bottom of the Home screen. In the Control Center, tap the Orientation Lock or Mute icon. Which icon appears in the Control Center depends on which Side switch setting you chose.

Getting to know the Home screen

The Home screen is Grand Central Station as far as the iPad is concerned. The iPad puts an icon on the Home screen for every app you install. Figure 1-4 shows the Home screen. Here is a summary list of things you can do in regard to the Home screen:

- ✔ *Open an app.* Tap an icon on the Home screen to open an app. Notice the Dock at the bottom of the Home screen (see Figure 1-4). You can put icons representing your favorite apps on the Dock and be able to open your favorite apps more easily (see Chapter 2).

- ✔ *Return to the Home screen.* Press the Home button *once* to return to the Home screen. Return to the Home screen, for example, when you're working with one app and you want to open another.

Swipe to see other Home screens

Figure 1-4:
The Home
screen.

Dock

✔ *Switch between open apps.* Press the Home button *twice* to see which apps are open. Each open app appears in a small window. Swipe to and tap an app window to switch to another app. Later in this chapter, "Switching between apps" explains this in detail.

✔ *Scroll the Home screens.* Because all icons can't fit on one Home screen, the Home screen comprises more than one screen. Swipe the right or left side of the Home screen to go from screen to screen.

✔ *Tell the time.* The top of the Home screen tells you the time.

✔ *Tell how charged the battery is.* A percentage figure in the upper-right corner of the Home screen tells you how charged the battery is and whether the battery needs recharging.

Chapter 2 explains how to customize the Home screen and put app icons on the Dock.

Changing the screen orientation

You must have noticed by now that the iPad screen is capable of reorienting itself. When you turn the iPad on its ear, the screen changes orientation. You can rotate the iPad from portrait view to landscape view and back again to get a better look at what's onscreen.

How does the screen know when to reorient itself? The iPad has a built-in gyroscope and accelerometer that tell it when the screen needs reorienting. I just tried looking at my iPad while standing on my head. Darned if my iPad's gyroscope didn't flip the screen the wrong direction for someone standing on his feet. Don't try this experiment at home.

Earlier in this chapter, the "Deciding what to do with the Side switch" side-bar explains how you can use the Side switch and Orientation Lock icon in the Control Center to prevent the screen from reorienting. Visit that sidebar if your screen isn't reorienting correctly. It'll show you what's wrong.

Understanding the Screen Gestures

Screen gestures take some getting used to if you're new to the iPad. Actions that are accomplished with the mouse on a desktop computer or laptop require fingers and thumbs on the iPad. The iPad, you could say, is all fingers and thumbs. Table 1-1 explains screen gestures.

Table 1-1	Screen Gestures	
Gesture	*Description*	*Mouse Equivalent*
Tap	Lightly tap the screen with your fingertip. Example: Tap an icon to open an app.	Clicking
Drag	Hold your fingertip to the glass and slide it to a different place onscreen. Example: In PowerPoint, move a shape to a different location.	Dragging
Slide/Swipe	Brush your fingertip horizontally or vertically across the screen. Example: Slide the Slide to Unlock notice when you start the iPad.	Scrolling
Pinch/Spread to zoom	With your thumb and index finger touching the screen, move your thumb and finger closer together (pinch); move them farther apart (spread). Example: Pinch to zoom in on a photo; spread to zoom out.	Clicking Zoom In/Out
Four-finger side swipe*	Place four fingers on the screen and swipe to the left or right to go to open apps. Example: Go from the Word app to the Excel app.	
Four-finger pinch*	Place four fingers on the screen, the fingertips spread apart, and pinch to go to the Home screen (equivalent to pressing the Home button once).	
Four-finger upward swipe*	Place four fingers on the screen and swipe upward to see the multitasking bar (equivalent to pressing the Home button twice).	

*To use this gesture, Multitasking Gestures must be turned on in the Settings app.

To use gestures marked with an asterisk (*) in Table 1-1, you must turn on the Multitasking Gestures feature. Follow these steps:

1. **On the Home screen, tap Settings.**

2. **On the Settings screen, tap General.**

3. **Turn on Multitasking Gestures.**

   In the Settings app, use the sliders to turn features on or off.

An iPad screen can get awfully dirty. To clean it, use a soft, lint-free cloth, the same cloth you use to clean your glasses or TV screen. *Do not* use ammonias or cleansers of any kind to wipe down the screen. Using cleansers damages the screen's protective coating.

Running Apps on the iPad

The iPad would be nothing more than an expensive paperweight were it not for the many apps you can run on it. These pages explain how to open apps, close apps, and switch between apps on the iPad.

The iPad can't run more than one app at the same time. Unlike a laptop or desktop computer, you can't listen to music with one program, for example, while you write a letter with another. What's more, you can't run one app on the left side of the screen and another app on the right. You can open many apps but run only one.

Opening an app

The Home screen is the place to go open an app. You will find one icon on the Home screen for each app that is installed on your iPad. Follow these steps to open an app:

1. **Go to the Home screen.**

   To get there, either press the Home button or use the four-finger pinch technique (refer to Table 1-1, earlier in this chapter).

2. **Tap the icon that represents the app you want to open.**

   If you can't find the icon, swipe from the right side of the Home screen to get to the next set of icons. If more than twenty apps are installed on your iPad, the device creates more Home screens for them.

Closing an app

Follow these steps to close an app:

1. **Press the Home button twice (or place four fingers on the screen and swipe upward).**

   As shown in Figure 1-5, you see thumbnail images of open apps. Below each image is an icon that tells you the name of the app that is open.

Swipe upward to close an app

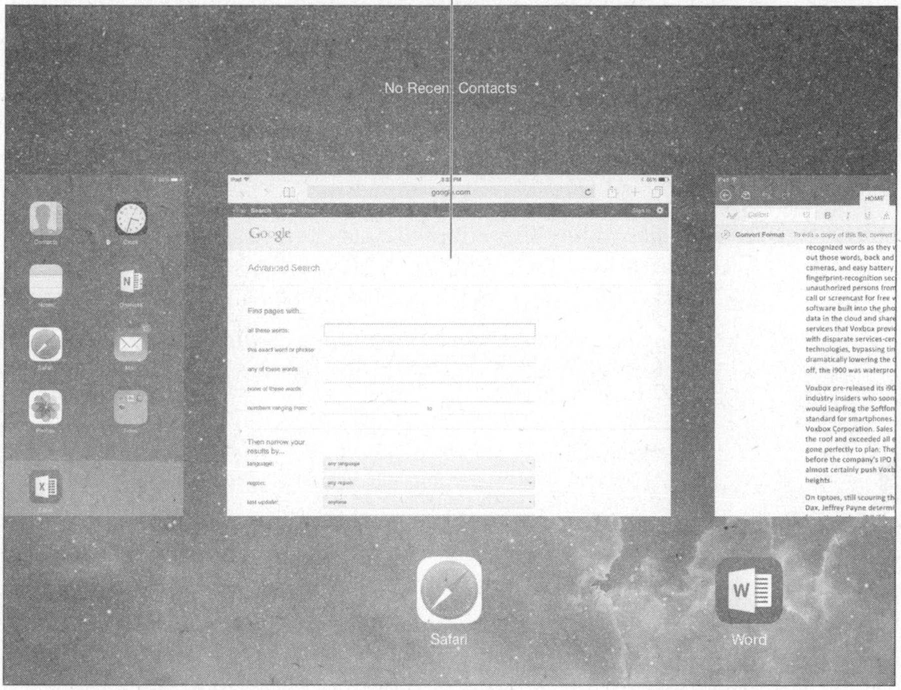

Figure 1-5:
Press the
Home but-
ton twice to
see which
apps are
running.

2. **If necessary, swipe left or right to find the app you want to close.**

3. **Swipe the app to the top of the screen.**

   After you close the app, you can tap the Home screen image to go to the
   Home screen.

Switching between apps

Follow these steps to go from one app to another:

1. **Press the Home button twice.**

   Thumbnail images of open apps appear (refer to Figure 1-5).

2. **If necessary, swipe left or right to find the app you're looking for.**

3. **Tap the app or its icon.**

Controlling the Volume

How do you control the volume on an iPad? Let me count the ways:

✔ *Press the Volume control buttons (located on the right side of the iPad).* Press the top of the control to turn the volume up; press the bottom to turn the volume down.

✔ *Press the Side switch down to mute sound effects, alerts, and notification sounds.* When the Side switch is down, an orange dot appears above the Side switch. (See "Getting the lay of the land," earlier in this chapter, to find out more about the Side switch and Volume control buttons.)

✔ *Drag the volume slider in the Control Center.* Figure 1-6 shows the Control Center. To make it appear, swipe from the bottom of the screen.

Volume slider

Airplane Mode

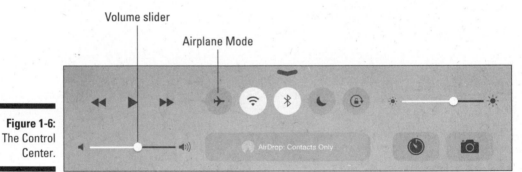

Figure 1-6:
The Control
Center.

AirDrop: Contacts Only

Handling Internet Wi-Fi Connections

The iPad is to the Internet what a tadpole is to muddy water. The iPad wants to be connected to the Internet at all times. Most apps require an Internet connection to do their stuff.

When you start your iPad for the first time, you provide the name of the Wi-Fi network that serves your home or place of work and the network's password. The iPad keeps this information on hand and uses it to connect automatically to the Internet whenever you start your device.

Suppose you take your iPad to a business conference or other place it hasn't gone before. The iPad can't connect automatically to the Internet. It doesn't know which Wi-Fi network to connect to. When you open an app like the Safari browser or the App Store that needs an Internet connection, you get a "cannot connect" message.

To handle all things that have to do with Internet connections, follow these steps to go to the Wi-Fi screen in the Settings app:

1. **On the Home screen, tap Settings.**

2. **In the Settings app, tap Wi-Fi.**

   You see a Wi-Fi screen similar to the one in Figure 1-7.

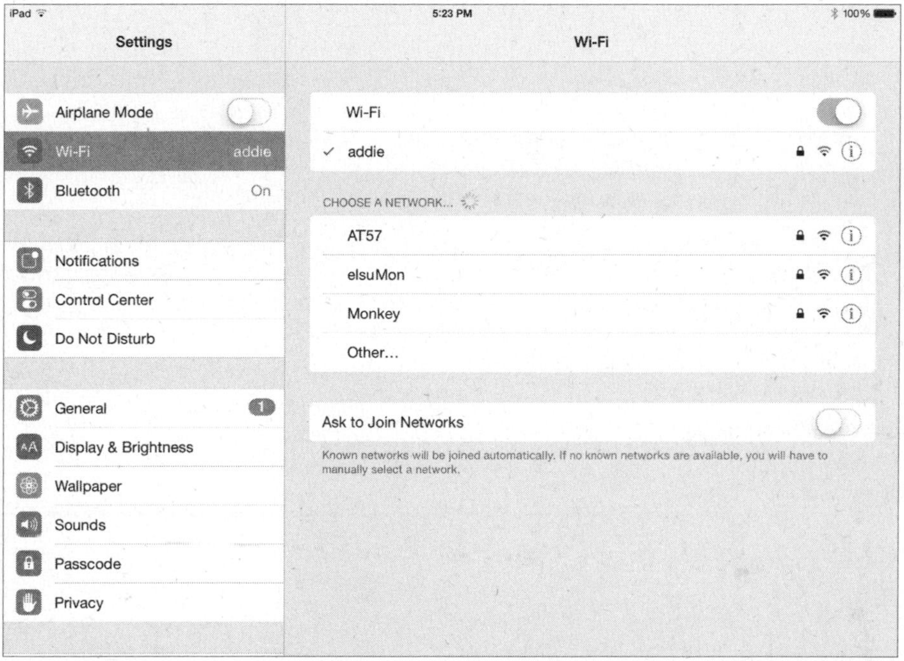

Figure 1-7: The Wi-Fi screen in the Settings app.

If your iPad is connected to a network, the network's name (with a check mark) appears in the Wi-Fi list.

The Choose a Network list shows nearby Wi-Fi networks whose presence your iPad has detected. You can connect to the Internet with one of these networks if you know its password. Get the password from the hotel clerk or business conference greeter or whoever happens to have it.

3. **Tap a network's name on the Wi-Fi screen to connect to a network.**

   If your iPad is already connected to the Internet but you want to connect using a different Wi-Fi network, tap its name in the Choose a Network list.

   The Enter Password screen appears.

4. Enter the password on the keypad and tap the Join key.

The iPad remembers network names and network passwords. Next time you want to connect using the Wi-Fi network you chose in Step 3, the iPad connects you automatically.

Flying in Airplane Mode

For safety's sake, the airlines don't want passengers to send or receive wireless data signals while the airplane is in flight. These signals can interfere with an airplane's communications systems. An iPad, however, sends wireless data signals when it's connected to the Internet.

So that you can use your iPad on airplanes, the iPad offers something called Airplane Mode. When the iPad is in Airplane Mode, it isn't connected to the Internet. You can use an iPad safely on an airplane when your iPad is in Airplane Mode.

Use either of these techniques to turn Airplane Mode on or off:

✔ Open the Control Center and tap the Airplane Mode icon. To open the Control Center, swipe from the bottom of the screen. Earlier in this chapter, Figure 1-6 shows the Airplane Mode icon in the Control Center.

✔ Tap Settings on the Home screen to open the Settings app. Then turn on Airplane Mode (the first setting on the Settings screen).

When the iPad is in Airplane Mode, a tiny airplane icon appears in the upper-left corner of the screen.

Chapter 2

Making the iPad Work Your Way

*T*his chapter explains how to make the iPad do your bidding. The little device is meant to serve you, not the other way around.

In this chapter, you discover tips and techniques for making your time with the iPad more productive and entertaining. You find out how to install and delete apps, customize the Home screen, and place icons on the Dock. You also see how to change the wallpaper design on the face of the Home screen and handle passcodes.

Downloading and Installing Apps

The App Store offers, at last count, 1.2 million applications that you can download and install on your iPad. These apps range from games to instant messengers to weather alerts. Some are free and some are not. Some are useful and some are downright silly.

Read on to discover how to visit the App Store, search for apps, and download and install apps on your iPad. (For information about downloading and installing Office apps, go to Chapter 1.)

Visiting the App Store

Follow these steps to pay a visit to the App Store:

1. **On the Home screen, tap the App Store icon.**

2. **If necessary, enter your Apple ID and password.**

   The Apple Store asks for your ID and password if you aren't already signed in. You see a screen similar to the one in Figure 2-1.

Searching for apps at the store

How do you find the app you want in a store that offers more than a million different apps? You use the tools at the top and bottom of the screen, that's how:

- ✔ *Browse for an app.* In the upper-left corner of the screen, tap Categories. A drop-down menu appears so that you can choose a browsing category. Scroll through the apps in the category to find one you like.

- ✔ *Search for an app.* Enter an app name in the Search box and tap Search on the keyboard. Go this route if you know the name of the app you want to install.

- ✔ *Browse in popular apps.* At the bottom of the screen, tap Featured, Top Charts, or Explore to examine popular applications. The Explore option is kind of interesting. It lists apps that are popular with people who live in your town or city, or if you're in transit, people in the area. (To use the Near Me option, the Settings ⇨ Privacy ⇨ Location Services option must be turned on.)

Tap Purchased on the App Store screen to see a list of apps you installed on your iPad. You can tap an Open button on the list to open an application you installed.

Installing an app

To investigate an app, tap its Details and Reviews buttons to discover more about it, as shown in Figure 2-2. To install an app, tap its price tag or tap Get to download it. After the app is installed, you can click the Open button to open it.

Browse for apps

Search for apps

Figure 2-1:
Paying a
visit to the
Apple Store.

See apps you installed

Find out more about it

Install the app

Close window

Figure 2-2:
Want to
install this
app?

 If the App Store doesn't recognize your credit card, go to Settings to set things right. Tap Settings on the Home screen, choose iTunes & App Store, tap your Apple ID, and tap View Apple ID. You come to the Account Settings screen, where you can reenter or revise your credit card information.

Tidying the Home Screen

The iPad places an icon on the Home screen for every app you install. After installing a number of apps, your Home screen (your Home screens, I should say) can get crowded. Finding an icon can be a chore. You want to open an app but you can't locate its icon. You hang your head in despair.

The iPad offers a few ways to make finding icons (and opening apps) easier. When your Home screen gets too crowded with icons, consider these techniques to prevent clutter on the Home screen:

✔ Arrange icons on the Home screen so that you can find them easily (see "Arranging icons on the Home screen").

✔ Put icons representing your favorite apps on the Dock, as shown in Figure 2-3. The *Dock* is located at the bottom of the Home screen. In Figure 2-3, Office for the iPad icons have been placed on the Dock. All I have to do to open Word, PowerPoint, or Excel is tap its icon on the Dock. (See "Putting an icon on the Dock," later in this chapter.)

✔ Put icons into folders. Then, to open an app, all you have to do is locate the folder where its icon is kept, open the folder, and tap the icon. Figure 2-3 shows what folders on the Home screen and Dock look like. (See "Creating folders for the Home screen.")

✔ Delete apps you no longer need. After you delete an app, its icon no longer appears on the Home screen. (See "Deleting an App," later in this chapter.)

The Home screen can comprise many different screens if you install a number of apps. To see how many Home screens you have, note how many dots appear above the Dock. You have one dot for every Home screen on your iPad. The dot that is illuminated indicates which Home screen you're currently viewing.

Arranging icons on the Home screen

Arrange icons on the Home screen so that you can find them in a hurry. For example, put the icons you click most often on the top row of the first Home screen so that you can find them quickly. As for the icons that don't matter as much to you, move them to a second or third Home screen.

Follow these steps to arrange icons on the Home screen:

1. **Place your finger on any icon on the Home screen and leave it there until the icons on the screen start to wiggle.**

   Odd, isn't it, to see icons wiggle like that? But this wiggling business is just the iPad's way of saying you can move icons on the Home screen.

While the icons are wiggling, you can swipe to go to a different Home screen.

2. Drag an icon to a different location on the Home screen.

As you drag, icons are rearranged on the screen. Go ahead, drag as many icons as you want until your Home screen looks just-so.

To move an icon to a different Home screen, carefully drag the icon to the left or right edge of the window. If you do this correctly, the previous or next Home screen appears and your icon lands in the previous or next screen. Drag your icon where you want it to be on the previous or next Home screen.

3. Press the Home button once.

Your icons stop wiggling.

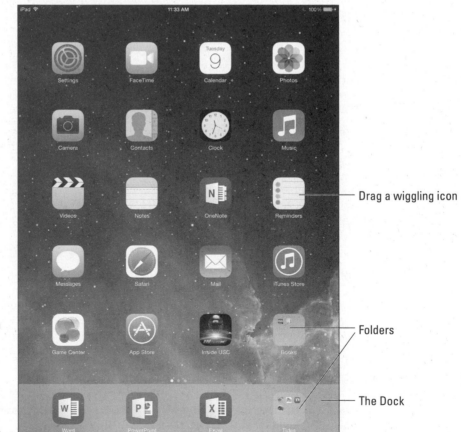

Figure 2-3: Arrange icons on the Home screen to your liking.

Want to create another Home screen? Make like you're arranging icons on the Home screen, and while the icons are wiggling, go to your last Home screen and drag an icon from this screen to the right as though you were moving it to another screen. The iPad will create another Home screen for you so that you can move your icon there.

Putting an icon on the Dock

The Dock is located at the bottom of the Home screen (refer to Figure 2-3). You can place up to six icons (or icons and folders) on the Dock. No matter which Home screen you're viewing, the Dock is always there so that you can tap an icon without having to scroll to it. Put the icons you tap most often on the Dock.

Follow these steps to put an icon (or folder) on the Dock:

1. **Place your finger on any icon on the Home screen and leave it there until the icons start wiggling.**

2. **Drag an icon (or folder) onto the Dock.**

   As long as the icons continue to wiggle, you can drag as many as six icons onto the Dock. Swipe to go to a different Home screen if you need to move an icon on another screen onto the Dock.

3. **Press the Home button once.**

   To move an icon off the Dock, set the icons to wiggling. While they wiggle, drag the icon from the Dock to the Home screen.

Creating folders for the Home screen

Especially if your Home screen is very crowded, folders are a neat way to organize icons on the Home screen. Put apps that are similar to one another in the same folder. Then, to open an app, open its folder and click its icon.

Creating a folder

Follow these steps to create a folder for storing icons on the Home screen:

1. **Place your finger on any icon on the Home screen and leave it there.**

   The icons start wiggling.

2. **Drag the icon you want to place in a folder over another icon you want to place in a folder.**

   As shown in Figure 2-4, the iPad creates a new folder for the two icons. What's more, the iPad gives the folder a name.

3. Tap the folder name to activate the keyboard.

4. Enter a descriptive name for your folder and tap the Done button.

5. Touch your screen, but not anywhere on the folder.

The folder shrinks to the size of an icon and you return to the Home screen. Do you recognize the tiny icons within your folder? They tell you which icons are stored there.

6. Press the Home button once.

Pressing the Home button makes the icons stop wiggling.

Figure 2-4: Creating and naming a folder for the Home screen.

Preventing automatic downloads

The iPad can download apps and music to every device that is logged into the same Apple account. To see how this works, suppose you have an iPod and an iPad. When you download music and apps to the one, you also download music and apps to the other. And if you are in a family whose members share the same Apple account, every time one family member downloads music and apps to his or her device, all other devices on the account also get the apps and the music.

If your iPad is being deluged by music files and apps, and mysterious icons keep appearing on your Home screen, the culprit is probably automatic downloading.

To choose whether to download music and apps automatically, follow these steps:

1. **On the Home screen, tap Settings.**

2. **On the left side of the Settings screen, scroll to and tap iTunes & App Store.**

3. **Under Automatic Downloads, choose whether to download music and apps automatically to your Apple devices.**

AUTOMATIC DOWNLOADS

Music

Apps

Updates

Automatically download new purchases (including free) made on other devices.

Caring for and feeding Home screen folders

To manage folders on the Home screen, start by placing your finger on an icon so that the icons wiggle. Then follow these instructions:

✔ **Moving a folder:** Drag the folder to a different location (see "Arranging icons on the Home screen," earlier in this chapter, for details.) You can move a folder to the Dock (see "Putting an icon on the Dock," earlier in this chapter).

✔ **Renaming a folder:** Open the folder and tap its name. Then enter a new name on the keyboard, click the Done button, and tap onscreen outside the folder.

✔ **Removing an icon from a folder:** Open the folder and then drag the icon outside the folder.

✔ **Adding an icon to a folder**: Drag the icon over the folder.

✔ **Deleting a folder:** Drag to remove all icons from the folder. The iPad deletes the folder when the last icon is removed.

Of course, be sure to press the Home button once after you finish manipulating folders. You need those icons to stop wiggling.

Deleting an App

Don't let apps you no longer need clutter the Home screen. By all means, delete them. Deleting an app is simply a matter of deleting its icon on the Home screen. The iPad won't let you, however, delete apps that came with the machine; only apps you installed yourself can be deleted.

Follow these steps to delete an app:

1. **Locate the icon (and app) you want to delete on the Home screen.**

2. **Place your finger on the icon and leave it there.**

   Icons on the Home screen start to wiggle. Notice that some icons have an *X* (a delete mechanism) on them, as shown in Figure 2-5. You can delete these icons.

3. **Tap the *X* in the upper-left corner of the icon you want to delete.**

   A confirmation screen appears.

4. **Select Delete on the confirmation screen.**

5. **Press the Home button once to make the icons stop wiggling.**

Figure 2-5:
Tap the *X*
to delete an
icon.

Hanging Some Wallpaper

In iPad terminology, *wallpaper* is the design or image that appears in the background of the Home screen. Real wallpaper is something else. Wallpaper is decorative paper that is hung and pasted to the interior walls of a house. I knew someone who used to say, to tell me how busy he was, "I'm busier than a one-armed paper hanger in a windstorm."

You're invited to trade the wallpaper on your Home screen for something more to your liking. You can use a design from Apple or a photo of your own as the wallpaper background, as shown in Figure 2-6. To use a photo, make sure that it's stored in the Photos app.

Follow these steps to change the wallpaper:

1. **Tap Settings on the Home screen.**

   The Settings screen opens.

2. **Choose Wallpaper.**

3. **Tap Choose a New Wallpaper.**

   The Choose screen appears.

4. **Choose a wallpaper design or photo.**

   You have come to a fork in the road:

   - *Choose a wallpaper design from Apple.* Under Apple Wallpaper, select a wallpaper design (Dynamic or Stills) to go to a screen with designs. Then select a design.

   - *Choose a photo.* Select Camera Roll or My Photo Stream. Then, on the next screen, select a photo.

5. **Choose Set Home Screen.**

   Be sure to visit the Home screen and see whether you like the design or photo you chose.

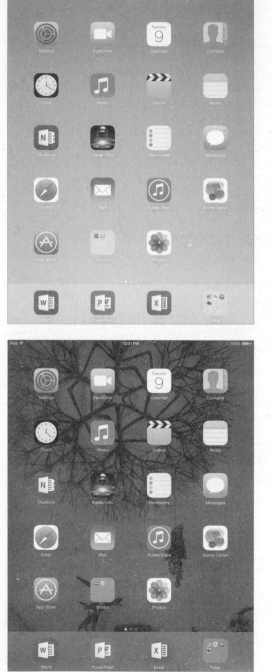

Figure 2-6:
A wallpaper design from Apple (top) and customized wallpaper (bottom).

Handling Passcodes

Be sure to protect your iPad with a passcode. A *passcode* is the four-digit code that must be entered before the iPad can run. By protecting your iPad with a passcode, you make it difficult for others to start your iPad without your permission.

You can change the passcode at any time as well as decide how long your iPad may remain idle before it shuts down (and you have to enter the passcode to resume using it). Follow these steps to handle passcodes:

1. **On the Home screen, tap Settings.**

   The Settings screen opens.

2. **Choose Passcode.**

   A screen appears so that you can enter your passcode. The iPad needs a correct passcode before it can change passcode settings.

3. **Enter your passcode on the keypad and tap Done (or tap the Return key).**

   The Passcode Lock screen opens, as shown in Figure 2-7.

4. **Choose options on the Passcode Lock screen.**

   The options are these:

   - **Turn Passcode Off:** Allows anyone to start your iPad without entering a passcode. This option is not recommended because it makes the data on your iPad vulnerable to theft and abuse.

   - **Change Passcode:** Opens a screen so that you can change your passcode.

   - **Require Passcode:** Opens a screen so that you can choose when you must enter your passcode after your iPad is awakened from Sleep mode. This setting is designed to prevent others from starting your iPad if you leave it unattended. Choose Immediately (the default) to require others to enter the passcode right away when the device is awakened.

   - **Simple Passcode:** Opens a screen so that you can use an advanced password with four numerals rather than a password with four digits.

   - **Allow Access When Locked:** Allows you or anyone else to view today's calendar events (Today) and reminders and notifications (Notifications view) without entering a passcode first.

   - **Erase Data:** Prevents others from cracking your passcode with software designed to repeatedly enter different passcodes. After the tenth attempt at entering a passcode fails, your personal information on the iPad is deleted on the idea that someone is trying to break into your iPad.

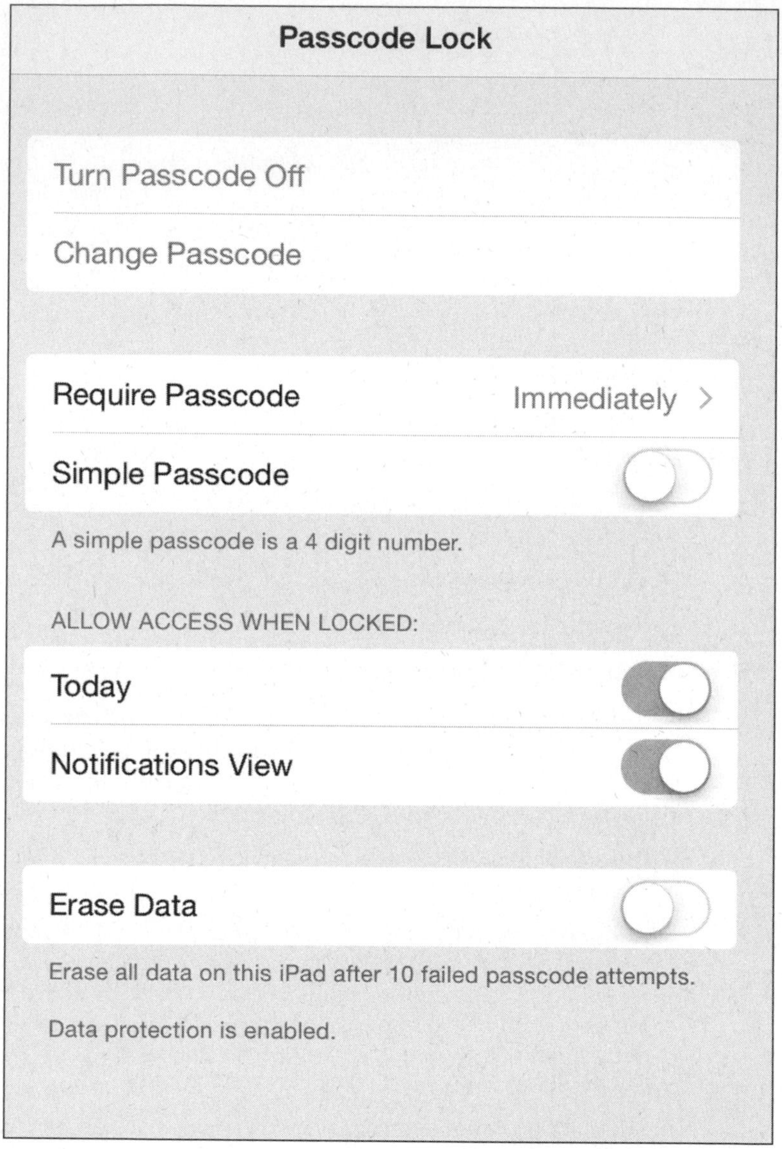

Passcode Lock

Turn Passcode Off

Change Passcode

Require Passcode   Immediately   >

Simple Passcode

A simple passcode is a 4 digit number.

ALLOW ACCESS WHEN LOCKED:

Today

Notifications View

Erase Data

Erase all data on this iPad after 10 failed passcode attempts.

Data protection is enabled.

Figure 2-7:
The
Passcode
Lock
screen.

To tell the iPad how long you want it to be idle before slipping into Sleep mode, tap Settings on the Home screen to open the Settings window. Then choose General➪Auto-Lock. You see the Auto-Lock screen. Choose an option (2 Minutes, 5 Minutes, 10 Minutes, 15 Minutes, or Never). Except for Never, these options are meant to preserve battery power. Turning the iPad off after a set amount of time keeps the battery from running down.

Chapter 3

Exploring Office for the iPad Basics

This chapter looks into a handful of tasks that you do whenever you use an Office for iPad app. It explains how to create and manage files, enter and format text, and make bulleted and numbered lists. You also find out how to find and replace text and plan ahead to work on files when your iPad isn't connected to the Internet.

I'm not telling you to read this chapter carefully, because I know how carefully you read everything. But if you read this carefully, you'll pick up some tips and tricks that come in very, very handy.

Working with Files (Documents, Workbooks, and Presentations)

Files go by different names in Office. A Word file is called a *document*; an Excel file is called a *workbook*; and a PowerPoint file is called a *presentation*. By any name, you'll be glad to know, the techniques for creating, opening, saving, and naming files are the same. These pages explain how Office for the iPad handles files and how to create, open, save, name, and duplicate files. You also find out how to work with files when your iPad isn't connected to the Internet.

How Office for the iPad handles files

Office for the iPad operates under the assumption that your iPad is always connected to the Internet and you want to store your files on OneDrive, Microsoft's online file storage facility. However, you can store files on the iPad itself. What's more, you can move files back and forth between the iPad and OneDrive.

In Word, Excel, and PowerPoint for the iPad, all file operations are done by way of the Office window and File menu, as shown in Figure 3-1. To handle files, look to the upper-left corner of the screen and tap the Office button or File button. Tapping Office opens the Office window; tapping File opens the File menu:

- **Office window:** Offers commands for signing in and out of OneDrive, creating files, and opening files (see Figure 3-1).
- **File menu:** Offers commands for naming, duplicating, restoring, and printing files, as well as viewing the properties of a file (see Figure 3-1).

Opening a file

When you start Word, Excel, or PowerPoint for the iPad, you also open the file that was open the last time you ran the app. Is this the file you want to work on? If it isn't, follow these steps to open a file:

1. Tap the Office button.

The Office window opens (see Figure 3-1).

2. Tap Open.

3. Go to where the file you want to open is stored.

It can be stored on OneDrive, on your iPad, or at another location.

- *OneDrive:* Tap One Drive. You may see some folder names. If the file is in a folder, tap the folder's name to open it. (Chapter 17 covers how to create and organize folders and files on OneDrive.)

    To open a file on OneDrive, you must have signed in to your Office 365 account. To sign in, tap the Office button, tap your name twice, and enter your user name and password.

- *iPad:* Tap iPad to open a file that is stored locally on your iPad device.

- *Another location:* If you added a location for keeping files, it is listed in the Office window. Find and open your file there.

4. Tap the name of the file you want to open.

TIP

Tap Recent in the Office window to see a list of files you opened recently. If the file you want to open is on the list, tap its name to open it. You can move a file permanently to the top of the list by tapping the pin icon next to a file's name. Pin a file to the top of the list if you open it often.

REMEMBER

In an Office for iPad app, only one file can be open at a time. You can't, for example, open two Excel workbooks and switch back and forth to compare the two. Office for the iPad is stubborn about not letting you open more than one file. The program is so stubborn, in fact, that it saves and closes the file that is open when you tap the Office button to open a different file.

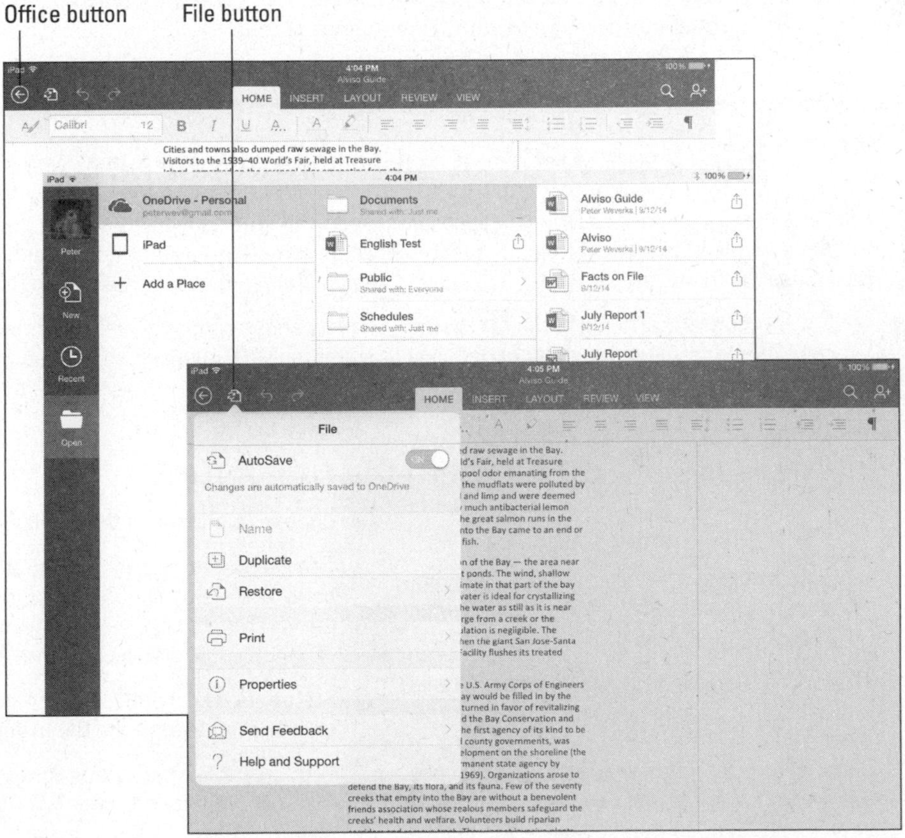

Office button   File button

Figure 3-1:
Open the Office window (left) or File menu (right) to handle files.

No Save button exists in the Office for iPad apps. That's because as changes are made to files, the changes are saved automatically, as long as AutoSave is turned on, that is. To see whether AutoSave is on:

- Tap the File button and note on the drop-down menu whether it's on.
- Note on the File button itself whether two little arrows appear. If they appear, AutoSave is turned on.

When AutoSave is off (and I see no reason for turning it off), save files by tapping the File button and choosing Save on the drop-down menu.

Closing a file

The only way to close a file is either to open a different file or close the app itself. Office for the iPad is peculiar about that. It doesn't offer a Close command for closing files. Because you can't open two files at the same time and because at least one file must always be open, the only way to close a file is to open another one or shut down everything.

Working without an Internet connection

Consider these scenarios and what happens in an Office for the iPad app when your iPad loses its connection to the Internet:

- You're boarding an airplane or going another place where Internet connections aren't allowed or aren't available. How do you open Office for iPad files that you store on OneDrive, seeing as how OneDrive is an online Internet location and you can't reach it unless your iPad is connected to the Internet?

- You're editing a file when suddenly the connection between your iPad and the Internet is broken.

To work on files when you know that an Internet connection won't be available, plan ahead. Before you take that flight or visit that obscure place where the Internet doesn't reach, copy the files you want to work on from OneDrive to your iPad. Then, on the flight or in the jungle, open the files on your iPad and get to work. Later, when an Internet connection becomes available, you can save the files to OneDrive.

Follow these steps to make a copy of a file stored on OneDrive and save the copy to your iPad:

1. **Open the file.**

2. **Tap the File button.**

3. **Choose Duplicate on the File menu.**

   The keyboard appears so that you can enter a name for the duplicate, or copy, of the file. The name text box shows the name of your file followed by the word *copy*.

4. **Swipe to the right, if necessary, and choose iPad to save the file to your iPad.**

   You have to swipe to the right to see the iPad option if your screen is in landscape mode.

5. **If you want, enter a name for the file and tap the Return key; otherwise, tap Save.**

When you have an Internet connection, follow these steps to move the file from your iPad to OneDrive:

1. **Tap the Office button.**

2. **Locate the file you want to move.**

   To do so, tap Recent or Open and navigate in the Office window until you see the name of the file you want to move.

3. **Tap the File icon to the right of the file's name.**

   The File icon shows an upward-pointing arrow. A drop-down menu appears after you tap the File icon.

4. **Choose Move to Cloud on the drop-down menu.**

5. **Choose a location on OneDrive to store your file.**

6. **Tap Save.**

Copying files back and forth between the iPad and OneDrive is a recipe for confusion. Soon files with similar names are in both places and it's hard to tell which files are up-to-date. When you swap files between the iPad and OneDrive, be careful about naming files and deleting outdated files.

When your iPad loses its connection to the Internet while you're working on an Office file, all is not lost because Office for the iPad retains a copy of open files in case the Internet goes down. This copy, called a *local copy*, is kept on the iPad itself. You can keep working without fear that your work will be lost. When the Internet connection is restored, Office for the iPad automatically copies the local copy of your file to OneDrive. You can tell when you're working on a local copy of a file by opening the File menu. If it says "Upload pending" under AutoSave, the changes you've made to your file have not been made to OneDrive yet. But they will be made to OneDrive when the Internet connection is restored.

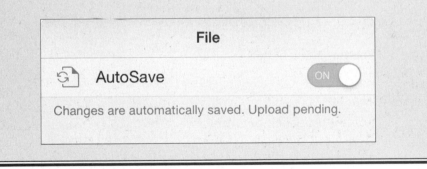

Creating a file

When you create a file, you are asked to choose a template to establish what your file will look like. A *template* is a preformatted file. Some of the templates are terribly spiffy; others are plain in case you want to do the formatting yourself. Figure 3-2 shows templates you can use to create a file in Word for the iPad.

Tap New   Choose a template

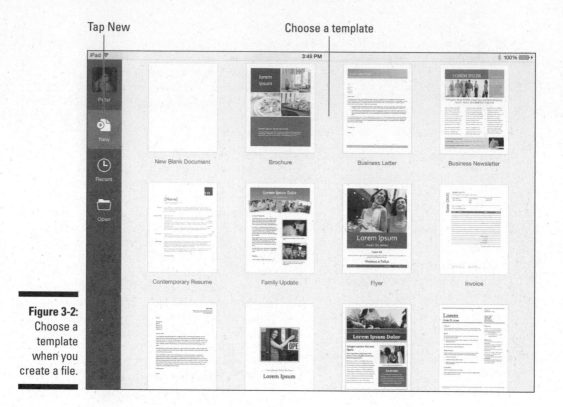

Figure 3-2:
Choose a
template
when you
create a file.

Follow these steps to create a file:

1. **Tap the Office button.**

   The Office window opens (see Figure 3-1).

2. **Tap New.**

   You see templates for creating files. The template names tell you something about what your file will look like after you create it.

3. **Tap a template name.**

   Your new file appears onscreen.

4. **Tap the File button and choose Name on the drop-down menu.**

   The Save As window and keyboard appear so that you can name your file and select a place to store it. By default, files are stored on OneDrive in the Documents folder. If this folder is where you want to keep the file, enter a name and tap Save; otherwise, proceed to step 5.

5. Choose where to store the file.

Select a OneDrive folder, select iPad to store the file on your iPad device, or select another location if you've designated one.

6. Tap the Name text box, enter a descriptive name for your file on the keyboard, and tap the Return key.

Renaming and moving files

Office for the iPad offers the Duplicate command for renaming and moving files. This command is located on the File menu. It's called "Duplicate" because duplicating a file — in other words, making a copy — is the only way to rename and move files:

- ✔ To rename a file, create a copy under a different name with the Duplicate command. Then delete the original file.
- ✔ To move a file, create a copy in a different location. Then delete the original.

Follow these steps to rename or move a file:

1. Open the file you want to rename or move.

See "Opening a file," earlier in this chapter, if you need help.

2. Tap the File button and choose Duplicate on the drop-down menu.

The Choose Name and Location window opens.

3. Move the file to a different location, enter a new name, or do both.

Here's how:

- *Choose a location:* Move the file to a OneDrive folder or to the iPad.
- *Enter a name:* Enter a name in the Name box and tap the Return key.

4. Tap Save.

5. Delete the original copy of the file.

See "Deleting a file in an Office for iPad app," the next topic in this chapter.

Deleting a file in an Office for iPad app

The easiest way to delete a file stored on OneDrive is to open the OneDrive website in a browser and delete the file inside the OneDrive website. How to delete and otherwise manage files on OneDrive by way of a browser is covered in Chapter 17. If you don't care to turn to that chapter to discover how to delete files, follow these steps to delete a file in an Office for iPad app:

1. **Tap the Office button.**

2. **Locate the file you want to delete.**

   To locate the file, tap Recent or Open and navigate to the file.

3. **Tap the File icon to the right of the file's name.**

   As shown in Figure 3-3, the File drop-down menu appears.

4. **Choose Delete.**

5. **Choose Delete in the confirmation message box.**

   That's all there is to it.

 Many computers have a Trash feature (Mac) or a Recycle Bin (Windows) where deleted files are kept in case you want to recover them. The iPad has no such thing. Files you delete are deleted permanently and irrevocably. For that reason, think twice before deleting a file.

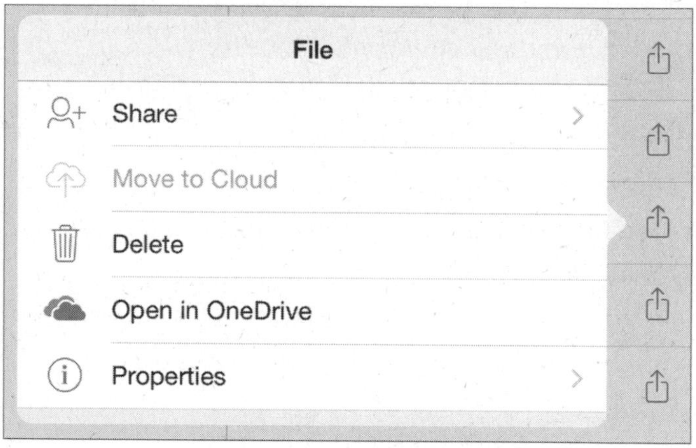

File	
⊗+ Share	>
☁ Move to Cloud	
🗑 Delete	
☁ Open in OneDrive	
ⓘ Properties	>

Figure 3-3:
Tap the File icon and choose Delete to delete a file.

A Quick Tour of the Office for iPad Interface

Interface is the computer term that describes how a software program presents itself to the people who use it. Figure 3-4 shows the PowerPoint for the iPad interface. You'll be glad to know that the interfaces of all the Office for the iPad apps — Word, Excel, and PowerPoint — are pretty much the same. The apps have these interface features in common:

- ✔ **Quick Access toolbar:** No matter where you go in an Office for iPad app, you see the *Quick Access toolbar* in the upper-left corner of the screen. It offers these buttons: Office, File, Undo, and Redo. Earlier in this chapter, "How Office for the iPad handles files" explains the Office and File buttons. The Undo button reverses your most recent action; Redo "redoes" what you "undid" in case you regret tapping the Undo button.

- ✔ **Ribbon:** Across the top of the screen is the *Ribbon,* an assortment of different tabs. Tap a tab to view a different set of commands and undertake a task.

- ✔ **Context-sensitive tabs:** To keep the Ribbon from getting too crowded with tabs, some tabs, called *context-sensitive tabs,* only appear in context. They appear on the Ribbon after you select or insert something. In Figure 3-4, I selected a chart, so an additional tab called Chart appears on the Ribbon.

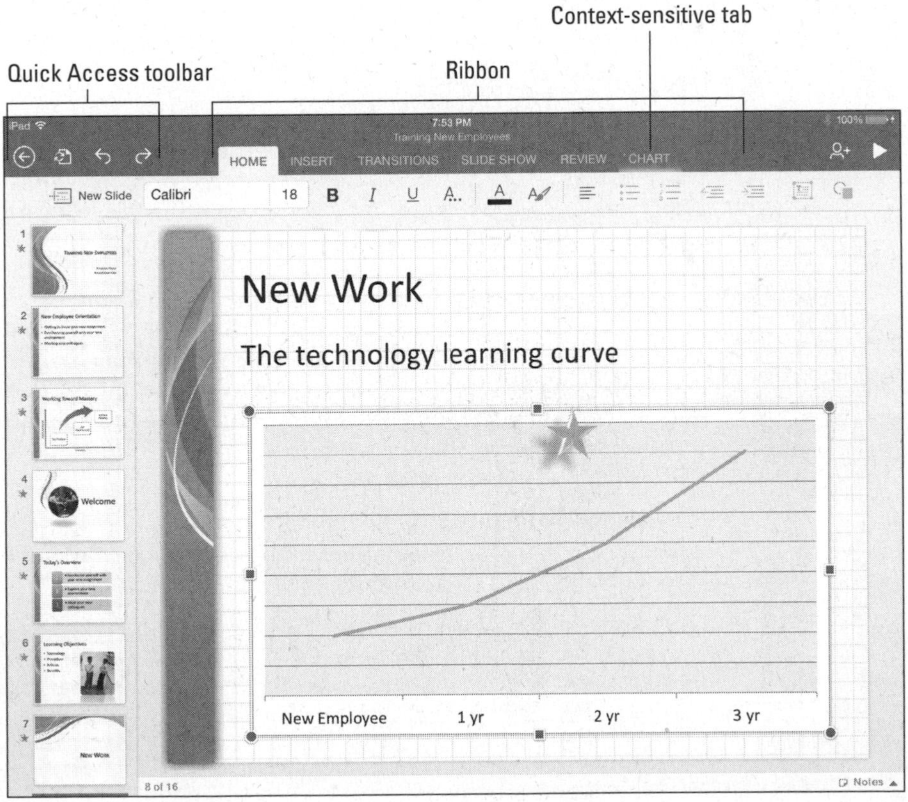

Figure 3-4: All the Office for iPad apps have the same interface.

Shrinking and Enlarging the Screen

In Office for the iPad apps, shrinking and enlarging what is on the screen is simply a matter of pinching. With thumb and forefinger touching the screen, move the two farther apart to enlarge what is on the screen; move your thumb and forefinger closer together to shrink it.

Don't pinch pennies when it comes to shrinking and enlarging what is on the screen. Do it often to spare your eyes and be able to see your work better.

Handling and Manipulating Text

You must have noticed by now that entering and editing text on an iPad keyboard takes some getting used to. These pages explain how the iPad keyboard works and what you can do to make entering and editing text a little easier. It also delves into selecting, moving, copying, deleting, and formatting text.

Keyboard basics

To bring up the keyboard, tap the screen. As long as you tap a part of the screen where text is located or can be entered, the keyboard appears. When you finish typing, tap the Keyboard button (located in the lower-right corner of the keyboard) to hide the keyboard.

Here is what everyone needs to know about the keyboard:

- **Capital letters:** Tap the Shift key (the upward-pointing arrow on either side of the keyboard's third row) to enter a capital letter. The key turns black until you finish typing the letter. Double-tap the Shift key to turn Caps Lock on and be able to type several capital letters at a time (tap Shift again to turn Caps Lock off).

- **Punctuation/Numbers:** Tap the Punctuation/Numbers key (.?123) to make the keyboard show numbers and punctuation marks. Type the Alphabet key (ABC) to see letters again.

- **Special characters:** After pressing the Punctuation/Numbers key, you can press the Special Characters key (#+=) to see special characters on the keyboard. Press the Numbers key (123) to see numbers and punctuation marks again or the Alphabet key (ABC) to see letters again.

Here is what the lucky few know about the keyboard:

- **Backspacing:** Tap the Backspace key once to delete a letter. Press and hold down this key to delete a word at a time.

- **Apostrophe:** Press and hold down the comma key and then drag your finger onto the pop-up menu to enter an apostrophe.

- **Accented and special characters:** Press and hold down a key to see a pop-up menu of accented and special characters. Then drag your finger to a character to enter it.

- **Period:** Besides pressing the period key, double-tap the spacebar to enter a period at the end of sentence.

To move the cursor with precision, press and hold down your finger on a word or sentence that needs editing. A magnifying glass image of the word or sentence appears. Drag to move the cursor in the image where you want to make an edit.

Office for the iPad "auto-corrects" some words as you enter them. For example, type the misspelling *truely* and Office corrects your error; it enters the word *truly*. Office also capitalizes the first word in sentences. If this behind-the-scenes skullduggery annoys you, you can turn off auto-correct and auto-capitalization in the Settings app. In Settings, choose General⇨Keyboard to find and turn off the settings.

Selecting text

Before you can do anything to text — move it, copy it, delete it, reformat it — you have to select it. Here are speed techniques for selecting text:

To select	Do this
A word	Double-tap
Several words	Double-tap and drag the selection handles, as shown in Figure 3-5
A paragraph	Triple-tap
All text	Tap and hold down your finger in text, and choose Select All on the pop-up menu (see Figure 3-5)

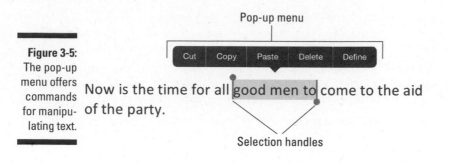

Figure 3-5:
The pop-up
menu offers
commands
for manipu-
lating text.

Moving, copying, and deleting text

In the course of human events, it often becomes necessary to move, copy, and delete text. Follow these steps to move, copy, or delete text:

1. **Select the text.**

   After you select text, a pop-up menu appears (see Figure 3-5). Selecting text is the previous topic in this chapter.

2. **Move, copy, or delete the text.**

   Here's how to do these little tasks:

   • *Move text:* Tap Cut on the pop-up menu and proceed to Step 3.

   • *Copy text:* Tap Copy on the pop-up menu and proceed to Step 3.

   • *Delete text:* Tap Delete on the pop-up menu.

3. **Tap where you want to move or copy the text.**

   A pop-up menu appears.

4. **Tap Paste on the pop-up menu.**

Formatting text

What text looks like is determined by its font, the size of the letters, the color of the letters, and whether text effects or font styles such as italic or boldface are in play.

Select text (if you've already entered it) and use these techniques on the Home tab to change the look of text:

  ✔ **Choosing a font:** Tap the Font button and choose a font on the drop-down menu.

✔ **Changing the font size:** Tap the Font Size button and choose a size on the drop-down menu. You can tap the current font size and enter a size with the keyboard.

✔ **Applying text styles:** Tap the Formatting button and choose Bold, Italic, or another style on the drop-down menu. The Formatting button is located to the right of the Font size button.

✔ **Changing the color of text:** Tap the Font Color button and choose a color on the drop-down menu.

Commands for formatting text become available when the keyboard is on the screen. Without the keyboard showing, these commands are null and void. To activate the keyboard, tap the screen or select text.

Making Bulleted and Numbered Lists

Everybody is fond of lists, and Office for the iPad gives you the opportunity to create two types of lists: bulleted and numbered, as shown in Figure 3-6. A *bulleted list* is an unranked list, with each item marked with a solid, hollow, or square bullet. Numbered lists order items by their importance or present step-by-step procedures.

Figure 3-6: A bulleted list (left) and numbered list (right).

▪ John	1.John
▪ Paul	2.Paul
▪ George	3.George
▪ Ringo	4.Ringo

Go to the Home tab and follow these instructions to create lists:

✔ **Bulleted list:** Tap the Bullets button, choose a bullet type on the drop-down menu, and write the list, pressing Return as you complete each item; or, if you already entered items for the list, select the list, tap the Bullets button, and choose a bullet type.

✔ **Numbered list:** Tap the Numbers button, choose a numbering style, and enter items for the list. As you press Return, the list is numbered. You can also select an unnumbered list, tap the Numbers button, and choose a numbering style to enter numbers all at one time.

To remove bullets or numbers from a list, select the list, tap the Bullets or Numbers button, and choose None.

Finding and Replacing Text

Use the Find command to locate a text or numbers. Use its twin, the powerful Find and Replace command, to find and replace text or numbers throughout a document, worksheet, or presentation.

Follow these steps to run a find or find-and-replace operation:

1. Tap the Search button.

This button is located in the upper-right corner of the screen, as shown in Figure 3-7. After you tap it, the Search bar appears.

2. Enter the text or numbers that you seek in the Find text box.

Office for the iPad scrolls to and selects the text or numbers if it can locate them.

A number on the right side of the Find text box tells you how many instances of the text or numbers were found. Click the Next (or Previous) button to go to the next (or previous) instance of the word or numbers.

You can narrow your search by tapping the Options button and choosing either or both of these options on the drop-down menu:

- *Match Case:* Searches for words with upper- and lowercase letters that exactly match those in the Find text box.

- *Whole Words:* Searches for words, not text strings, that match what you entered in the Find Text box. For example, a search for *bow* finds that word only, not all instances of the letters *bow*. Without choosing Whole Words, a search for *bow* finds that word as well as *elbow, bowler,* and *bow-wow.*

In find-and-replace operations, always choose the Whole Words option. Failure to do so can produce gobbledygook. For example, replacing *bow* with *kneel,* can produce *elkneel, kneeller, and kneel-wow* (to use examples from the previous paragraph in this book).

3. To expand your find operation into a find-and-replace operation, tap the Options button and choose Find and Replace.

The Replace text box appears on the Search bar (see Figure 3-7).

4. Enter the replacement term in the Replace text box.

5. **Replace the search term one instance at a time or replace all instances.**

Review each replacement before making it or be bold and daring:

- *Replace one at a time:* Note the search term that is highlighted. To replace it, tap Replace on the Search bar; tap Next or Previous to pass it by.

- *Replace all:* Tap All on the Search bar. The Search bar tells you how many replacements were made.

6. **Double-tap onscreen to close the Search bar.**

If you regret conducting your find-and-replace operation, you can always tap the Undo button to reverse it, although you may have to tap the Undo button many times.

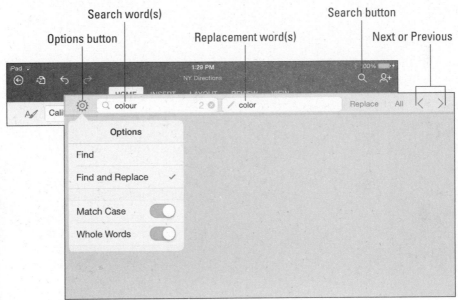

Figure 3-7:
Conducting
a find-and-
replace
operation.

Part II
Word

Prior to the 1849 California Gold Rush, San Francisco Bay was a third again larger than it is now. During the Gold Rush, profuse amounts of mud and sludge washed down creeks and rivers from the High Sierra to the Bay as a result of hydraulic mining techniques. In hydraulic mining, water is blasted at high pressure into the sides of mountains to dislodge soil and rocks so the gold can be extracted. So much muddy sediment was unearthed in the mountains, the floor of San Francisco Bay rose several feet. Meanwhile, dykes and levees were built to capture tidal marshes from the Bay and turn the marshes into farmland. Cities and towns dumped their refuse in the Bay, and when the refuse rose to sea level, it was filled in and paved over so the Bay could receive still more refuse.

Page Numbers

Numbering

Show # on First Page

Position   Bottom of page (Footer) >

Alignment   Right >

Format   1, 2, 3, ... >

Go to www.dummies.com/extras/officeipadmac to see how to place watermarks — pale images or words — behind text on the page.

In this part . . .

- ✔ Explore Word for the iPad — applying styles, laying out pages, using footnotes, and tracking revisions to documents.

- ✔ Take Word to another level with tips for selecting text, getting around in documents, handling breaks, numbering pages, and managing headers and footers.

- ✔ Find out how to apply styles and save a ridiculous amount of time formatting Word documents.

- ✔ Master Word tables and present data in the best possible light.

- ✔ Use the Word features — cross-referencing, table of contents, indexing, and footnotes — that can make your reports and papers better.

Chapter 4

Word for the iPad

This chapter takes on Word for the iPad, the word processor in the Office for the iPad family. It explains why formatting documents with styles saves time and gives documents a professional look. This chapter delves into page layouts and how to handle page margins, page numbers, and headers and footers.

If, like me, you're not a good speller, you'll be glad to know that this chapter covers spell checking. It also looks into footnotes and how to track and identify editorial changes made to a document with several co-authors.

By the way, Chapter 3 explains how to create, open, and close Word for the iPad documents.

Applying Styles

Styles save time because when you apply a *style,* you apply several formatting commands at one time. The Heading 1 style, for example, applies formats that are suitable for headings — a heavier font, a larger font size. Styles give you the opportunity to make headings and other parts of a document consistent with one another. All the first-level headings look the same when you apply the Heading 1 style to all first-level headings.

Every document comes with built-in styles inherited from the template with which it was created. These styles are available on the Styles menu on the Home tab, as shown in Figure 4-1. (Chapter 6 explains in detail how styles work.)

In Word 2011 (the desktop version of Word), you can tell right away whether a style is a paragraph or character style because symbols on the Styles menu tell you as much. Word for the iPad isn't that sophisticated, though. Its Style menu doesn't tell you which styles are paragraph or character styles. All you can do is take a hint from the style's name (maybe) to understand what kind of style you're dealing with. For example, a style called Emphasis is likely to be a character style that italicizes words, whereas Heading 3 is almost certainly a style that applies to entire paragraphs.

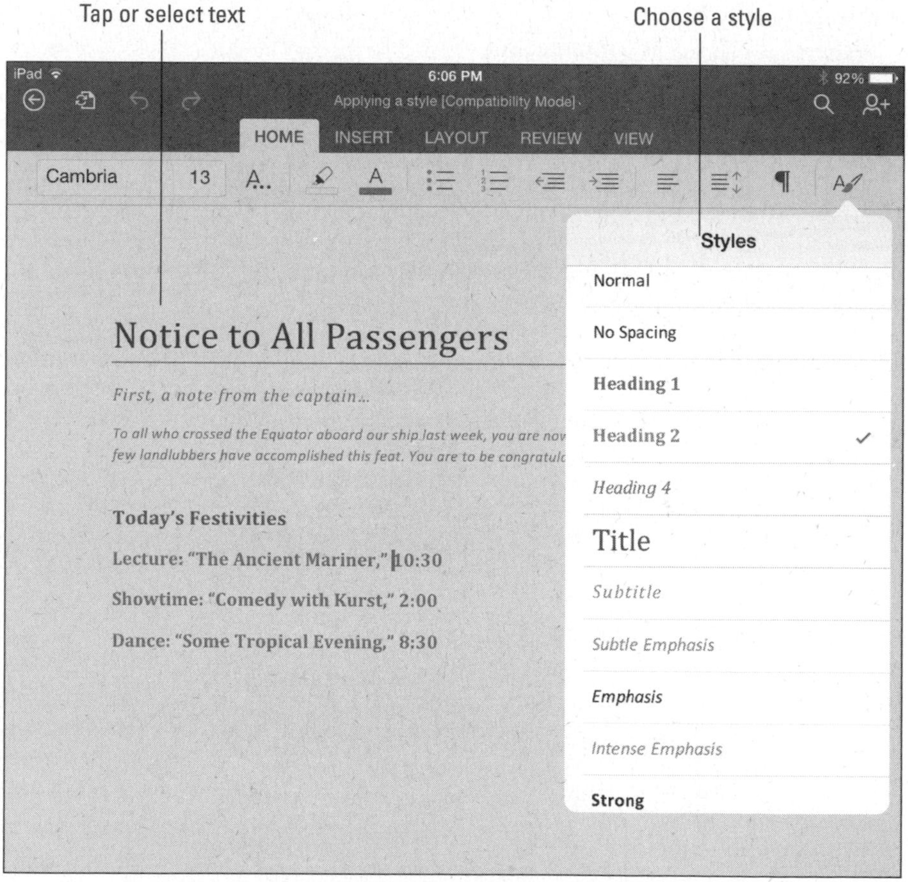

Tap or select text   Choose a style

Notice to All Passengers

First, a note from the captain...

To all who crossed the Equator aboard our ship last week, you are now few landlubbers have accomplished this feat. You are to be congratul

Today's Festivities

Lecture: "The Ancient Mariner," 10:30

Showtime: "Comedy with Kurst," 2:00

Dance: "Some Tropical Evening," 8:30

Styles

Normal
No Spacing
Heading 1
Heading 2 ✓
Heading 4
Title
Subtitle
Subtle Emphasis
Emphasis
Intense Emphasis
Strong

Figure 4-1: Apply styles with the Styles menu on the Home tab.

Follow these steps to apply a style:

1. **Tap or select the part of your document that you want to apply the style to.**

   What you select depends on the type of style you want to apply.

   - *A word or phrase (character style)*: Select the word or phrase. The style you choose will be applied only to the word or phrase you selected.
   - *A paragraph (paragraph style)*: Tap in the paragraph. Paragraph styles apply to the entire paragraph that the cursor is in. All you have to do is tap in a paragraph to apply a paragraph or linked style throughout.
   - *More than one paragraph (paragraph style)*: Select all or part of the paragraphs. Because paragraph styles apply throughout a paragraph, you can select part of a paragraph. You don't have to select all of it.

2. **On the Home tab, tap the Styles button and choose a style on the drop-down menu.**

   Figure 4-1 shows the Styles drop-down menu.

Don't like the style you selected? Tap the Undo button and start all over.

You can't create or change styles in Word for the iPad. If you want to do that, open your document in Word 2011 for Mac or another edition of Word.

Laying Out the Page

Word for the iPad offers the Layout tab for laying out pages. Go to the Layout tab when you want to change the size, margins, and orientation of the pages in a document. The Layout tab also offers commands for numbering pages and creating headers and footers, as I explain in the following pages of this book.

Determining the page margins

Page margins are the empty spaces along the top, bottom, right side, and left side of the page. Margins serve to frame the text on the page. As every college student knows, you can make a term paper longer by widening the margins. Wide margins leave less room for text and push text onto subsequent pages, making the term paper longer and making the student seem a little smarter than he or she really is.

Section breaks for layout changes

To lay out pages in different ways in a document, divide the document into sections. For example, to make page margins wider in the first four pages of a document, create a section for the first four pages and apply margin commands to the first section only. Layout commands in Word for the iPad apply to the entire document or, if the document is divided into sections, the section where the cursor is when you give a layout command.

Create a section by inserting a *section break* where you want the new section to begin.

Section breaks occur at the top of pages. Follow these steps to insert a section break and create a new section:

1. **Place the cursor where you want the new section to start.**

2. **Go to the Layout tab.**

3. **Tap the Breaks button.**

4. **Choose Next Page on the drop-down menu.**

Follow these steps to change page margins:

1. **Go to the Layout tab.**

2. **Tap the Margins button.**

3. **Choose an option on the drop-down menu.**

   The Mirrored option is for documents that will be bound and on which text will be printed on both sides of the page. The page margins on the binding side of the page are made wider to accommodate the binding.

Numbering the pages

It almost goes without saying, but a document more than a few pages long needs page numbers. Unless you number the pages, how can you put your document together again if you drop it on the sidewalk and the wind scatters the pages hither and yon?

Follow these steps to number the pages in a document:

1. **Go to the Insert tab.**

2. **Tap the Page Numbers button.**

   The Page Numbers drop-down menu appears, as shown in Figure 4-2.

3. **Turn on Numbering.**

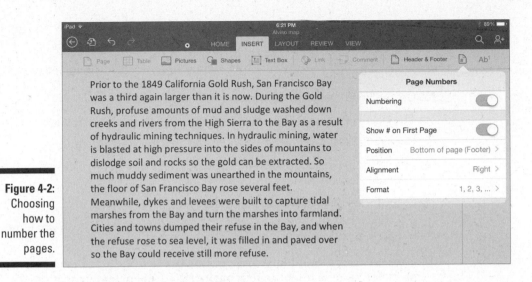

Figure 4-2: Choosing how to number the pages.

4. **Choose options to determine how the pages are numbered and what page numbers look like:**

   Your choices are as follows:

   - *Show # on First Page:* Typically, the title page of a report isn't numbered. Turn this option off to keep a page number from appearing on the first page.

   - *Position:* On the submenu, choose whether to put page numbers on the top or bottom of the page.

   - *Alignment:* On the submenu, choose where in the header or footer you want the page number to appear. The Inside and Outside options are for bound, two-sided documents in which text is printed on both sides of the page. The Inside option places page numbers next to the binding; the Outside option places page numbers away from the binding.

   - *Format:* On the submenu, choose a format for numbering pages.

   To remove page numbers, return to the Page Numbers menu and turn off the Numbering option.

Creating headers and footers

A *header* is descriptive text along the top of the page; a *footer* is descriptive text along the bottom. Headers and footers identify the subject of a document, its author, which page is which, and other essential stuff.

(To include page numbers in a header or footer, use the Page Numbers command; see "Numbering the pages," earlier in this chapter.)

Follow these steps to enter (or edit) a header or footer on a document:

1. **On the Insert tab, tap the Header & Footer button.**

   The Header & Footer drop-down menu appears, as shown in Figure 4-3.

2. **Choose Edit Header or Edit Footer on the drop-down menu.**

   The Header pane or Footer pane opens. A fast way to open either pane is to double-tap the header or footer.

3. **Enter (or edit) your header or footer.**

   You can call on the formatting commands on the Home tab as you enter the text. For example, you can italicize or boldface text.

4. **Turn on the Different First Page option if you don't want your header or footer to appear on the first page of your document or section.**

   Typically, headers and footers don't appear on the title page of reports and white papers.

5. **Tap the Close button.**

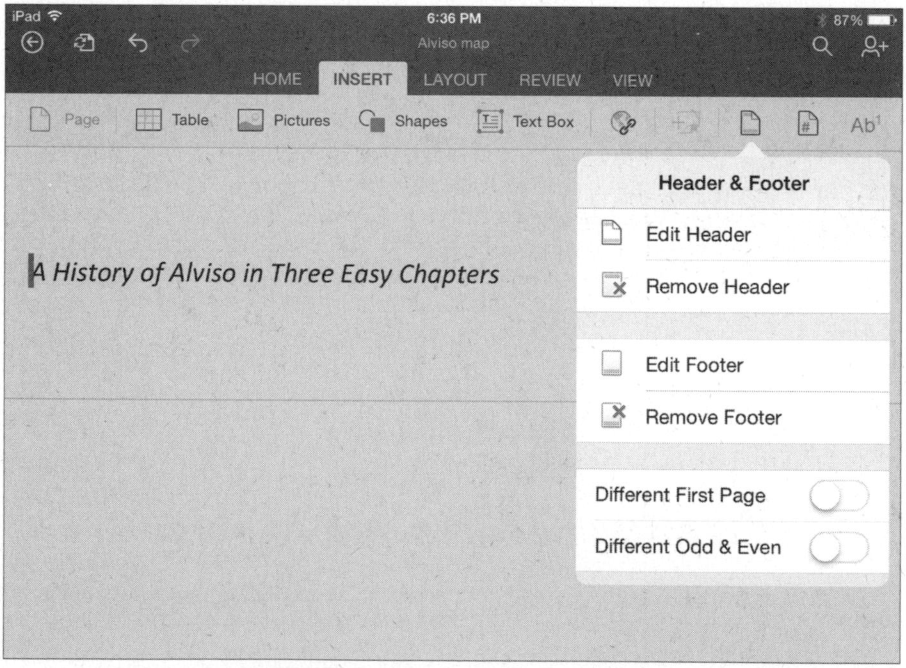

Figure 4-3:
Entering a
header in
the Header
pane.

To remove a header or footer, open the Header & Footer menu and choose Remove Header or Remove Footer.

The final option on the Header & Footer menu is for two-sided documents. Choose this option to have a different header or footer on the left and right side of the page spread, the two pages that readers see when they lay a bound document flat on the table.

Spell Checking Your Work

For those of us who can't spell, Word for the iPad provides a spell checker, but not an especially good one. The only way to spell check words is to check them one at a time.

Spelling errors are underlined in red. To correct these errors, tap a redlined word and choose an alternative spelling on the pop-up list, as shown in Figure 4-4.

Tapping Learn on the pop-up list enters the word in the iPad's spelling dictionary so that it is no longer considered a misspelling. Tap Learn to prevent a word from being mistaken for a misspelling.

If Word for the iPad isn't flagging misspelled words and you want it to do so, go to the Review tab, tap the Spelling button, and turn on the Spelling option.

Figure 4-4:
Correcting a
misspelling.

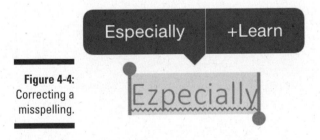

Putting Footnotes in Documents

Scholarly papers require footnotes, the notes that tell readers where information came from or refer readers to other sources of information. In Word for the iPad, footnote citations are numbered in the text; footnotes appear at the bottom of the page. Word for the iPad renumbers footnotes as you enter and delete them, which spares you the terrible task of having to renumber footnotes yourself.

Follow these steps to write a footnote:

1. **Place the cursor where you want the numbered footnote citation to appear.**

   Citations usually appear at the end of sentences.

2. **On the Insert tab, tap the Footnote button.**

   This button is shown in Figure 4-5. The keyboard appears, and you scroll to the bottom of the page so that you can enter the note, as shown in Figure 4-5.

3. **Enter the footnote.**

4. **Scroll upward on the page to resume writing your document.**

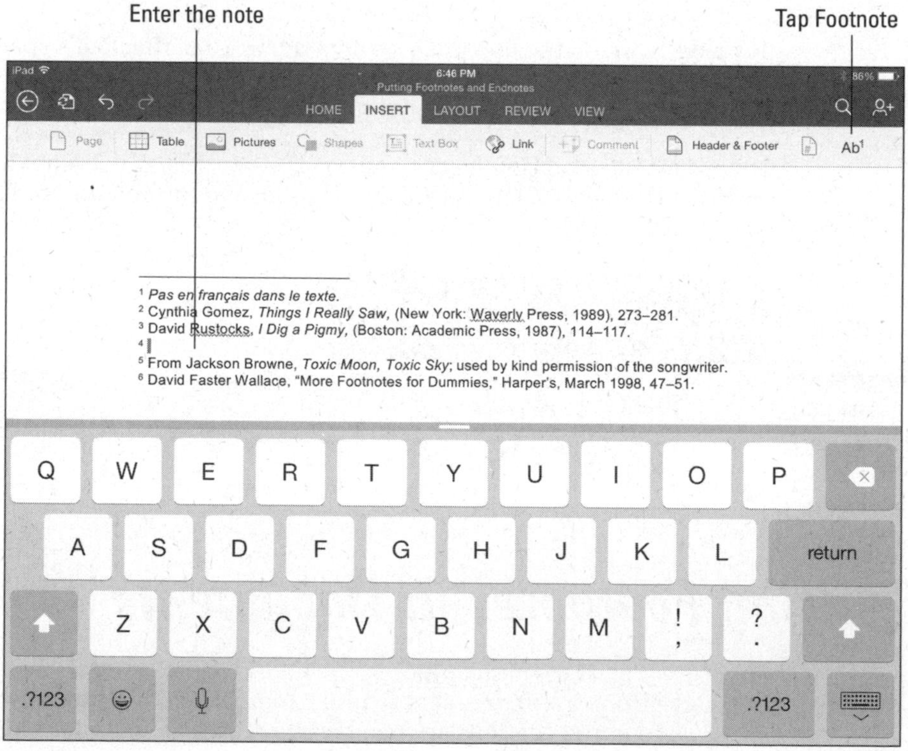

Enter the note   Tap Footnote

Figure 4-5: Entering a footnote.

To remove a footnote, backspace over its numbered citation in the text. The number and the footnote at the bottom of the page are deleted.

To edit a footnote, scroll to the bottom of the screen where the footnote is and edit it there.

Tracking Editorial Changes

When more than one person works on a document, how can you tell who contributed what? How can you review the document to see where changes were made and whether the changes made by Tom, Dick, and Harry are valid?

To track changes to a document, use the tools on the Review tab, as shown in Figure 4-6. The Review tab offers the means to comment on a document, track where words were added and deleted, and view editorial changes in different ways. You can even prevent people from editing a document.

Telling Word to track changes

Go to the Review tab and turn on the Track Changes option to be able to see where changes to a document are made. When Track Changes is turned on:

✔ Changes to a document are recorded in a different color, with one color for each reviewer.

✔ New text is underlined; deleted text is crossed out (see Figure 4-6).

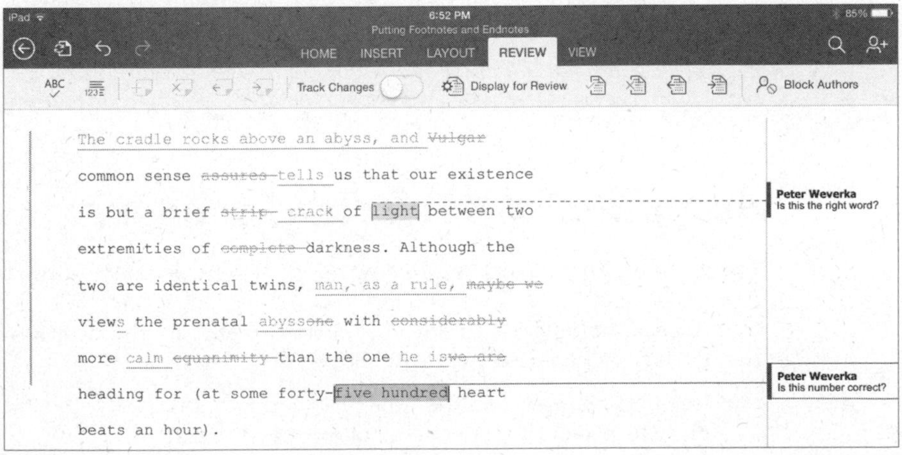

Figure 4-6:
The Review tab, where you can track changes to documents, write comments, and review comments.

Suppose you're co-authoring a document that you share on OneDrive and you want to prevent others from working on a paragraph while you work on your document. In that case, tap in the paragraph and then tap the Block Authors button. The block symbol appears to the left of the paragraph to show that no one but you can edit it. Blocking other authors is useful when you're working on a shared document and you don't want to be distracted. Chapter 18 describes sharing documents.

Reviewing editorial changes

Besides gazing at underlined and crossed-out words, you can find and examine editorial changes to a document by using these techniques:

✔ Tap the Previous Revision or Next Revision button to highlight changes one at a time. When you tap these buttons, the previous or next revision on the page is highlighted so that you can see it clearly. (While a revision is highlighted, you can accept or reject it by tapping the Accept Change or Reject Change button.)

✔ Tap the Display for Review button and choose an option on the drop-down menu to examine the document in different ways:

• *See where additions and deletions were made.* Choose All Markup. Additions are underlined and deleted text is crossed through, as in Figure 4-6.

• *See what the document would look like if you accepted all changes.* Choose No Markup. All change marks are stripped away and you see what your document would look like if you accepted all changes made to it.

• *See more clearly where text was inserted in the document.* Choose Original with Markup.

• *See what the document would look like if you rejected all changes.* Choose Original. You get the original, pristine document back.

Accepting and rejecting changes

Use these techniques on the Review tab to accept or reject editorial changes:

✔ **Accept a change:** Tap the Accept button and, on the drop-down menu, choose Accept Change or Accept & Move to Next.

✔ **Reject a change:** Tap the Reject button and, on the drop-down menu, choose Reject Change or Reject & Move to Next.

- ✔ **Accept all changes:** Tap the Accept button and, on the drop-down menu, choose Accept All.

- ✔ **Reject all changes:** Tap the Reject button and, on the drop-down menu, choose Reject All.

Commenting on documents

The Review tab also offers a means of writing comments about a document. The comments appear in boxes to the right of the text to which they apply (refer to Figure 4-6). Use these techniques to write and otherwise make use of comments to trade ideas with your collaborators:

- ✔ **Writing a comment:** Tap in the text you want to comment on and then tap the Comment button. A comment box appears so that you can enter your comment.

- ✔ **Reading comments:** Tap the Previous Comment or Next Comment button to go from comment to comment.

- ✔ **Deleting comments:** Tap the comment you want to delete, tap the Delete Comment button, and choose Delete Comment on the drop-down menu. Choose Delete All Comments in Document to delete every comment.

Chapter 5

Creating Sophisticated Documents with Word 2011

*T*his chapter explains shortcuts and commands that can help you become a speedy user of Word 2011 on your Mac. Everything in this chapter was put here so that you can get off work earlier and take the slow, scenic route home.

Starting here, you discover how to create and change your view of documents. You find out how to select text, get from place to place, and mark your place in long documents. You also explore how to insert one document into another, change the page layouts, number documents, handle headers and footers, make lists, and hyphenate.

Introducing the Word Screen

Seeing the Word 2011 screen for the first time is like trying to find your way through Tokyo's busy Ikebukuro subway station. It's intimidating. To help you get going, Figure 5-1 shows you the different parts of the screen. Here are shorthand descriptions of these screen parts:

- **Title bar:** At the top of the screen, the title bar tells you the name of the document you're working on.

- **Quit/Minimize/Maximize buttons:** In the upper-left corner of the screen, these buttons close Word, minimize the Word window, and maximize the Word window.

- **Standard toolbar:** This toolbar offers a handful of buttons that are useful no matter what you're doing in Word. The Standard toolbar is always available along the top of the screen.

- **The Ribbon:** Select a tab on the Ribbon to undertake a new task. Each tab offers different commands and features.

- **Collapse/Expand Ribbon button:** Click this button to hide or display the Ribbon. Collapsing the Ribbon leaves you more room onscreen to work on documents.

- **View buttons:** Click one of these buttons — Draft view, Outline view, Publishing Layout view, Print Layout view, Notebook Layout view, or Focus view — to change your view of a document.

- **Status bar:** The status bar gives you basic information about where you are and what you're doing in a document. It tells you what view you're in, the section and page you're in, and the total number of pages and words in your document.

- **Zoom slider:** Use this slider to zoom in and out on your work.

The same commands are found on the Word menu bar and the Ribbon. For example, to choose a font for text, go to the Home tab on the Ribbon and choose a font or open the Font menu on the Word menu bar and choose a font there.

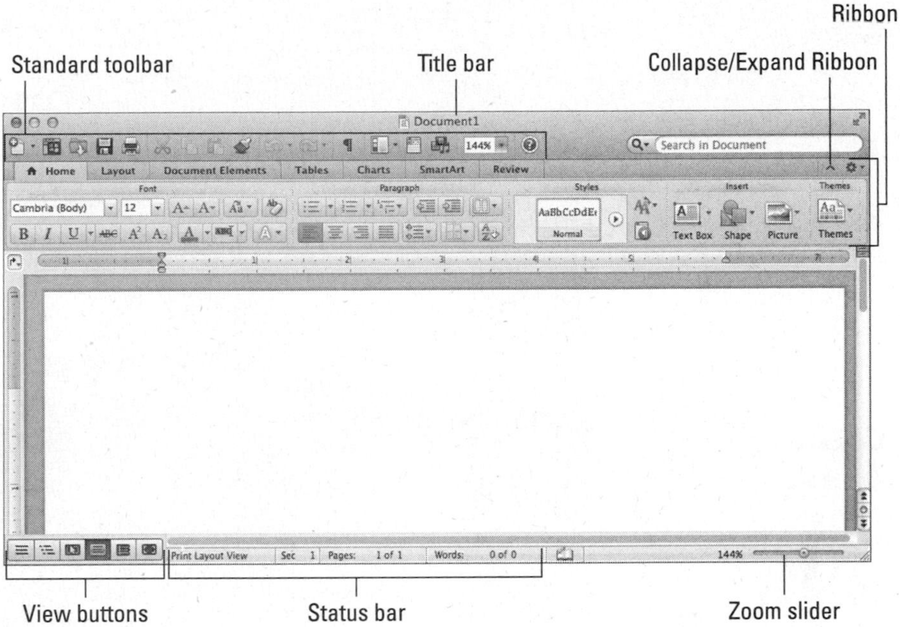
Ribbon
Standard toolbar
Title bar
Collapse/Expand Ribbon
Document1
Search in Document
Home
Layout
Document Elements
Tables
Charts
SmartArt
Review
Print Layout View
View buttons
Status bar
Zoom slider

Figure 5-1: The Word screen.

Creating a New Document

Document is just a fancy word for a letter, report, announcement, or proclamation that you create with Word. When you start Word, you see the *Word Document Gallery*, where you have the opportunity to create a new document, and you can create a document whenever you please. Figure 5-2 shows the Word Document Gallery.

The two types of documents

Word offers two types of documents:

- **A new blank document.** This is a bare-bones document with few formatting styles. Create a new blank document when you want a plain document or want to do most of the formatting yourself.
- **A document made from a template.** A *template* is a special kind of file that is used as the starting point for creating documents. Each template comes with many preformatted styles. If your aim is to create an academic report, flyer, newsletter, calendar, résumé, or other sophisticated document, see if you can spare yourself the formatting work by choosing the appropriate template when you create your document.

Choose a category

Choose a template

Preview and modify the template

Open or close the Preview pane

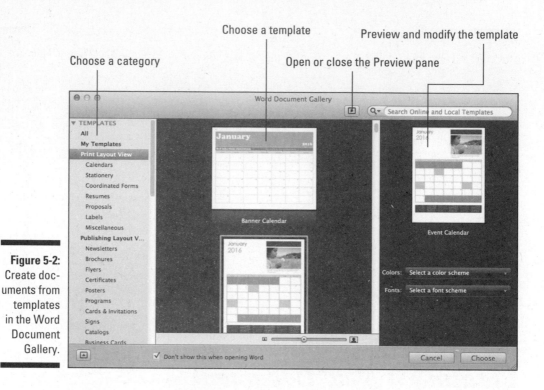

Figure 5-2:
Create doc-
uments from
templates
in the Word
Document
Gallery.

Creating a blank document

Use one of these techniques to create a blank document:

- ✔ Click the Create a New Word Document button on the Standard toolbar.
- ✔ Choose File⇨New Blank Document.
- ✔ Press Command+N.

Creating a document from a template

Follow these steps to create a document from a template:

1. **Open the Word Document Gallery (see Figure 5-2).**

   Open the gallery with one of these techniques:

   • Click the New From Template button on the Standard toolbar.

Choosing what you see when you start Word

When you start Word, you see the Word Document Gallery (refer to Figure 5-2), where you can create a new, blank document or create a document from a template. Do you want to see the Word Document Gallery each time you start Word? Maybe you prefer to open a document when you start the program rather than get the opportunity to create a new one.

Follow these steps to keep the Word Document Gallery from appearing when you start Word:

1. **Choose Word ⇨ Preferences to open the Word Preferences dialog box.**

2. **Choose General (it's the first option under Authoring and Proofing Tools).**

3. **Deselect the Open Word Document Gallery When Application Opens check box.**

4. **Click OK or press Return.**

Next time you start Word, you'll see a blank document or the previous document you worked on instead of the Word Document Gallery.

- Choose File ⇨ New From Template.
- Press Command+Shift+P.

2. **Select a templates category.**

   Scroll to the bottom of the category list to see categories that Microsoft makes available online. The My Templates category holds templates you create yourself.

3. **Select a template.**

   The Preview pane on the right side of the gallery gives you a better look at the template you chose. To see the Preview pane, you may have to click the Open or Close Right Pane button.

4. **Select a color scheme and font for your template in the Preview pane.**

5. **Click the Choose button.**

   Your new document appears onscreen.

Getting a Better Look at Your Documents

A computer screen can be kind of confining. There you are, staring at the darn thing for hours at a stretch. Do you wish the view were better? The Word screen can't be made to look like the Riviera, but you can examine documents in different ways and work in two places at one time in the same document. Better read on.

Of course, you can always get a better view of your documents by zooming in and out. Word provides the Zoom slider in the lower-right corner of the screen for that very purpose.

Viewing documents in different ways

In word processing, you want to focus sometimes on the writing, sometimes on the layout, and sometimes on the organization of your work. To help you stay in focus, Word offers different ways of viewing a document. Figure 5-3 shows these views.

Use one of these techniques to change views:

- Click a View button in the lower-left corner of the screen.
- Open the View menu and choose a view (Web Layout view is available only from the View menu).

Table 5-1 compares and contrasts the different views.

Splitting the screen

You can be two places at one time in a Word document by splitting the screen. One reason you might do this: You're writing a long report and want the introduction to support the conclusion, and you want the conclusion to fulfill all promises made by the introduction. That's difficult to do sometimes, but you can make it easier by splitting the screen so that you can be two places at the same time as you write your introduction and conclusion.

Splitting a window means to divide it into north and south halves, as shown in Figure 5-4. In a split screen, two sets of scroll bars appear so that you can travel in one half of the screen without disturbing the other half.

Follow these steps to split the screen:

1. **Move the mouse pointer to the *split box* at the top of the scroll bar on the right**

   Do this correctly and you see the pointer turn into double-arrows.

2. **Drag the split box down the screen.**

   As you drag, you see a line that shows where the split will be.

3. **Release the mouse button where you want to split the screen.**

   You can adjust the split by dragging the line north or south.

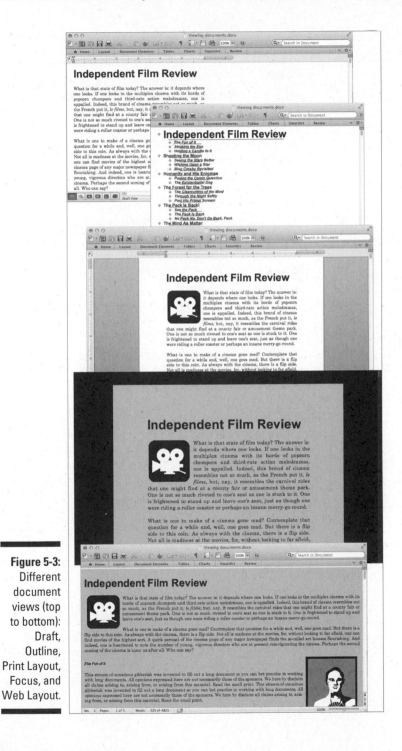

Table 5-1	Ways of Viewing Documents
View	*Purpose*
Draft	Focus on writing your document. Clip-art images, shapes, and other objects don't appear. Draft view is best for writing first drafts.
Outline	See how your work is organized. You can see only the headings in a document. You can get a sense of how your document unfolds and easily move sections of text backward and forward in a document. In other words, you can reorganize a document in Outline view. Chapter 8 explains outlines in torturous detail.
Publishing Layout	Create sophisticated documents such as newsletters and brochures using tools provided by Word. Word asks you to create a new document when you switch to this view.
Print Layout	See what your document will look like when you print it. You can see graphics, headers, footers, and even page borders in Print Layout view. You can also see clearly where page breaks occur (where one page ends and the next begins).
Notebook Layout	Take notes on a document you're working on. Word asks you to create a new document when you switch to this view.
Focus	Focus on the text itself and proofread your documents. Everything gets stripped away — the Ribbon, scroll bars, status bar, and all. All you see is the text and artwork in your documents. Press Esc to leave Focus view.
Web Layout	See what your document would look like as a web page. (This view is available from the View menu.)

When you tire of this split-screen arrangement, drag the line that divides the screen to the top or bottom of the screen. You can also double-click the line that splits the screen in two.

In a split screen, you can choose a different view for the different halves. For example, click in the top half of the screen and choose Outline view to see your document in outline form, and click the bottom half and choose Draft view to see the other half in Draft view. This way, for example, you can see the headings in a document while you write the introduction.

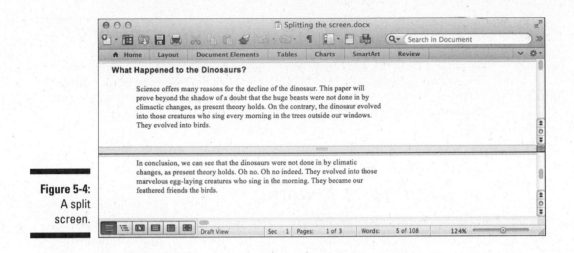

Figure 5-4:
A split
screen.

Selecting Text in Speedy Ways

After you enter text, you inevitably have to reformat, copy, move, or delete it, but you can't do those tasks until you select it first. Table 5-2 describes shortcuts for selecting text. To select text by clicking or dragging in the left margin, move the pointer into the left margin and click or drag when the pointer turns into an arrow.

Table 5-2	Shortcuts for Selecting Text
To Select This	*Do This*
A word	Double-click the word.
A line	Click in the left margin next to the line.
Some lines	Drag the mouse pointer over the lines or drag it down the left margin.
A sentence	Command+click the sentence.
A paragraph	Double-click in the left margin next to the paragraph.
A mess of text	Click at the start of the text, hold down the Shift key, and click at the end of the text.
A document	Triple-click in the left margin, press Command+A, or choose Edit⇨Select All.

Moving Around Quickly in Documents

Besides sliding the scroll bar, Word offers a handful of very speedy techniques for jumping around in documents: clicking a heading or page in the sidebar, browsing in the Select Browse Object menu, and using bookmarks. Read on to discover how to get there faster, faster, faster.

Navigating from page to page or heading to heading

In lengthy documents such as the one in Figure 5-5, the best way to get from place to place is to make use of the *sidebar.* Click a heading or thumbnail page in the sidebar and Word takes you there in the twinkling of an eye.

Click a heading

Click a page thumbnail

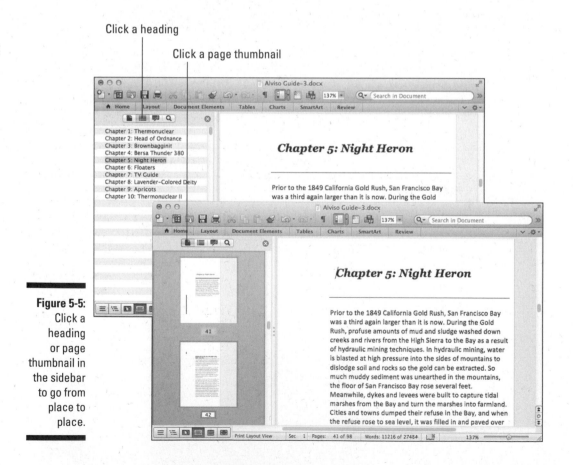

Figure 5-5:
Click a heading or page thumbnail in the sidebar to go from place to place.

To display the sidebar, click the Show/Hide the Sidebar button on the Standard toolbar or choose View ⇨ Sidebar ⇨ Document Map Pane. Then select a tab in the sidebar and go to it:

- **Going from heading to heading:** Select the Document Map tab. Headings in your document appear (provided that you assigned heading styles to headings). You can use the Document Map like a table of contents and click headings to get from place to place. Right-click a heading and choose a heading-level option on the shortcut menu to tell Word which headings to display. You can also right-click a heading and choose Expand or Collapse to see or hide lower-level headings.

- **Going from page to page:** Select the Thumbnail Pane tab. A thumbnail image of each page in the document appears. To quickly move from page to page, use the scroll bar in the sidebar or click a page thumbnail. Each thumbnail is numbered so that you always know which page you are viewing.

"Browsing" around a document

A really fast way to move around is to click the Select Browse Object button in the lower-right corner of the screen. When you click this little round button, Word presents 12 *Browse By* icons, including Browse by Heading, Browse by Table, and Browse by Page. Select the icon that represents the element you want to go to, and Word takes you there immediately. For example, click the Browse by Heading icon to get to the next heading in your document (provided that you assigned heading styles to headings).

After you select a Browse By icon, the navigator buttons — the double arrows directly above and below the Select Browse Object button — change purpose. Click a navigator button to get to the next example or the previous example of the element you chose. For example, if you selected the Browse by Heading icon, all you have to do is click the navigator buttons to get from heading to heading, backward or forward in your document.

Bookmarks for hopping around

Rather than press PgUp or PgDn or click the scroll bar to thrash around in a long document, you can use *bookmarks*. All you do is put a bookmark in an important spot in your document that you'll return to many times. To return to that spot, open the Bookmark dialog box and select a bookmark name, as shown in Figure 5-6. True to the craft, the mystery writer whose bookmarks are shown in Figure 5-6 wrote the end of the story first and used bookmarks to jump back and forth between the beginning and end to make all the clues fit together.

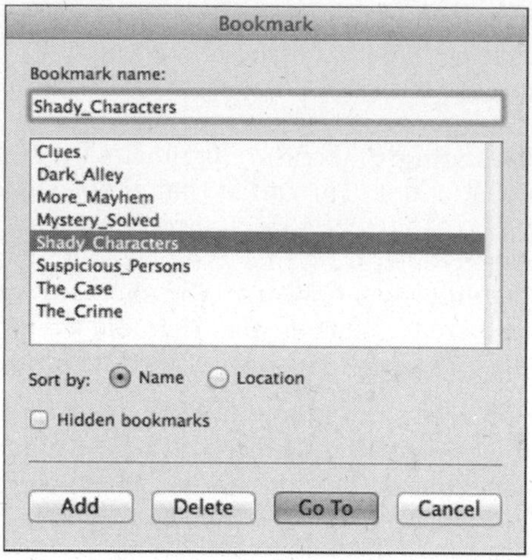

Bookmark

Bookmark name:

Shady_Characters

Clues
Dark_Alley
More_Mayhem
Mystery_Solved
Shady_Characters
Suspicious_Persons
The_Case
The_Crime

Sort by: ● Name   ○ Location

☐ Hidden bookmarks

[Add]   [Delete]   [**Go To**]   [Cancel]

Figure 5-6:
The
Bookmark
dialog box.

Follow these instructions to handle bookmarks:

- ✔ **Adding a bookmark:** Click where you want the bookmark to go and choose Insert⇨Bookmark. Then, in the Bookmark dialog box, type a descriptive name in the Bookmark Name box, and click the Add button. Bookmarks can't start with numbers or include blank spaces. You can also open the Bookmark dialog box by pressing Command+Shift+F5.

- ✔ **Going to a bookmark:** Choose Insert⇨Bookmark, and in the Bookmark dialog box, select a bookmark and click the Go To button.

- ✔ **Deleting a bookmark:** Select the bookmark in the Bookmark dialog box and click the Delete button.

Word uses bookmarks for many purposes. For example, bookmarks indicate where cross-references are located in a document.

Inserting a Whole File into a Document

One of the beautiful things about word processing is being able to recycle documents. Say that you wrote an essay on the Scissor-Tailed Flycatcher that would fit very nicely in a broader report on North American birds. You can insert the Scissor-Tailed Flycatcher document into your report document:

Paragraphs and formatting

Back in English class, your teacher taught you that a paragraph is a part of a longer composition that presents one idea or, in the case of dialogue, presents the words of one speaker. Your teacher was right, too, but for word-processing purposes, a paragraph is a lot less than that. In word processing, a paragraph is simply what you put onscreen before you press the Return key.

For instance, a heading is a paragraph. If you press Return on a blank line to go to the next line, the blank line is considered a paragraph.

If you type **Dear John** at the top of a letter and press Return, "Dear John" is a paragraph.

It's important to know this because paragraphs have a lot to do with formatting. When you monkey around with the paragraph formatting commands, your changes affect everything in the paragraph where the cursor is located. To make format changes to a whole paragraph, all you have to do is place the cursor there. You don't have to select the paragraph. And if you want to make format changes to several paragraphs, all you have to do is select those paragraphs first.

1. **Place the cursor where you want to insert the document.**
2. **Choose Insert⇨File.**

   You see the Insert File dialog box.
3. **Find and select the file you want to insert.**
4. **Click the Insert button.**

Inserting Line, Page, and Section Breaks

I know what you're thinking. You're thinking, "Give me a break," and the following pages do just that. They explain how to insert line breaks, page breaks, and section breaks.

Breaking a line

To break a line of text before it reaches the right margin without starting a new paragraph, press Shift+Return. Figure 5-7 shows how you can press Shift+Return to make lines break better. The paragraphs are identical, but I broke lines in the right-side paragraph to make the text easier to read. Line breaks are marked with the ↵ symbol. To erase line breaks, click the Show All Nonprinting Characters button on the Standard toolbar to see these symbols and then backspace over them.

Figure 5-7:
Break lines
to make
reading
easier.

"A computer in every home and a chicken in every pot is our goal!" stated Rupert T. Verguenza, president and CEO of the New Technics Corporation International at the annual shareholder meeting yesterday.	"A computer in every home and a chicken in every pot is our goal!" stated Rupert T. Verguenza, president and CEO of the New Technics Corporation International at the annual shareholder meeting yesterday.

Starting a new page

Word gives you another page so that you can keep going when you fill up one page. But what if you're impatient and want to start a new page right away? Whatever you do, *don't* press Return again and again until you fill up the page. Instead, create a *hard page break* by doing one of the following on the Insert tab:

- On the Layout tab, click the Break button and choose Page on the drop-down menu.
- Choose Insert ⇨ Break ⇨ Page Break.

In Draft view, you can click the Show All Nonprinting Characters button on the Standard toolbar and tell where you inserted a hard page break because you see the words `Page Break` onscreen. You can't tell where hard page breaks are in Print Layout view.

To delete a hard page break, switch to Draft view, click the Show All Nonprinting Characters button, click the words `Page Break`, and press the Delete key.

Inserting a section break for formatting purposes

When you want to change page numbering schemes, headers and footers, margin sizes, and page orientations in a document, you have to create a *section break* to start a new section. Word creates a new section for you when you create newspaper-style columns or change the size of margins.

Follow these steps to create a new section:

1. **Click where you want to insert a section break.**
2. **On the Layout or Document Elements tab, click the Break button.**

   You open a drop-down menu.
3. **Under Section Breaks on the drop-down menu, select a section break.**

All four section break options create a new section, but they do so in different ways:

- **Next Page:** Inserts a page break as well as a section break so that the new section can start at the top of a new page (the next one). Select this option to start a new chapter, for example.

- **Continuous:** Inserts a section break in the middle of a page. Select this option if, for example, you want to introduce newspaper-style columns in the middle of a page.

- **Even Page:** Starts the new section on the next even page. This option is good for two-sided documents in which the headers on the left- and right-side pages are different.

- **Odd Page:** Starts the new section on the next odd page. You might choose this option if you have a book in which chapters start on odd pages. (By convention, that's where they start.)

To delete a section break, make sure that you are in Draft view. Then drag over the break to select it and press the Delete key.

In the same way that paragraph marks store formats for a paragraph, section breaks store formats for an entire section. When you delete a section break, you apply new formats, because the section is folded into the section that formerly followed it and the section you deleted adopts that next section's formats. Because it's easy to accidentally delete a section break and create havoc, I recommend working in Draft view when your document has many section breaks. In Draft view, you can tell where a section ends because `Section Break` and a double line appear onscreen.

Setting Up and Changing the Margins

Margins are the empty spaces along the left, right, top, and bottom of a page, as shown in Figure 5-8. Headers and footers fall, respectively, in the top and bottom margins. And you can put graphics, text boxes, and page numbers in the margins as well. Margins serve to frame the text and make it easier to read.

When you start a new document, give a moment's thought to the margins. Changing the size of margins after you have entered the text, clip art, graphics, and whatnot can be disastrous. Text is indented from the left and right margins. Pages break on the bottom margin. If you change margin settings, indents and page breaks change for good or ill throughout your document. By setting the margins carefully from the beginning, you can rest assured that text will land on the page where you want it to land.

Outside margin   Inside margins   Outside margin

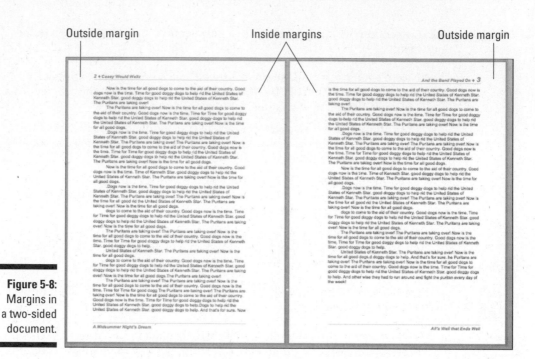

Figure 5-8:
Margins in
a two-sided
document.

Don't confuse margins with indents. Text is indented from the margin, not from the edge of the page. If you want to change how far text falls from the page edge, indent it. To change margin settings in the middle of a document, you have to create a new section.

To set up or change the margins, go to the Layout tab and click the Margins button. You see a drop-down list with margin settings. Either choose a setting or select Custom Margins to open the Margins tab of the Document dialog box and choose among these commands for handling margins:

- **Changing the size of the margins:** Enter measurements in the Top, Bottom, Left, and Right boxes to tell Word how much blank space to put along the sides of the page.

- **Making room for the gutter:** The *gutter* is the part of the paper that the binding eats into when you bind a document. If you intend to bind your document, enter a measurement in the Gutter box to increase the left or inside margin and make room for the binding. You can see on the pages of the printed version of this book, for example, that the margin closest to the binding is wider than the outside margin.

- **Using mirror margins (inside and outside margins) in two-sided documents:** In a bound document in which text is printed on both sides of the pages, the terms *left margin* and *right margin* are meaningless. What matters instead is in the *inside margin*, the margin in the middle of the page spread next to the bindings, and the *outside margin*, the margin on the outside of the page spread that isn't affected by the bindings (refer to Figure 5-8). Select the Mirror Margins check box and adjust the margins accordingly if you intend to print on both sides of the paper.

✔ **Applying margin changes:** On the Apply To drop-down list, choose Whole Document to apply your margin settings to the entire document; This Section to apply them to a section; or This Point Forward to change margins in the rest of a document. When you choose This Point Forward, Word creates a new section.

Indenting Paragraphs and First Lines

An *indent* is the distance between a margin and the text, not the edge of the page and the text. Word offers a handful of ways to change the indentation of paragraphs. You can change the indentation of first lines as well as entire paragraphs. To start, select all or part of the paragraphs you want to re-indent (just click in a paragraph if you want to re-indent only one paragraph). Then use one of these techniques to indent:

✔ **Left-indent with an Indent button.** On the Home tab, click the Increase Indent or Decrease Indent button. This is the fastest way to indent text, although you can't indent first lines or indent from the right margin this way. The Increase Indent and Decrease Indent buttons are located in the Paragraph area of the Home tab.

✔ **"Eye-ball it" with the ruler.** You can also change indentations by using the ruler to "eyeball it." This technique requires some dexterity with the mouse, but it allows you to see precisely where paragraphs and the first lines of paragraphs are indented. If necessary, display the ruler by choosing View➪Ruler. Then click in or select the paragraph or paragraphs that need indenting and use one of these techniques to re-indent them:

• *Indenting an entire paragraph from the left margin:* Drag the *left-indent marker* on the ruler to the right. Figure 5-9 shows where this marker is located. Dragging the left-indent marker moves the first-line indent marker as well.

• *Indenting the first line of a paragraph:* Drag the *first-line indent marker* to the right (refer to Figure 5-9). This marker determines how far the first line of the paragraph is indented.

• *Making a hanging indent:* Drag the *hanging indent marker* to the right of the first-line indent marker (refer to Figure 5-9). A *hanging indent* is one in which the first line of a paragraph appears to "hang" into the margin because the second and subsequent lines are indented to the right of the start of the first line. Bulleted and numbered lists sometimes employ hanging indents.

- • **Indenting an entire paragraph from the right margin:** Drag the *right-indent marker* to the left (refer to Figure 5-9).

✔ *Indent using the Paragraph dialog box.* Press Option+Command+M to open the Paragraph dialog box. Then, on the Indents and Spacing tab of the dialog box, change the indentation settings. If you want to indent the first line or create a hanging indent, choose First Line or Hanging on the Special drop-down list and enter a measurement in the By box.

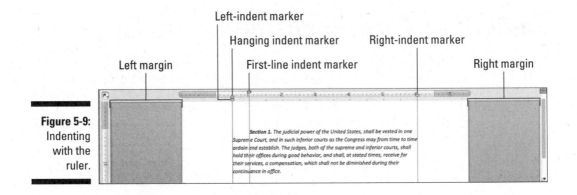

Left-indent marker

Hanging indent marker

Right-indent marker

Left margin

First-line indent marker

Right margin

Figure 5-9:
Indenting
with the
ruler.

Section 1. The judicial power of the United States, shall be vested in one Supreme Court, and in such inferior courts as the Congress may from time to time ordain and establish. The judges, both of the supreme and inferior courts, shall hold their offices during good behavior, and shall, at stated times, receive for their services, a compensation, which shall not be diminished during their continuance in office.

Numbering the Pages

How do you want to number the pages in your document? You can number them in sequence starting with the number 1; start numbering pages with a number other than 1; use Roman numerals or other number formats; and include chapter numbers in page numbers. What's more, you can number the pages differently in each section of your document as long as you divided your document into sections.

When it comes to numbering pages, you can proceed in two ways, as shown in Figure 5-10:

✔ Put a page number by itself on the pages of your document.

✔ Include the page number in the header or footer.

After you enter a page number, you can format it in different ways in the Page Number Format dialog box (refer to Figure 5-10) and the Header and Footer tab.

Choose page number format options

Page number by itself   Page number included in a header

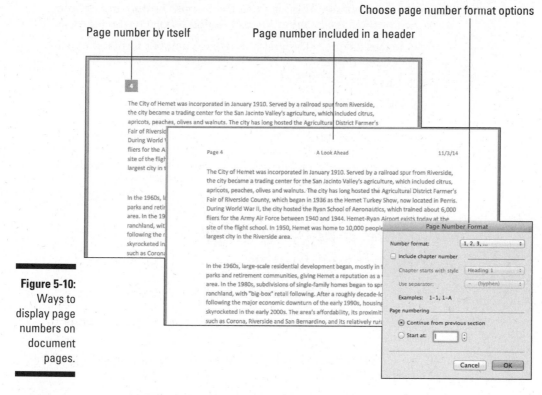

Figure 5-10:
Ways to
display page
numbers on
document
pages.

To handle page numbers (as well as headers and footers), you must be in Print Layout view. Click the Print Layout view button on the status bar or choose View ➪ Print Layout.

Numbering with page numbers only

Follow these steps to insert a page number by itself in the header or footer of the pages:

1. **On the Document Elements tab, click the Page # button.**

   You see the Page Numbers dialog box.

2. **Under Position, choose Top of Page or Bottom of Page.**

3. **Under Alignment, choose where on the top or bottom of pages to put the page number.**

 4. **To choose a number format, click the Format button and choose a format in the Page Number Format dialog box (refer to Figure 5-10).**

 Later in this chapter, "Understanding page number formats" explains page number formats.

 5. **Click OK.**

 Click OK twice if you chose a number format in Step 4.

To remove a page number, double-click in the header or footer where the page number is displayed. Then move the pointer over the page number and, when you see the four-headed arrow, click. This selects the frame where the page number is. With the frame selected, press the Delete key.

Including a page number in a header or footer

Follow these steps to put the page number in a header or footer:

 1. **Click in the header or footer where you want the page number to appear.**

 Later in this chapter, "Putting Headers and Footers on Pages" explains headers and footers.

 2. **On the Header and Footer tab, click the Page # button.**

 The page number appears.

Understanding page number formats

Change page number formats in the Page Number Format dialog box (refer to Figure 5-10). Use this dialog box to make your page numbers just so:

 ✔ **Choosing a different number format:** Open the Number Format drop-down list and choose a page-numbering format. You can use numbers, letters, or Roman numerals.

 ✔ **Including chapter numbers in page numbers:** If your document generates chapter numbers automatically from headings that have been assigned the same style (a subject not covered in this book), you can include the chapter number in the page number. Click the Include Chapter Number check box, choose a style, and choose a separator to go between the chapter number and page number.

✔ **Numbering each section separately:** You can number each section differently if your document is divided into sections (see "Inserting a section break for formatting purposes," earlier in this chapter, for information about sections). Click the Start At option button (not the Continue from Previous Section button) and enter **1** in the text box to begin counting pages anew at each section in your document.

✔ **Start numbering pages at a number other than 1:** Click the Start At option button and enter a number other than 1.

To keep some pages in a document from being numbered, create a section for those pages and then remove page numbers from the section. To paginate your document, Word skips the section you removed the page numbers from and resumes numbering pages in the following section.

Putting Headers and Footers on Pages

A *header* is a little description that appears along the top of a page so that the reader knows what's what. Usually, headers include the page number and a title, and often the author's name appears in the header as well. A *footer* is the same thing as a header except that it appears along the bottom of the page, as befits its name.

These pages explain everything a mere mortal needs to know about headers and footers. Meanwhile, here are the ground rules for managing them:

✔ **Switching to Print Layout view:** To enter, read, edit or delete headers and footers, you must be in Print Layout view. You can't see headers and footers in the other views.

✔ **Displaying the Header and Footer tab:** As shown in Figure 5-11, you manage headers and footers by way of buttons on the Header and Footer tab. To display this tab after you create a header or footer, switch to Print Layout view and double-click a header or footer.

✔ **Closing the Header and Footer tab:** Click the Close button on the header or footer.

✔ **Using different headers and footers:** To use different headers and footers in the same document, you have to create new sections, one for each set of pages that is to have a different header and footer. See "Fine-tuning a header or footer," later in this chapter.

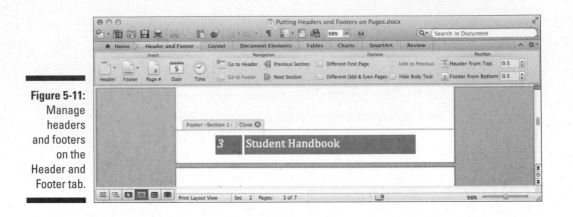

Figure 5-11:
Manage
headers
and footers
on the
Header and
Footer tab.

Creating, editing, and removing headers and footers

Follow these instructions to create, edit, and delete headers and footers:

- ✔ **Creating a header or footer:** On the Document Elements tab, click the Header or the Footer button and click a header or footer style in the gallery. The gallery presents headers or footers with preformatted page numbers, dates, and places to enter a document title and author's name.

- ✔ **Choosing a different header or footer:** Don't like the header or footer you chose? If necessary, double-click your header or footer to display the Header and Footer tab. Then click the Header or Footer button and click a different header or footer style in the gallery.

- ✔ **Removing a header or footer:** Select the header or footer and press the Delete key.

To switch back and forth between the header and footer, click the Go to Header or Go to Footer button on the Header and Footer tab.

As you work away on your header and footer, you can call on most of the text-formatting commands on the Home tab. You can change the text's font and font size, click an alignment button, and paste text from the Clipboard. Tabs are set up in most headers and footers to make it possible to center, left-align, and right-align text.

Fine-tuning a header or footer

To insert a page number, see "Including a page number in a header or footer" and "Understanding page number formats," earlier in this chapter. Additionally, here is advice for making a perfect header on the Header and Footer tab:

- **Inserting the date and time:** Click the Date button and Time button.

- **Changing headers and footers from section to section:** Use the Link to Previous check box to determine whether headers and footers are different from section to section (you must divide a document into sections to have different headers and footers). Deselecting this check box tells Word that you want your header or footer to be different from the header or footer in the previous section of the document; selecting this check box tells Word that you want your header or footer to be the same as the header or footer in the previous section of your document. To make a different header or footer, deselect the Link to Previous check box and enter a different header or footer.

  When the header or footer is the same as that of the previous section, the Header or Footer box reads `Same as Previous`; when the header or footer is different from that of the previous section, the words `Same as Previous` don't appear. You can click the Previous Section or Next Section button to examine the header or footer in the previous or next section.

- **Different headers and footers for odd and even pages:** Click the Different Odd & Even Pages check box to create different headers and footers for odd and even pages. As "Setting Up and Changing the Margins" explains earlier in this chapter, documents in which text is printed on both sides of the page can have different headers and footers for the left and right side of the page spread. The Header or Footer box reads `Odd Page Header` or `Even Page Header` to tell you which side of the page spread you're dealing with as you enter your header or footer.

- **Removing headers and footers from the first page:** Click the Different First Page check box to remove a header or footer from the first page of a document or section. Typically, the first page of letters and reports is not numbered.

Adjusting the Space between Lines

To change the spacing between lines, select the lines whose spacing you want to change, or simply put the cursor in a paragraph if you're changing the line spacing throughout a paragraph (if you're just starting a document, you're ready to go). Then, on the Home tab, click the Line Spacing button and choose an option on the drop-down list.

To take advantage of more line-spacing options, click the Line Spacing button on the Home tab and choose Line Spacing Options on the drop-down list (or press Option+Command+M). You see the Paragraph dialog box shown in Figure 5-12. The first three options on the Line Spacing drop-down list are self-explanatory. Here's what the options are about:

- **At Least:** Choose this one if you want Word to adjust for tall symbols or other unusual text. Word adjusts the lines but makes sure there is, at minimum, the number of points you enter in the At box between each line.

- **Exactly:** Choose this one and enter a number in the At box if you want a specific amount of space between lines.

- **Multiple:** Choose this one and put a number in the At box to get triple-spaced, quadruple-, quintuple-, or any other number of spaced lines.

To quickly double-space text, select the text and press Command+2. Press Command+5 to put one and a half lines between lines of text.

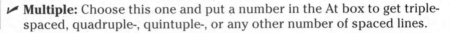

Figure 5-12:
Press
Option+
Command+
M to
open the
Paragraph
dialog box.

Adjusting the Space between Paragraphs

Rather than press Return to put a blank line between paragraphs, you can open the Paragraph dialog box (see Figure 5-12) and enter a point-size measurement in the Before or After text box. To open the Paragraph dialog box, press Option+Command+M. The Before and After measurements place a specific amount of space before and after paragraphs. The Don't Add Space between Paragraphs of the Same Style check box tells Word to ignore Before and After measurements if the previous or next paragraph is assigned the same style as the paragraph that the cursor is in.

Truth be told, the Before and After options are for use with styles (a subject of Chapter 6). When you create a style, you can tell Word to always follow a paragraph in a certain style with a paragraph in another style. For example, a paragraph in the Chapter Title style might always be followed by a paragraph in the Chapter Intro style. In a case like this, when you know that paragraphs assigned to one type of style will always follow paragraphs assigned to another style (remember that any line that ends with a Return is considered a paragraph), you can confidently put space before and after paragraphs. But if you use the Before and After styles indiscriminately, you can end up with large blank spaces between paragraphs.

Creating Numbered and Bulleted Lists

What is a document without a list or two? It's like an emperor with no clothes. Numbered lists are invaluable in manuals and books like this one that present a lot of step-by-step procedures. Use bulleted lists when you want to present alternatives to the reader. A *bullet* is a black, filled-in circle or other character. These pages explain numbered lists and bulleted lists.

Simple numbered and bulleted lists

The fastest, cleanest, and most honest way to create a numbered or bulleted list is to enter the text without any concern for numbers or bullets. Just press Return at the end of each step or bulleted entry. When you're done, select the list, go to the Home tab, and click the Numbered List or Bulleted List button. You can also click the Numbered List or Bulleted List button and start typing the list. Each time you press Return, Word enters the next number or another bullet.

Meanwhile, here are some tricks for handling lists:

- ✔ **Ending a list:** Press the Return key twice after typing the last entry in the list.
- ✔ **Removing the numbers or bullets:** Select the list and click the Numbered List or Bulleted List button.

Constructing lists of your own

If you're an individualist and want numbered and bulleted lists to work your way, follow these instructions for choosing unusual bullet characters and number formats:

- ✔ **Choosing a different numbering scheme:** On the Home tab, open the drop-down list on the Numbered List button and choose a numbering scheme. You can also choose Define New Number Format. As shown in Figure 5-13, you see the Customize Numbered List dialog box, where you can choose a number format, choose a font for numbers, and toy with number alignments.

- ✔ **Choosing a different bullet character:** On the Home tab, open the drop-down list on the Bulleted List button and choose a different bullet character on the drop-down list. You can also choose Define New Bullet to open the Customize Bulleted List dialog box, shown in Figure 5-13, and click the Bullet button to choose a bullet character in the Symbol dialog box. The dialog box also offers opportunities for indenting bullets and the text that follows them in unusual ways.

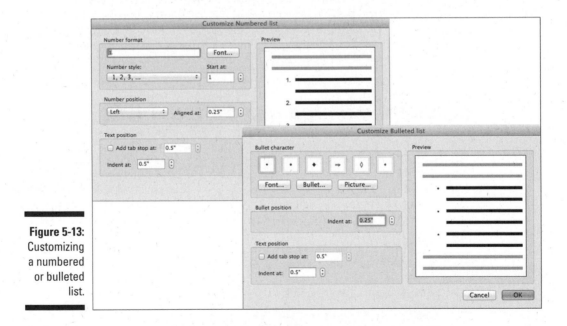

Figure 5-13: Customizing a numbered or bulleted list.

Hyphenating Text

The first thing you should know about hyphenating words is that you may not need to do it. Text that hasn't been hyphenated is much easier to read, which is why the majority of text in this book, for example, isn't hyphenated. It has a *ragged right margin,* to borrow typesetter lingo. Hyphenate only when text is trapped in columns or in other narrow places, or when you want a very formal-looking document.

Do not insert a hyphen simply by pressing the hyphen key, because the hyphen will stay there even if the word moves to the middle of a line and doesn't need to be broken in half. Instead, when a big gap appears in the right margin and a word is crying out to be hyphenated, put the cursor where the hyphen needs to go and press Command+hyphen. This way, you enter what is called a *soft hyphen* or *optional hyphen,* and the hyphen appears only if the word breaks at the end of a line. (To remove a soft hyphen, click the Show All Nonprinting Characters button on the Standard toolbar so that you can see it, and then backspace over it.)

Automatically and manually hyphenating a document

Select text if you want to hyphenate part of a document, not all of it, and use one of these techniques to hyphenate words that break on the end of a line of text:

- **Automatic hyphenation:** On the Layout tab, click the Hyphenation button to open the Hyphenation dialog box, shown in Figure 5-14. Choose Automatically Hyphenate Document and click OK. Word hyphenates your document (or a portion of your document, if you selected it first).

  You can tell Word how to hyphenate automatically in the Hyphenation dialog box. Deselect the Hyphenate Words in CAPS check box if you don't care to hyphenate words in uppercase. Words that fall in the hyphenation zone are hyphenated, so enlarging the hyphenation zone means a less ragged right margin but more ugly hyphens, and a small zone means fewer ugly hyphens but a more ragged right margin. You can limit how many hyphens appear consecutively by entering a number in the Limit Consecutive Hyphens To box.

- **Manual hyphenation:** On the Layout tab, click the Hyphenation button to open the Hyphenation dialog box (see in Figure 5-14), and click the Manual button. Word displays a box with some hyphenation choices in it, as shown in Figure 5-14. The cursor blinks on the spot where Word suggests putting a hyphen. Click Yes or No to accept or reject Word's suggestion. Keep accepting or rejecting Word's suggestions until the text is hyphenated.

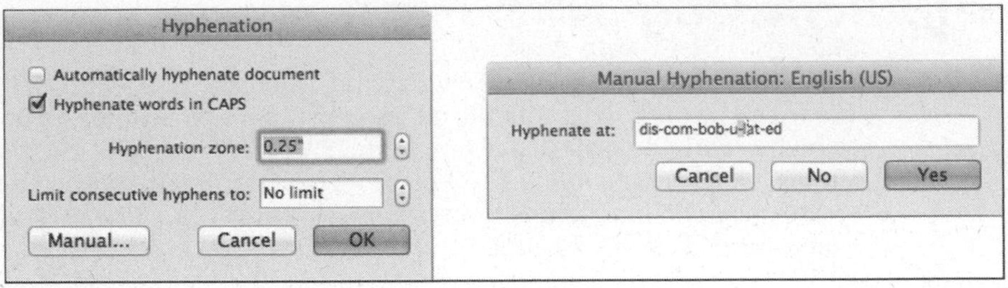

Figure 5-14:
Telling
Word how
to hyphen-
ate (left)
and decid-
ing where
a hyphen
goes (right).

Unhyphenating and other hyphenation tasks

More hyphenation esoterica:

- ✔ **Unhyphenating:** To "unhyphenate" a document or text that you hyphen-ated automatically, open the Hyphenation dialog box (see Figure 5-14), deselect the Automatically Hyphenate Document check box, and click OK.

- ✔ **Preventing text from being hyphenated:** Select the text and press Option+Command+M to open the Paragraph dialog box. Then, on the Line and Page Breaks tab, select the Don't Hyphenate check box. (If you can't hyphenate a paragraph, it's probably because this box was selected unintentionally.)

Em and en dashes

Here is something about hyphens that editors and typesetters know, but the general public does not know: There is a difference between hyphens and dashes. Most people insert a hyphen where they ought to use an em dash or an en dash:

- ✔ An *em dash* looks like a hyphen but is wider — it's as wide as the letter *m*. The previous sentence has an em dash in it. Did you notice?

- ✔ An *en dash* is the width of the letter *n*. Use en dashes to show inclusive numbers or

time periods, like so: pp. 45–50; Aug.–Sept. 1998; Exodus 16:11–16:18. An en dash is a little bit longer than a hyphen.

To place an em or en dash in a document and impress your local typesetter or editor, not to mention your readers, press Command+Option+– (the minus-sign key on the numeric keypad) to enter an em dash, or Command+– (on the numeric keypad) to enter an en dash. You can also choose Insert ➪ Symbol ➪ Advanced Symbol and choose Em Dash or En Dash in the Symbol dialog box.

Chapter 6

Word Styles

*I*f you want to be stylish, at least where Word is concerned, you have to know about styles. Styles can save a ridiculous amount of time that you would otherwise spend formatting and wrestling with text. And many Word features rely on styles. You can't create a table of contents or use the Document Map pane unless each heading in your document has been assigned a heading style. Nor can you take advantage of Outline view and the commands for moving text around in that view. You can't cross-reference headings or number the headings in a document.

All about Styles

A *style* is a collection of formatting commands assembled under one name. When you apply a style, you give many formatting commands simultaneously, and you spare yourself the trouble of visiting numerous tabs and dialog boxes to format text. Styles save time and make documents look more professional. Headings assigned the same style — Heading 1, for example — all look the same. When readers see that headings and paragraphs are consistent with one another across all the pages of a document, they get a warm, fuzzy feeling. They think that the person who created the document really knew what he or she was doing.

Styles and templates

Every document comes with built-in styles that it inherits from the template with which it was created. You can create your own styles to supplement styles from the template. For that matter, you can create a template, populate it with styles that you design, and use your new template to create distinctive letters or reports for your company.

A simple document created with the Blank Document template — a document that you create by pressing Command+N — has only a few styles, but a document that was created with a sophisticated template comes with many styles. The template shown in Figure 6-1, for example, comes with styles for formatting titles, subtitles, headings, and quotations. Figure 6-1 illustrates how choosing styles from a template changes text formatting. Notice how choosing style options in the Styles toolbox reformats the text.

Types of styles

In the Styles toolbox (refer to Figure 6-1), the symbol next to each style name tells you what type of style you're dealing with. Word offers two style types you need to know about:

- ✔ **Paragraph styles:** Determine the formatting of entire paragraphs. A paragraph style can include these settings: font, paragraph, tab, border, language, bullets, numbering, and text effects. Paragraph styles are marked with the paragraph symbol (¶) next to their names.

- ✔ **Character styles:** Apply to text, not to paragraphs. You select text before you apply a character style. Create a character style for text that is hard to lay out and for foreign-language text. A character style can include these settings: font, border, language, and text effects. When

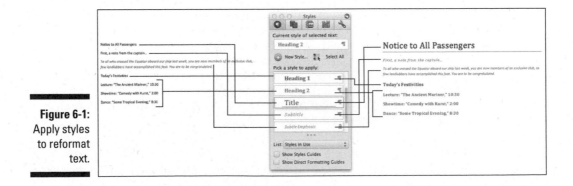

Figure 6-1:
Apply styles
to reformat
text.

you apply a character style to text, the character-style settings override the paragraph-style settings. For example, if the paragraph style calls for 14-point Arial font but the character style calls for 12-point Times Roman font, the character style wins. Character styles are marked with the letter *a* next to their names.

Applying Styles to Text and Paragraphs

Word offers several ways to apply a style, and you are invited to choose the one that works best for you. These pages explain how to apply a style and tell Word how to present style names in the various places where style names are presented for your enjoyment and pleasure.

Applying a style

The first step in applying a style is to select the part of your document that needs a style change:

- **A paragraph or paragraphs:** Because paragraph styles apply to all the text in a paragraph, you need only click in a paragraph before applying a style to make a style apply throughout the paragraph. To apply a style to several paragraphs, select all or part of them.

- **Text:** To apply a character style, select the letters whose formatting you want to change.

Next, apply the style with one of these techniques:

- **Quick Style gallery:** On the Home tab, choose a style in the Quick Style gallery. Figure 6-2 shows where the Quick Style gallery is located. Either scroll in the gallery to locate a style or click the down-arrow to open the gallery in full. The formatted letters above each style name in the gallery show you what your style choice will do to paragraphs or text.

- **Styles toolbox:** Choose a style in the Styles toolbox, as shown in Figure 6-2. To open the Styles toolbox, go to the Home tab and click the Manage Styles That Are Used in This Document button (or choose View⇨Styles). For viewing convenience, you can drag the Styles toolbox to different locations on your screen. It remains onscreen after you leave the Home tab.

To strip a paragraph or text of its style and give it the generic Normal style, select it and choose Clear Formatting in the Styles gallery or Clear All at the top of the Styles pane.

Styles toolbox   Quick Style gallery

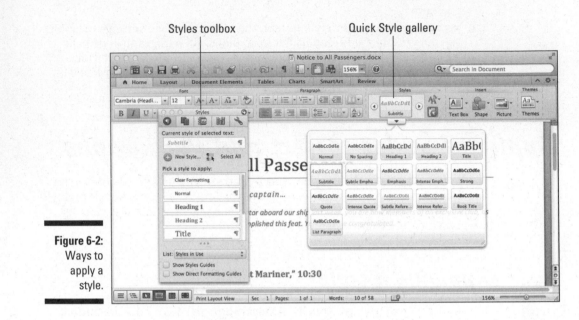

Figure 6-2:
Ways to
apply a
style.

Experimenting with style sets

A *style set* is a slight variation on the styles in the template you chose when you created your document. Style sets include Classic, Elegant, Fancy, and Modern. Choosing a style set imposes a slightly different look on your document — you make it classier, more elegant, fancier, or more modern. Style sets are a convenient way to experiment with the overall look of a document.

To experiment with style sets, go to the Home tab, click the Change Quick Style Settings button, and do one of the following on the submenu that appears:

✔ **Choose a new style set:** Select a style set on the submenu.

✔ **Use the original styles in the template:** Choose Reset to Quick Styles from Template on the submenu.

Choosing which style names appear on the Style menus

One of the challenges of applying styles is finding the right style to apply in the Quick Style gallery or Styles toolbox (refer to Figure 6-2). The gallery and toolbox can become crowded with style names. To make finding and

Determining which style is in use

How can you tell which style has been applied to a paragraph or text? Sometimes you need to know which style is in play before you decide whether applying a different style is necessary.

Click the paragraph or text and use these techniques to find out which style was applied to it:

✔ **Glance at the Quick Style gallery or Styles toolbox to see which style is selected.** The selected style is the one that was applied to your paragraph or text.

✔ **Click the Show Styles Guides check box in the Styles toolbox.** Numbers appear next to style names in the toolbox, with one number for each style; corresponding numbers appear on the left side of your document to show which style is in play.

✔ **Choose Format ⇨ Style.** The Style dialog box appears. Note which style is selected in the dialog box.

choosing styles names easier, you can decide for yourself which names appear on these two style menus.

You can put the name of a style you create in the Quick Style gallery and Styles toolbox. See "Creating a New Style," later in this chapter.

Quick Style gallery

In the Quick Style gallery, remove a style name by right-clicking it and choosing Remove from Quick Style Gallery. If you regret removing style names, click the Change Quick Styles Settings button and choose Reset to Quick Styles from Template.

Styles toolbox

To decide for yourself which style names appear in the Styles toolbox, open the toolbox (click the Manage Styles That Are Used in This Document button to do so). Then, on the list menu, choose All Styles to show all style names or one of the other options to place a subset of names in the toolbox. The Recommended option puts style names that Microsoft thinks you need most often in the toolbox.

Creating a New Style

Create a new style to make formatting easier. After you create your style, you can make it part of the template that you're currently working in as well as copy it to other templates (later in this chapter, "Creating Templates" explains templates).

To get a head start on creating a style, format text or a paragraph with the font and other elements you want for the style. Then open the Styles toolbox and click the New Style button. You see the New Style dialog box shown in Figure 6-3. Fill in the dialog box and click OK.

Here's a rundown of the options in the New Style dialog box:

- ✔ **Name:** Enter a descriptive name for the style.

- ✔ **Style Type:** On the drop-down list, choose a style type ("Types of styles," earlier in this chapter, describes the style types).

- ✔ **Style Based On:** If your new style is similar to a style that is already part of the template with which you created your document, choose the style to get a head start on creating the new one. Be warned, however, that if you or someone else changes the Based On style, your new style will inherit those changes and be altered as well.

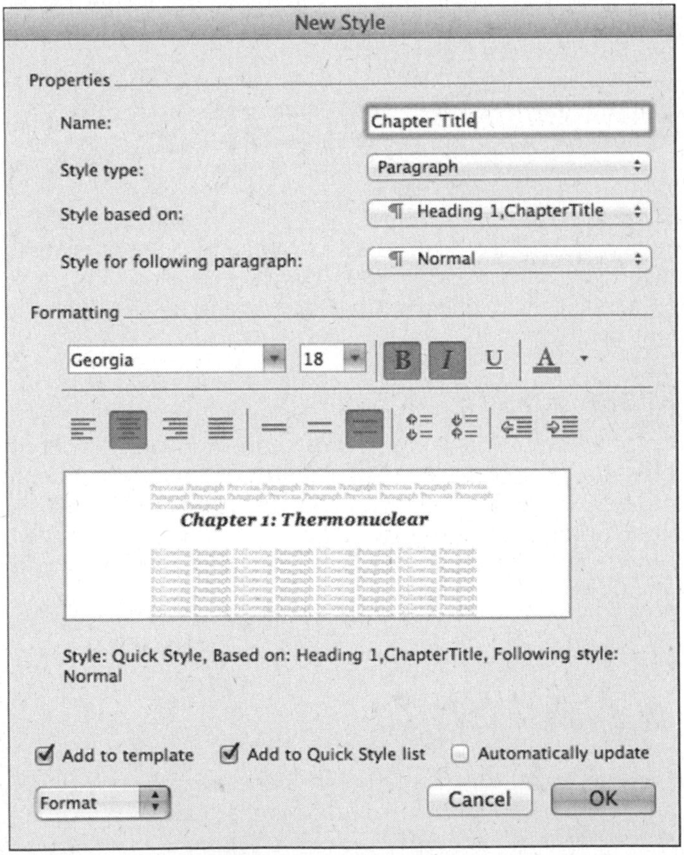

New Style	
Properties	
Name:	Chapter Title
Style type:	Paragraph
Style based on:	¶ Heading 1,ChapterTitle
Style for following paragraph:	¶ Normal

Formatting

Georgia   18   **B** *I* U A

Previous Paragraph Previous Paragraph Previous Paragraph Previous Paragraph Previous Paragraph Previous Paragraph Previous Paragraph Previous Paragraph Previous Paragraph Previous Paragraph

Chapter 1: Thermonuclear

Following Paragraph Following Paragraph Following Paragraph Following Paragraph Following Paragraph Following Paragraph Following Paragraph Following Paragraph Following Paragraph Following Paragraph Following Paragraph Following Paragraph Following Paragraph Following Paragraph Following Paragraph Following Paragraph Following Paragraph Following Paragraph Following Paragraph Following Paragraph

Style: Quick Style, Based on: Heading 1,ChapterTitle, Following style: Normal

☑ Add to template   ☑ Add to Quick Style list   ☐ Automatically update

Format   Cancel   OK

Figure 6-3:
Creating a brand-spanking-new style.

- **Style for Following Paragraph:** Choose a style from the drop-down list if the style you're creating is always followed by an existing style. For example, a new style called Chapter Title might always be followed by a style called Chapter Intro Paragraph. For convenience, someone who applies the style you're creating and presses Return automatically applies the style you choose here on the next line of the document. Applying a style automatically to the following paragraph saves you the trouble of having to apply the style yourself.

- **Formatting:** Choose options from the menus or click buttons to fashion or refine your style. (You can also click the Format button to do this.)

- **Add to Template:** Select this check box to make your style a part of the template from which you created your document as well as the document itself. This way, new documents you create that are based on the template you are using can also make use of the new style.

- **Add to Quick Style List:** Select this check box to make the style's name appear in the Quick Style gallery and Styles toolbox.

- **Automatically Update:** Normally, when you make a formatting change to a paragraph, the style assigned to the paragraph does not change at all, but the style does change if you select this box. Selecting this box tells Word to alter the style itself each time you alter a paragraph to which you've assigned the style. With this box selected, all paragraphs in the document that were assigned the style are altered each time you change a single paragraph that was assigned the style.

- **Format:** This is the important one. Click the button and make a formatting choice. Word takes you to dialog boxes so that you can create or refine the style.

Modifying a Style

What if you decide at the end of an 80-page document that all 35 introductory paragraphs to which you assigned the Intro Para style look funny? If you clicked the Automatically Update check box in the New Style dialog box when you created the style, all you have to do is alter a paragraph to which you assigned the Intro Para style to alter all 35 introductory paragraphs. However, if you decided against updating styles automatically, you can still change the introductory paragraphs throughout your document.

Follow these steps to modify a style that isn't updated automatically:

1. Choose Format⇨Style.

You see the Style dialog box.

2. **In the Styles menu, select the name of the style you want to modify.**

3. **Click the Modify button.**

   You see the Modify Style dialog box. Does the dialog box look familiar? It is nearly identical to the New Style dialog box that you used to create the style in the first place (refer to Figure 6-3). The only difference is that you can't choose a style type in the Modify Style dialog box.

4. **Change the settings in the Modify Style dialog box and click OK.**

   The previous section in this chapter explains the settings.

After you modify a style, all paragraphs or text to which the style was assigned are instantly changed. You don't have to go back and reformat text and paragraphs throughout your document.

Creating Templates

As I explain at the start of this chapter, every document you create is fashioned from a *template*. The purpose of a template is to store styles for documents. In the act of creating a document, you choose a template, and the styles on the template become available to you when you work on your document. (Chapter 4 explains how to choose a template when you create a new document.)

To save time formatting your documents, you are invited to create templates with styles that you know and love. You can create a new template from scratch, create a template from a document, or create a template by assembling styles from other templates and documents. Styles in templates, like styles in documents, can be modified, deleted, and renamed.

How do you want to create a new template? You can create a new template from a document or other template, or you can assemble styles from other templates. Read on.

To create a document from a template that you created yourself, open the Word Document Gallery (click the New From Template button on the Standard toolbar) and click My Templates. Your self-made templates appear in the gallery. Select a template and click the Choose button.

Creating a template from a document

If a document has all or most of the styles you want for a template, convert the document into a template so you can use the styles in documents you create in the future. Follow these steps to create a Word template from a Word document:

1. **Open the Word document you will use to create a template.**

2. **Choose File ⇨ Save As.**

   The Save As dialog box appears.

3. **Enter a name for your template.**

4. **Open the Format menu and choose Word Template.**

   After you choose Word Template, the Where option in the dialog box changes to My Templates. Word templates are kept in the My Templates folder. Next time you create a document, you can go to the My Templates folder in the Word Document Gallery and create a document with your new template.

5. **Click the Save button.**

Probably your new template includes text that it inherited from the document it was created from. Delete the text (unless you want it to appear in documents you create from your new template).

Assembling styles from other documents and templates

Use the Organizer to copy styles from a document to a template or from one template to another. After making a style a part of a template, you can call upon the style in other documents. You can call upon it in each document you create or created with the template. Follow these steps to copy a style between templates and documents:

1. **Open the document or template with the styles you want to copy.**

   To copy styles from a document, open the document. To copy styles from a template, create a new document using the template with the styles you want to copy.

2. **Choose Tools ⇨ Templates and Add-Ins.**

   The Templates and Add-Ins dialog box appears.

3. **Click the Organizer button.**

   You see the Organizer dialog box, shown in Figure 6-4. Styles in the document or template that you opened in Step 1 appear in the In list box on the left side.

Select the styles you want to copy

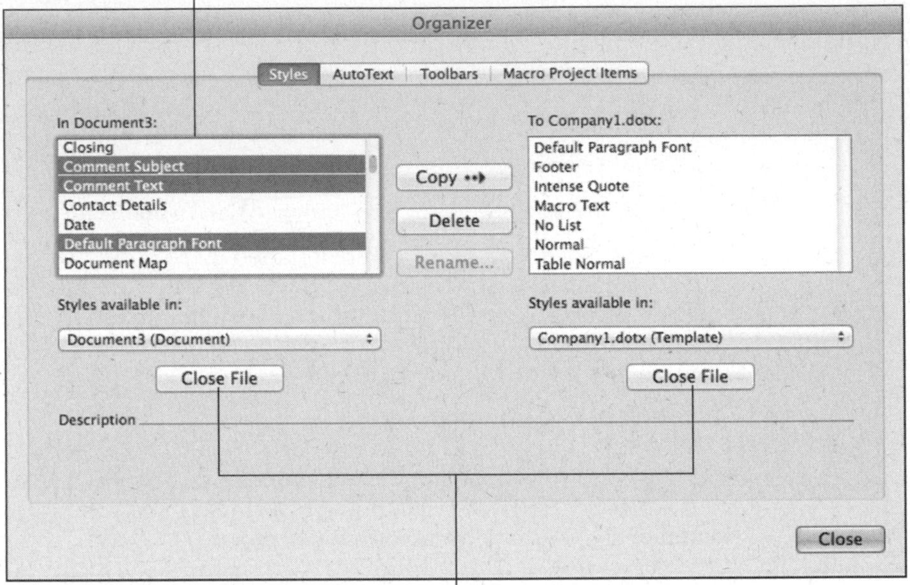

Figure 6-4:
Copying
styles to a
template.

Click to close one template and open another

Attaching a different template to a document

It happens in the best of families. You create or are given a document, only to discover that the wrong template is attached to it. For times like those, Word gives you the opportunity to switch templates. Follow these steps:

1. **Choose Tools ⇨ Templates and Add-Ins.**

   You see the Templates and Add-Ins dialog box.

2. **Click the Attach button to open the Choose a File dialog box.**

3. **Find and select the template you want and click the Open button.**

You return to the Templates and Add-ins dialog box, where the name of the template you chose appears in the Document Template box.

4. **Click the Automatically Update Document Styles check box.**

   Doing so tells Word to apply the styles from the new template to your document.

5. **Click OK.**

4. Click the Close File button on the right side of the dialog box.

The button changes names and becomes the Open File button.

5. Click the Open File button and, in the Open dialog box, find and select the template to which you want to copy styles; then, click the Open button.

The names of styles in the template you chose appear on the right side of the Organizer dialog box.

6. In the Organizer dialog box, Command+click to select the names of styles on the left side of the dialog box that you want to copy to the template listed on the right side of the dialog box.

As you click the names, they become highlighted.

7. Click the Copy button.

The names of styles that you copied appear on the right side of the Organizer dialog box.

8. Click the Close button and click Save when Word asks whether you want to save the new styles in the template.

Chapter 7

Constructing the Perfect Table

- -

In This Chapter

▶ Understanding table jargon

▶ Creating a table and entering the text and numbers

▶ Aligning table text in various ways

▶ Merging and splitting cells to make interesting layouts

▶ Changing the size of rows and columns

▶ Decorating a table with table styles, colors, and borders

▶ Doing math calculations in a Word table

- -

The best way to present a bunch of data at one time is to do it in a table. Viewers can compare and contrast the data. They can compare Elvis sightings in different cities or income from different businesses. They can contrast the number of socks lost in different washing machine brands. A table is a great way to plead your case or defend your position. Readers can refer to your table to get the information they need.

As everyone who has worked on tables knows, however, creating tables is a chore. Getting all the columns to fit, making columns and rows the right width and height, and editing the text in a table isn't easy. This chapter explains how to create tables, enter text in tables, change the number and size of columns and rows, lay out tables, format tables, and do the math in tables.

Talking Table Jargon

As with much else in Computerland, tables have their own jargon. Figure 7-1 describes this jargon. Sorry, but you need to catch up on these terms to construct the perfect table:

> ✔ **Cell:** The box that is formed where a row and column intersect. Each cell holds one data item.

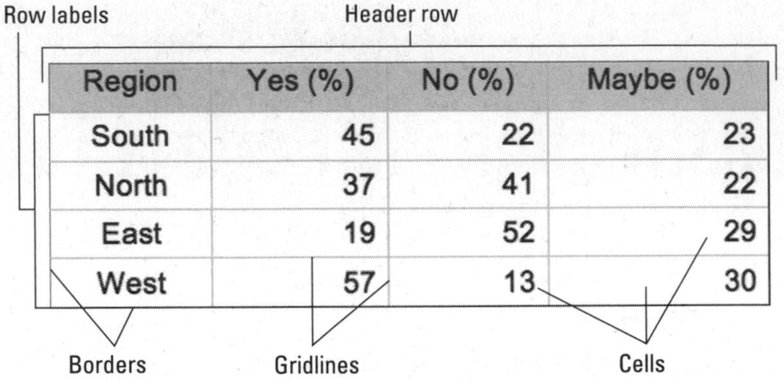

Row labels   Header row

Region	Yes (%)	No (%)	Maybe (%)
South	45	22	23
North	37	41	22
East	19	52	29
West	57	13	30

Figure 7-1:
The parts of
a table.

Borders   Gridlines   Cells

✔ **Header row:** The name of the labels along the top row that explain what is in the columns below.

✔ **Row labels:** The labels in the first column that describe what is in each row.

✔ **Borders:** The lines in the table that define where the rows and columns are.

✔ **Gridlines:** The gray lines that show where the columns and rows are. Unless you've drawn borders around all the cells in a table, you can't tell where rows and columns begin and end without gridlines. To display or hide the gridlines, go to the Table Layout tab and click the Gridlines button.

Creating a Table

Word offers several ways to create a table:

✔ **Drag on the Table menu.** On the Tables tab, click the Insert or Draw a Table button, point in the drop-down list to the number of columns and rows you want, click, and let go of the mouse button.

✔ **Use the Insert Table dialog box.** On the Tables tab, click the Insert or Draw a Table button and then choose Insert Table on the drop-down list. The Insert Table dialog box appears. Enter the number of columns and rows you want and click OK.

✔ **Draw a table.** On the Tables tab, click the Draw button. The pointer changes into a pencil. Draw the table and press the Esc key when you finish drawing.

✔ **Convert text in a list into a table.** Press Tab or enter a comma in each list item where you want the columns in the table to be. For example, to turn an address list into a table, put each name and address on its own line and press Tab or enter a comma after the first name, the last name, the street address, the city, the state, and the ZIP code. For this feature to work, each name and address — each line — must have the same number of tab spaces or commas in it. Select the text you'll convert to a table, click the Insert or Draw a Table button on the Tables tab, and choose Convert Text to Table. Under Separate Text At in the Convert Text to Table dialog box, choose Tabs or Commas to tell Word how the columns are separated. Then click OK.

After you create a table, you get a new tab on the Ribbon called the Table Layout tab. It offers commands for changing around the rows and columns.

Entering the Text and Numbers

After you've created the table, you can start entering text and numbers. All you have to do is click in a cell and start typing. Select your table and take advantage of these techniques to make the onerous task of entering table data a little easier:

✔ **Quickly changing a table's size:** Drag the selection handle (the square in the lower-right corner) to change the table's overall size. You can also go to the Table Layout tab, click the AutoFit button, and choose AutoFit to Window to make the table stretch from margin to margin.

✔ **Moving a table:** In Print Layout view, drag the table selector (the square in the upper-left corner of the table).

✔ **Quickly inserting a new row:** Click in the last column of the last row in your table and press the Tab key to quickly insert a new row at the bottom of the table.

Selecting Different Parts of a Table

It almost goes without saying, but before you can reformat, alter, or diddle with table cells, rows, or columns, you have to select them:

✔ **Selecting cells:** To select a cell, click in it. You can select several adjacent cells by dragging the pointer over them.

✔ **Selecting rows:** Move the pointer just to the left of the row and click when you see the right-pointing arrow; click and drag to select several rows.

✔ **Selecting columns:** Move the pointer above the column and click when you see the down-pointing arrow; click and drag to select several columns.

✔ **Selecting a table:** Click the table selector (the square in the upper-left corner of the table).

Another way to select parts of a table is to go to the menu bar. Choose Table ⇨ Select and choose an option on the submenu.

Aligning Text in Columns and Rows

Aligning text in columns and rows is a matter of choosing how you want the text to line up vertically and how you want it to line up horizontally. Follow these steps to align columns and rows:

1. **Select the cells, columns, or rows that contain text that you want to align (or select your entire table).**

2. **Visit the Table Layout tab.**

3. **Click the Align button.**

4. **Choose an alignment option.**

To align a column with numbers, choose Top Right, Center Right, or Bottom Right to make the numbers line up.

Merging and Splitting Cells

Merge and split cells to make your tables a little more elegant than run-of-the-mill tables. *Merge* cells to break down the barriers between cells and join them into one cell; *split* cells to divide a single cell into several cells (or several cells into several more cells). In the table shown in Figure 7-2, cells in rows and columns have been split or merged to create a curious-looking little table.

Select the cells you want to merge or split, go to the Table Layout tab, and follow these instructions to merge or split cells:

✔ **Merging cells:** Click the Merge button.

✔ **Splitting cells:** Click the Split Cells button. In the Split Cells dialog box, declare how many columns and rows you want to split the cell into and then click OK.

Merge and split table cells

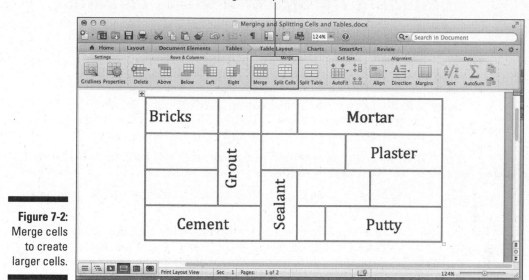

Figure 7-2:
Merge cells
to create
larger cells.

You can merge and split cells by clicking the Draw and Erase buttons on the Tables tab. Click the Draw button and then draw lines through cells to split them. Click the Erase button and drag over or click the boundary between cells to merge cells. Press Esc when you're finished drawing or erasing table cell boundaries. You can click the Lines button and choose a color on the drop-down list to draw in a particular color.

Need to split a table? Place the cursor in what you want to be the first row of the new table, go to the Table Layout tab, and click the Split Table button.

Laying Out Your Table

Very likely, you created too many or too few columns or rows for your table. Some columns are probably too wide and others too narrow. If that's the case, you have to change the table layout by deleting, inserting, and changing the size of columns and rows, not to mention changing the size of the table itself. In other words, you have to modify the table layout. (Later in this chapter, "Decorating your table with borders and colors" shows how to put borders around tables and embellish them in other ways.)

Changing the size of a table, columns, and rows

The fastest way to adjust the width of columns, the height of rows, and the size of a table itself is to "eyeball it" and drag the mouse:

- **Column or row:** Move the pointer onto a gridline or border, and when the pointer changes into a double-headed arrow, start dragging. Tug and pull, tug and pull until the column or row is the right size.

- **A table:** Select your table and use one of these techniques to change its size in Word and PowerPoint:

  - *Dragging:* Drag the selection handle (the square in the lower-right corner).

  - *Table Properties dialog box:* On the Table Layout tab, click the Properties button. Then, in the Table Properties dialog box under Size, enter a measurement in inches or by percentage of the page width.

Adjusting column and row size

Resizing columns and rows can be problematic. For that reason, Word offers special commands on the Table Layout tab for adjusting the width and height of rows and columns:

- **Making all columns the same width:** Click the Distribute Columns button. Select columns before giving this command to make only the columns you select the same width.

- **Making all rows the same height:** Click the Distribute Rows button. Select rows before clicking the button to make only the rows you select the same height.

You can also click the AutoFit button on the Table Layout tab and take advantage of these commands on the drop-down list for handling columns and rows:

- **AutoFit to Contents:** Make each column wide enough to accommodate its widest entry.

- **AutoFit to Window:** Stretch the table so that it fits across the page between the left and right margin.

- **Fixed Column Width:** Fix the column widths at their current settings.

Inserting and deleting columns and rows

The trick to inserting and deleting columns and rows is to correctly select part of the table first. You can insert more than one column or row at a time by selecting more than one column or row before giving the Insert command. To insert two columns, for example, select two columns and choose an Insert command; to insert three rows, select three rows and choose an Insert command. Earlier in this chapter, "Selecting Different Parts of a Table" explains how to make table selections.

Go to the Table Layout tab and follow these instructions to insert and delete columns and rows:

- **Inserting columns:** Select a column or columns and click the Left or Right button. If you want to insert just one column, click in a column and then click the Insert Left or Insert Right button.

- **Inserting rows:** Select a row or rows and click the Above or Insert button. If you want to insert just one row, click in a row and click the Above or Below button. You can also right-click, choose Insert, and choose an Insert Rows command on the shortcut menu.

  To insert a row at the end of a table, move the pointer into the last cell in the last row and press the Tab key.

- **Deleting columns:** Click in the column you want to delete, click the Delete button, and choose Delete Columns on the drop-down list. Select more than one column to delete more than one. (Pressing the Delete key deletes the data in the column, not the column itself.)

- **Deleting rows:** Click in the row you want to delete, click the Delete button, and choose Delete Rows. Select more than one row to delete more than one. (Pressing the Delete key deletes the data in the row, not the row itself.)

Moving columns and rows

Because there is no elegant way to move a column or row, you should move only one at a time. If you try to move several simultaneously, you open a can of worms that is best left unopened. To move a column or row:

1. **Select the column or row you want to move.**

   Earlier in this chapter, "Selecting Different Parts of a Table" explains how to select columns and rows.

2. Press Command+X.

The column or row is moved to the Clipboard (a temporary storage area).

3. Insert a new column or row where you want the column or row to be.

Earlier in this chapter, "Inserting and deleting columns and rows" explains how.

4. Move the column or row:

- **Column:** Click in the topmost cell in your new column and then press Command+V.

- **Row:** Click in the first column of the row you inserted and then press Command+V.

Sorting, or reordering, a table

On the subject of moving columns and rows, the fastest way to rearrange the rows in a Word table is to sort the table. *Sorting* means to rearrange all the rows in a table on the basis of data in one or more columns. For example, a table that shows candidates and the number of votes they received could be sorted in alphabetical order by the candidates' names or in numerical order by the number of votes they received. Both tables present the same information, but the information is sorted in different ways.

The difference between ascending and descending sorts is as follows:

- Ascending arranges text from A to Z, numbers from smallest to largest, and dates from earliest to latest.

- Descending arranges text from Z to A, numbers from largest to smallest, and dates from latest to earliest.

When you rearrange a table by sorting it, Word rearranges the formatting as well as the data. Do your sorting before you format the table.

Follow these steps to sort a table:

1. **On the Table Tools Layout tab, click the Sort button.**

   You see the Sort dialog box. Depending on the size of your screen, you may have to click the Data button before you see the Sort button.

2. **In the first Sort By drop-down list, choose the column you want to sort with.**

3. **If necessary, open the first Type drop-down list and choose Text, Number, or Date to describe what kind of data you're dealing with.**

4. **Select the Ascending or Descending option button to declare whether you want an ascending or descending sort.**

5. **If necessary, on the first Then By drop-down list, choose the tiebreaker column.**

   If two items in the Sort By columns are alike, Word looks to your Then By column choice to break the tie and place one row before another in the table.

6. **Click OK.**

When you sort a table, Word ignores the *header row* — the first row in the table — and doesn't move it. However, if you want to include the header row in the sort, click the No Header Row option button in the Sort dialog box.

Sort		
Sort by		
City	Type: Number	● Ascending ○ Descending
Then by		
State	Type: Number	● Ascending ○ Descending
Then by		
	Type: Text	● Ascending ○ Descending
My list has		
● Header row	○ No header row	
Options...	Cancel	OK

Formatting Your Table

After you enter text in the table, lay out the columns and rows, and make them the right size, the fun begins. Now you can dress up your table and make it look snazzy. You can change fonts, choose colors for columns and rows, and choose borders. You can also play with the borders that divide the columns and rows and shade columns, rows, and cells by filling them with gray shades or a black background. Read on to find out how to do these tricks.

Designing a table with a table style

The fastest way to get a good-looking table is to select a table style in the Table Styles gallery on the Tables tab, as shown in Figure 7-3. A *table style* is a ready-made assortment of colors and border choices. You can save yourself a lot of formatting trouble by selecting a table style. After you select a table style, you can modify it by selecting or deselecting check boxes in the Table Options group on the Tables tab.

Click anywhere in your table and follow these steps to choose a table style:

1. **Go to the Tables tab.**

2. **Open the Table Styles gallery and select a table style.**

   To remove a table style, open the Table Styles gallery and choose Plain Tables.

Modify your table   Select a table style

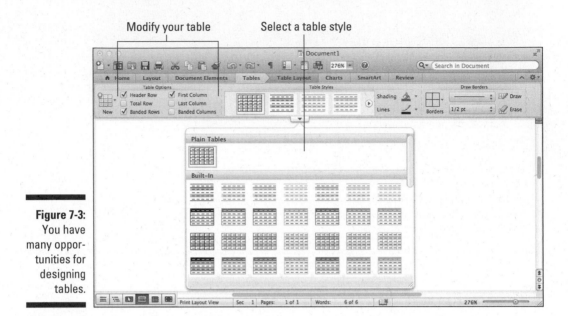

Figure 7-3:
You have
many oppor-
tunities for
designing
tables.

For consistency's sake, choose a similar table style — or better yet the same table style — for all the tables in your document. This way, your work doesn't become a showcase for table styles.

Calling attention to different rows and columns

On the Tables tab, Word offers Table Style Options check boxes for calling attention to different rows or columns (refer to Figure 7-3, in the previous section). For example, you can make the first row in the table, called the header row, stand out by selecting the Header Row check box. If your table presents numerical data with total figures in the last row, you can call attention to the last row by selecting the Total Row check box. Select or deselect these check boxes on the Tables tab to make your table easier to read and understand:

✔ **Header Row and Total Row:** These check boxes make the first row and last row in a table stand out. Typically, the header row is a different color or contains boldface text because it is the row that identifies the data in the table. Click the Header Row check box to make the first row stand out; if you also want the last row to stand out, click the Total Row check box.

✔ **Banded Columns and Banded Rows:** *Banded* means "striped" in Office lingo. For striped columns or striped rows — columns or rows that alternate in color — select the Banded Columns or Banded Rows check box.

✔ **First Column and Last Column:** Often, the first column stands out in a table because it identifies what type of data is in each row. Select the First Column check box to make it a different color or to boldface its text. Check the Last Column check box if you want the rightmost column to stand out.

Decorating your table with borders and colors

Rather than rely on a table style, you can play interior decorator on your own. You can slap color on the columns and rows of your table, draw borders around columns and rows, and choose a look for borders. Figure 7-4 shows the drop-down lists on the Tables tab that pertain to table decoration. Use these drop-down lists to shade table columns and rows and draw table borders.

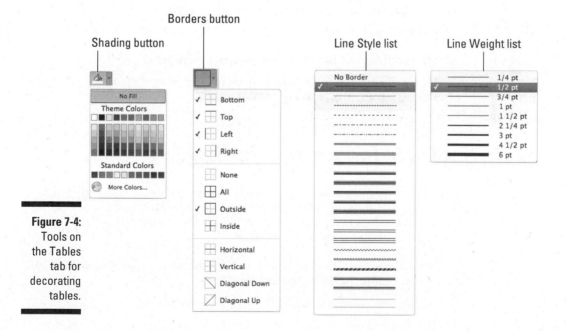

Figure 7-4:
Tools on the Tables tab for decorating tables.

Designing borders for your table

Follow these steps to fashion a border for your table or a part of your table:

1. **Go to the Tables tab.**

2. **Select the part of your table that needs a new border.**

3. **Open the Line Style drop-down list and choose a line style for the border.**

   Stay away from the dotted and dashed lines unless you have a good reason for choosing one. These lines can be distracting and keep others from focusing on the data presented in the table.

4. **Open the Line Weight drop-down list and choose a thickness for the border.**

5. **Open the drop-down list on the Borders button and choose where to place borders on the part of the table you selected in Step 2.**

   This is the tricky part. The Borders commands have different effects, depending on which part of the table you selected. For example, if you selected two rows and you choose the Top Border command, the command applies only to the top of the uppermost row. If you are anywhere near typical, you have to repeat Step 5 until you get it right.

Selecting colors for columns, rows, or your table

Follow these steps to paint columns, rows, or your table a new color:

1. **Select the part of the table that needs a paint job.**

2. **On the Tables tab, open the drop-down list on the Shading button and choose a color (refer to Figure 7-4).**

Using Math Formulas in Tables

No, you don't have to add the figures in columns and rows yourself; Word gladly does that for you. Word can perform other mathematical calculations as well. Follow these steps to perform mathematical calculations and tell Word how to format sums and products:

1. **Put the cursor in the cell that will hold the sum or product of the cells above, below, to the right, or to the left.**

2. **On the Table Layout tab, click the AutoSum button.**

   The Formula dialog box appears, as shown in Figure 7-5. In its wisdom, Word makes an educated guess about what you want the formula to do and places a formula in the Formula box.

3. **If this isn't the formula you want, delete everything except the equal sign in the Formula box, open the Paste Function drop-down list, and choose another function for the formula.**

   For example, choose PRODUCT to multiply figures. You may have to type **left**, **right**, **above**, or **below** in the parentheses within the formula to tell Word where the figures that you want it to compute are.

4. **In the Number Format drop-down list, choose a format for your number.**

5. **Click OK.**

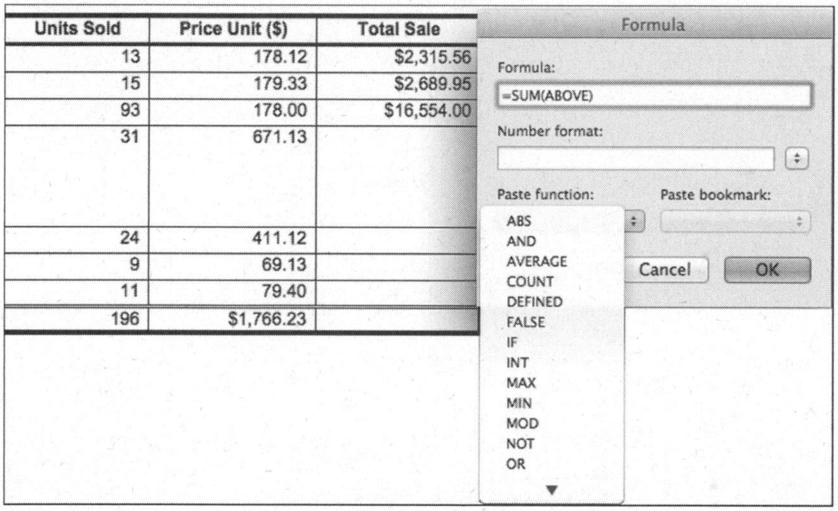

Units Sold	Price Unit ($)	Total Sale
13	178.12	$2,315.56
15	179.33	$2,689.95
93	178.00	$16,554.00
31	671.13	
24	411.12	
9	69.13	
11	79.40	
196	$1,766.23	

Formula

Formula:

`=SUM(ABOVE)`

Number format:

Paste function:
- ABS
- AND
- AVERAGE
- COUNT
- DEFINED
- FALSE
- IF
- INT
- MAX
- MIN
- MOD
- NOT
- OR

Paste bookmark:

Cancel   OK

Figure 7-5:
A math formula in a table.

Word doesn't calculate blank cells in formulas. Enter 0 in blank cells if you want them to be included in calculations. You can copy functions from one cell to another to save yourself the trouble of opening the Formula dialog box.

Chapter 8

Getting the Most Out of Word

*T*his chapter is hereby dedicated to everyone who has had to delve into the unknown and write a report about it. Writing reports, manuals, and scholarly papers is not easy. You have to explore uncharted territory. You have to contemplate the ineffable. And you have to write footnotes and maybe an index, too. Word cannot take you directly to uncharted territory, but it can take some of the sting out of it.

This chapter explains how to handle footnotes and endnotes, generate a table of contents, index a document, include cross-references in documents, and use Outline view to organize your thoughts and ideas. It also explains spell checking and the thesaurus. For people who have the onerous chore of sending out mass mailings, this chapter explains how to get Word's help for that task.

Correcting Your Spelling Errors

Office keeps a dictionary in its hip pocket, which is a good thing for you. Who wants to be embarrassed by a spelling error? Office consults its dictionary when you enter text in Word (and PowerPoint and Excel). To correct misspellings, you can either address them one at a time or start the spell checker and proof many pages simultaneously.

Don't trust the smell checker to be accurate all the time. It doesn't really locate misspelled words — it locates words that aren't in its dictionary. For example, if you write "Nero diddled while Rome burned," the spell checker doesn't catch the error. Nero *fiddled* while Rome burned, but because *diddle* is a legitimate word in the spelling dictionary, the spell checker overlooks the error. The moral: Proofread your files carefully and don't rely on the spell checker to catch all your smelling errors.

Correcting misspellings one at a time

Figure 8-1 shows the one-at-a-time method of spell checking. Under this method, you right-click each word that is underlined in red and choose a correct spelling from the shortcut menu. After you choose a word from the shortcut menu, it replaces the misspelling that you right-clicked.

Words entered twice are also flagged in red, in which case the shortcut menu offers the Delete Repeated Word option so that you can delete the second word. You can also click Ignore All to tell Office when a word is correctly spelled and shouldn't be flagged, or click Add, which adds the word to the Office spelling dictionary and declares it a correctly spelled word.

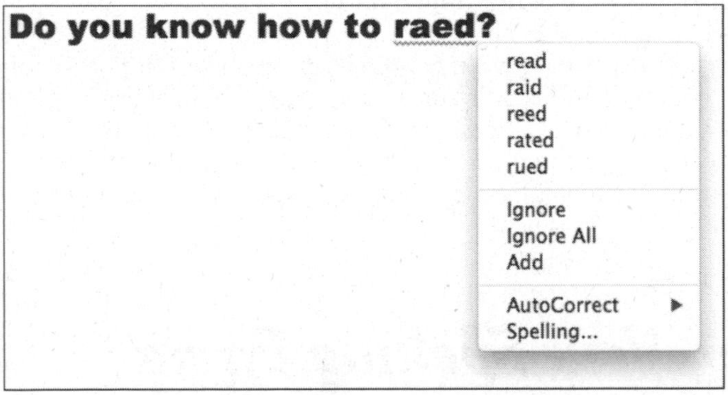

Figure 8-1:
Right-click a
word under-
lined in red
to correct
a typo or
repeated
word.

Do you know how to raed?

read
raid
reed
rated
rued

Ignore
Ignore All
Add

AutoCorrect ▶
Spelling...

Getting rid of the squiggly red lines

More than a few people think that the squiggly red lines that appear under misspelled words are annoying. To keep those lines from appearing, press Option+Command+L to open the Spelling dialog box; then click the Options button. You see the Spelling and Grammar dialog box. Deselect the Check Spelling As You Type check box.

Even with the red lines gone, you can do a quick spell check of a word that you suspect has been misspelled. To do so, select the word (double-click it) and press F7. The Spelling dialog box appears if the word has indeed been misspelled. Select a word in the Suggestions box and click the Change button.

Running a spell check

Instead of correcting misspellings one at a time, you run a spell-check on your work. Start your spell-check with one of these methods:

✔ Press Option+Command+L.

✔ Choose Tools ➪ Spelling and Grammar.

✔ Click the Spelling and Grammar Status button on the status bar. (A red *X* appears on this button when there are misspelled words in your document; a check mark appears when the document has been spell checked.)

You see the Spelling and Grammar dialog box, as shown in Figure 8-2. Misspellings appear in the Not In Dictionary text box. Here are options for correcting known misspellings in the Spelling and Grammar dialog box:

✔ Select the correct spelling in the Suggestions box and click the Change button.

✔ Click in the page you're working on and correct the spelling there; then click the Resume button, located where the Ignore or Ignore Once button used to be.

✔ Correct the spelling inside the Not in Dictionary text box and then click the Change button. (In PowerPoint, correct the spelling in the Change To box and then click the Change button.)

If the word in question isn't a misspelling, tell your program how to handle the word by clicking one of these buttons:

✔ **Ignore:** Ignores this instance of the misspelling but stops on it again if the same misspelling appears later.

✔ **Ignore All:** Ignores the misspelling throughout the document you're working on.

✔ **Add:** Adds the misspelling to the Office spelling dictionary. By clicking the Add button, you tell Office that the misspelling is a legitimate word or name.

✔ **Change/Delete:** Enters the selected word in the Suggestions box where the misspelling used to be. When the same word appears twice in a row, the Delete button appears where the Change button was. Click the Delete button to delete the second word in the pair.

✔ **Change All/Delete All:** Replaces all instances of the misspelled word with the word that you selected in the Suggestions box. Click the Change All button to correct a misspelling that occurs throughout a document. When two words appear in a row, this button is called Delete All. Click the Delete All button to delete the second word in the pair throughout your document.

✔ **AutoCorrect:** Adds the spelling correction to the list of words that are corrected automatically. If you find yourself making the same typing error over and over, place the error on the AutoCorrect list and never have to correct it again.

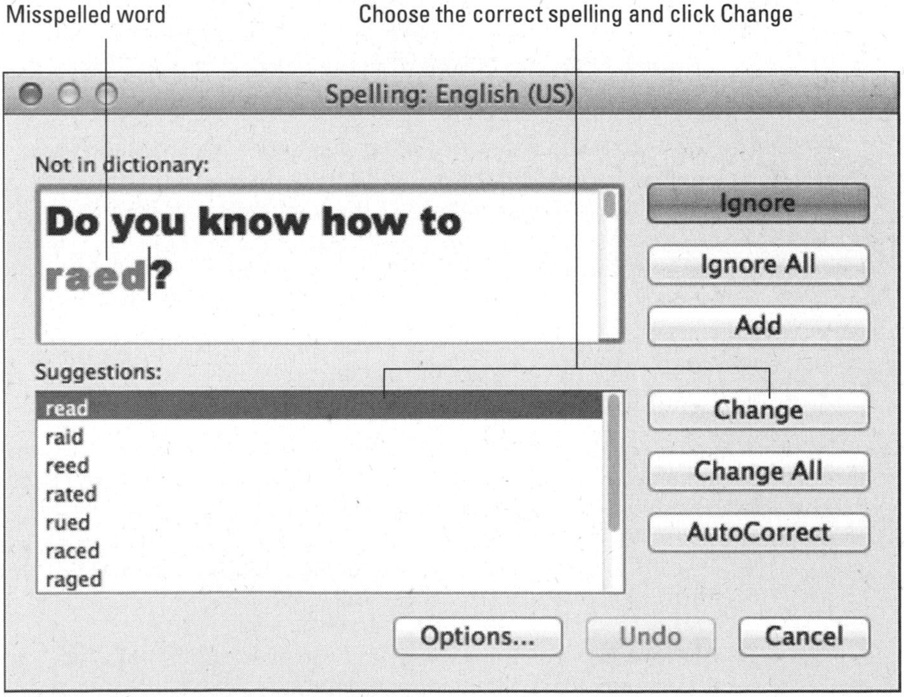

Misspelled word   Choose the correct spelling and click Change

Figure 8-2: Correcting a misspelling in the Spelling and Grammar dialog box.

Office programs share the same spelling dictionary. For example, words you add to the spelling dictionary in Word documents are deemed correct spellings in PowerPoint presentations and Excel spreadsheets.

Finding the Right Word with the Thesaurus

If you can't find the right word or if the word is on the tip of your tongue but you can't quite remember it, you can always give the thesaurus a shot. To find synonyms for a word, start by right-clicking the word and choosing Synonyms on the shortcut menu, as shown in Figure 8-3. With luck, the synonym you're looking for appears on the submenu, and all you have to do is click to enter the synonym. Usually, however, finding a good synonym is a journey, not a Sunday stroll.

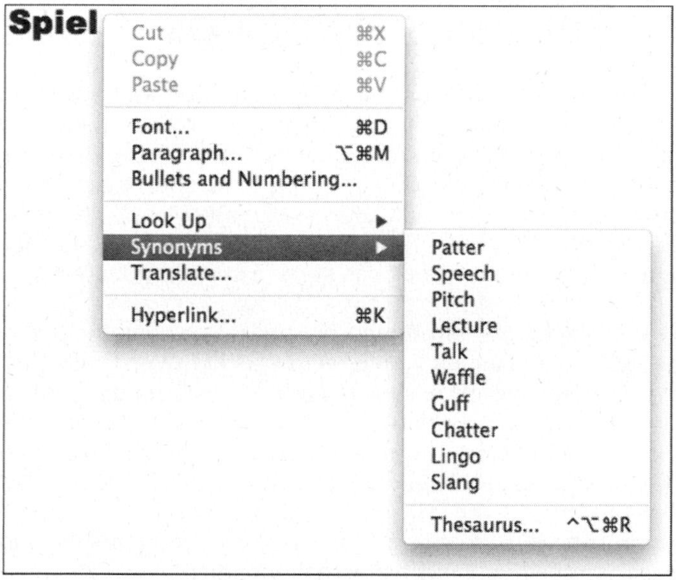

Spiel

Cut	⌘X
Copy	⌘C
Paste	⌘V
Font...	⌘D
Paragraph...	⌥⌘M
Bullets and Numbering...	
Look Up	▶
Synonyms	▶
Translate...	
Hyperlink...	⌘K

Synonyms submenu:

Patter
Speech
Pitch
Lecture
Talk
Waffle
Guff
Chatter
Lingo
Slang

Thesaurus...   ^⌥⌘R

Figure 8-3:
Searching
for a
synonym.

To search for a good synonym, click the word in question and open the thesaurus with one of these techniques:

- Choose Tools ⇨ Thesaurus.
- Right-click the word and choose Synonyms ⇨ Thesaurus.

✔ Click the Show or Hide the Toolbox button on the Standard toolbar and, in the Reference Tools dialog box, click the Thesaurus button.

✔ Press Shift+Option+Command+R.

The Thesaurus opens. It offers a list of synonyms and sometimes includes an antonym or two at the bottom. Now you're getting somewhere:

✔ **Choosing a synonym:** Select a synonym and choose Insert.

✔ **Searching for synonyms:** Select a word under Meanings to turn your search in a different direction.

✔ **Revisit a word:** Open the Recent Searches drop-down list and choose a word to backtrack. This drop-down list is located to the left of the synonym at the top of the dialog box.

Churning Out Letters, Envelopes, and Labels for Mass Mailings

Thanks to the miracle of computing, you can churn out form letters, labels, and envelopes for a mass mailing in the privacy of your home or office, just as the big companies do. Churning out form letters, envelopes, and labels is easy, as long as you take the time to prepare the source file. The *recipients list* is the file that the names and addresses come from. A Word table, an Excel worksheet, a FileMaker Pro database table or query, an Office Address Book, or an Apple Address Book can serve as the recipients list.

To generate form letters, envelopes, or labels, you combine the form letter, envelope, or label document with a recipients list. Word calls this process *merging.* During the merge, names and addresses from the recipients list are plugged into the appropriate places in the form letter, envelope, or label document. When the merge is complete, you can either save the form letters, envelopes, or labels in a new file or start printing right away.

The following pages explain how to prepare the recipients list and merge addresses from the recipients list with a document to create form letters, labels, or envelopes. Then you discover how to print the form letters, labels, or envelopes after you have generated them.

Preparing the recipients list

If you intend to get addresses for your form letters, labels, or envelopes from an Office Address Book or Apple Address Book on your computer, you're ready to go. However, if you haven't entered the addresses yet or you are keeping them in a Word table, Excel worksheet, or FileMaker Pro database table or query, make sure that the data is in good working order:

- ✔ **Word table:** Save the table in its own file and enter a descriptive heading at the top of each column. In the merge, when you tell Word where to plug in address and other data, you do so by choosing a heading name from the top of a column. In Figure 8-4, for example, the column headings are Last Name, First Name, Street, and so on. (Chapter 7 explains how to construct a Word table.)

- ✔ **Excel worksheet:** Arrange the worksheet in table format with a descriptive heading atop each column and no blank cells in any columns. Word will plug in address and other data by choosing heading names.

- ✔ **FileMaker Pro table or query:** Make sure that you know the field names in the database table or query where you keep the addresses. During the merge, you will be asked for field names. By the way, if you're comfortable in FileMaker Pro, query a database table for the records you will need. As you find out shortly, Word offers a technique for choosing only the records you want for your form letters, labels, or envelopes. However, by querying first in FileMaker Pro, you can start off with the records you need and spare yourself from having to choose records in Word.

A Word table, Excel worksheet, or FileMaker Pro table or query can include more than address information. Don't worry about deleting information that isn't required for your form letters, labels, and envelopes. As you find out soon, you get to decide which information to include from the Word table, Excel worksheet, or FileMaker Pro table or query.

Figure 8-4: A Word source table for a mail merge.

Last Name	First Name	Street	City	State	ZIP	Birthday
Creed	Hank	443 Oak St.	Atherton	CA	93874	31-Jul
Daws	Leon	13 Spruce St.	Colma	CA	94044	1-Apr
Maves	Carlos	11 Guy St.	Reek	NV	89201	28-Feb
Ng	Winston	1444 Unger Ave.	Colma	CA	94404	12-Nov
Smith	Jane	121 First St.	Colma	CA	94044	10-Jan
Weiss	Shirley	441 Second St.	Poltroon	ID	49301	4-May

Merging the recipients list with the source file

After you prepare the recipients list, the next step in generating form letters, labels, or envelopes for a mass mailing is to merge the document with the recipients list. Follow these general steps to do so:

1. **Choose Tools⇨Mail Merge Manager.**

   The Mail Merge Manager dialog box opens. It lists the six steps you need to complete for the mass mailing.

2. **Click Select Document Type.**

   The Create New button appears in the dialog box.

3. **Create (or open) a document.**

   - *Form letters:* If you haven't written the text of the form letter yet, click the Create New button and choose Form Letters, as shown in Figure 8-5. Otherwise, if you've written the form letter, close the Word document you're working in now. Then open the form letter you've written, choose Tools⇨Mail Merge Manager, click the Create New button, and choose Form Letters.

   - *Labels:* Click the Create New button and choose Labels (see Figure 8-5).

   - *Envelopes:* Click the Create New button and choose Envelopes (see Figure 8-5).

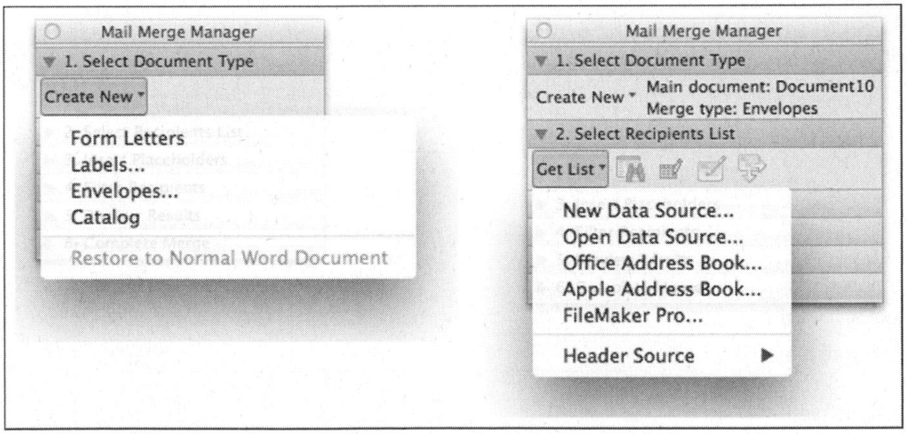

Figure 8-5:
Steps 1
and 2 of a
mail merge.

4. **Prepare the groundwork for creating form letters, labels, or envelopes for a mass mailing.**

   What you do next depends on what kind of mass mailing you want to attempt:

   - *Form letters:* You're ready to go. The text of your form letter already appears onscreen if you already wrote your letter.

   - *Labels:* You see the Label Options dialog box, where you tell Word what size labels to print on. Choose a label product and then, after consulting the box your labels came in, a product number. If you don't know the name of the company that produced your labels or you can't find a product number, click the New Label button and describe your label in the New Custom dialog box.

   - *Envelopes:* You see the Envelope dialog box. This is where you tell Word what size envelopes to print on and how envelopes are fed to your printer. Click the Page Setup button to open the Page Setup dialog box and describe the envelopes you intend to use. Click the Custom button to open the Custom Page Options dialog box and describe how your printer receives envelopes. While you're here, you can type a return address in the Return Address box.

5. **Click Select Recipients List, click the Get List button, and choose an option on the drop-down list (see Figure 8-5) to direct Word to your source file or the source of your address and data information.**

   Earlier in this chapter, "Preparing the recipients list" explains what a source file is. Your options are as follows:

   - *Addresses from a Word table or Excel worksheet:* Choose Open Data Source. You see the Choose a Data File dialog box. Locate the Word file or Excel worksheet, select it, and click Open.

   - *Addresses from an Office or Apple Address Book:* Choose Office Address Book or Apple Address Book. Field names from the address book appear.

   - *Addresses from a FileMaker Pro database:* Choose FileMaker Pro. Then, in the Choose a File dialog box, select a database or query and click the Choose button.

6. **Enter the placeholders you need for your letters, labels, or envelopes.**

   This part can be tricky. At the very least, you'll need these fields (or fields with similar names): First_Name, Last_Name, Street, City, Zip_Code.

   - *Form letters:* As shown in Figure 8-6, you drag fields into your Word document where they are needed to construct addresses. You can enter punctuation marks between these placeholders, copy and paste them, and delete them until your representative addresses are just so.

- *Labels:* In the Edit Labels dialog box, choose fields from the Insert Merge Field dialog box to construct a representative address for your labels. You can enter punctuation marks (such as commas). Press the Return key to enter a second or third line in the address.

- *Envelopes:* Drag fields on to the envelope to create a representative address. You need to press the Return key and spacebar many times to land the address square in the middle of the envelope.

7. **Click Preview Results (step 5 in the Mail Merge Manager dialog box) and then click the ABC button.**

   Clicking the ABC button (its official name is View Merged Data) replaces placeholder names with real names from the recipients list. Now you can see whether you landed the fields correctly in your Word form letter, labels sheet, or representative envelope. If necessary, click the ABC button again to see the fields, go into the document, and move placeholder fields until the addresses and other variable material look right.

At last — you're ready to print the form letters, envelopes, or labels. Take a deep breath and keep reading.

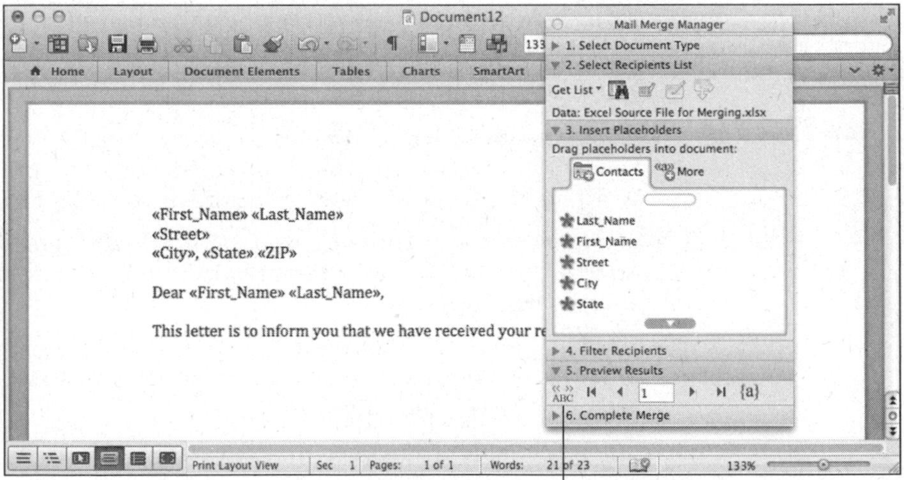

Figure 8-6:
Step 3 of a mail merge: Placing field names in your document.

Click to see real data

Printing form letters, envelopes, and labels

After you have gone to the trouble to prepare the data file and merge it with the document, you're ready to print your form letters, envelopes, or labels. Start by loading paper, envelopes, or sheets of labels in your printer:

- ✔ **Form letters:** Form letters are easiest to print. Just put the paper in the printer.

- ✔ **Labels:** Load the label sheets in your printer.

- ✔ **Envelopes:** Not all printers are capable of printing envelopes one after the other. Sorry, but you probably have to consult the dreary manual that came with your printer to find out the correct way to load envelopes.

Click Complete Merge (Step 6 in the Mail Merge dialog box) to print the form letters, envelopes, or labels. After you click Complete Merge, you can save the material in a new document or send it straight to the printer:

- ✔ **Saving in a new document:** Click the Merge to New Document button. Save this document and then print it. You can go into the document and make changes here and there before printing. In form letters, for example, you can write a sentence or two in different letters to personalize them.

- ✔ **Printing right away:** Click the Merge to Printer button to print the form letters, envelopes, or labels without saving them in a document. The Print dialog box appears so that you can direct Word on how to print the letter, envelopes, or labels.

Save the form letters, labels, or envelopes in a new document if you intend to print them at a future date or ink is running low on your printer and you may have to print in two or more batches. Saving in a new document permits you to generate the mass mailing without having to start all over again with the merge process and all its tedium.

Outlines for Organizing Your Work

Outline view is a great way to see at a glance how your document is organized and whether you need to organize it differently. To take advantage of this feature, you must have assigned heading styles to the headings in your document. (Chapter 6 explains styles.) In Outline view, you can see all the headings in your document. If a section is in the wrong place, you can move it simply by dragging an icon or by clicking one of the buttons on the Outlining tab. To change the rank of a heading, simply click a button to promote or demote it.

To switch to Outline view, click the Outline View button in the lower-left corner of the screen or choose View⇨Outline. Outlining tools appear on the Home tab, as shown in Figure 8-7. Rather than see text, you see the headings in your document, as well as the first line underneath each heading. Now you get a sense of what is in your document and whether it is organized well. By choosing an option from the Show Level drop-down list, you can decide which headings to see onscreen.

Choose which headings to see

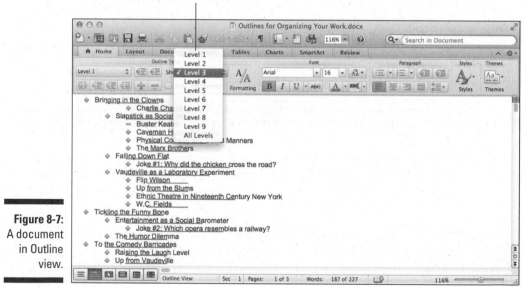

Figure 8-7: A document in Outline view.

Viewing the outline in different ways

Before you start rearranging your document in Outline view, get a good look at it:

> ✔ **View some or all headings:** Choose an option from the Show Level drop-down list to tell Word which level headings to see. To see only first-level headings, for example, choose Level 1. To see first-, second-, and third-level headings, choose Level 3. Choose All Levels to see all the headings.

- **View heading formats:** Click the Formatting button. When this button is selected, you can see how headings were formatted and get a better idea of their ranking in your document.

- **View or hide the subheadings in one section:** To see or hide the subheadings and text in one section of a document, select that section by clicking the plus sign beside its heading; then, click the Expand button to see the subheadings, or click the Collapse button to hide the subheadings. You can also double-click the plus sign beside a heading to view or hide its subheadings.

- **View or hide paragraph text:** Click the Show First Line Only check box. When this check box is selected, you see only the first line in each paragraph. First lines are followed by an ellipsis (. . .) so that you know that more text follows.

Notice the plus and minus icons next to the headings and the text. A plus icon means that the item has subheadings and text under it. For example, headings almost always have plus icons because text comes after them. A minus icon means that nothing is found below the item in question. For example, body text usually has a minus icon because body text is lowest on the Outline totem pole.

Rearranging document sections in Outline view

Outline view is mighty convenient for moving sections in a document and for promoting and demoting sections. Use these techniques to rearrange and reorganize your document:

- **Move a section:** To move a section up or down in the document, select it and click the Move Up or Move Down button. You can also drag the plus sign to a new location. If you want to move the subheadings and subordinate text along with the section, be sure to click the Collapse button to tuck all the subheadings and subtext into the heading before you move it.

- **Promote and demote headings:** Click the heading and then click the Promote button or Demote button. For example, you can promote a Level 3 heading to Level 2 by clicking the Promote button. Click the Promote To Heading 1 button to promote any heading to a first-level heading; click the Demote to Body Text button to turn a heading into prose.

- **Choose a new level for a heading:** Click the heading and choose a new heading level from the Outline Level drop-down list.

Generating a Table of Contents

A book-size document or long report isn't worth very much without a table of contents (TOC). How else can readers find what they're looking for? Generating a table of contents with Word is easy, as long as you give the headings in the document different styles — Heading 1, Heading 2, and so on (Chapter 6 explains styles). The beautiful thing about Word TOCs is the way they can be updated nearly instantly. If you add a new heading or erase a heading, you can update the TOC with a snap of your fingers. Moreover, you can quickly go from a TOC entry to its corresponding heading in a document by clicking the entry.

Before you create your TOC, create a new section in which to put it and number the pages in the new section with Roman numerals. (Chapter 5 explains sections and how to number pages.) TOCs, including the TOC in this book, are usually numbered in this way. The first entry in the TOC should cite page number 1. If you don't heed my advice and create a new section, the TOC will occupy the first few numbered pages of your document, and the numbering scheme will be thrown off.

Creating a TOC

To create a table of contents, place the cursor where you want the TOC to go, visit the Document Elements tab and open the Table of Contents gallery. In the gallery, choose one of Word's automatic TOC options. You can also click the Options button to fashion a TOC on your own in the Table of Contents dialog box. (Later in this chapter, "Customizing a TOC" explains how to fashion a TOC of your own in the Table of Contents dialog box.)

Updating and removing a TOC

Follow these instructions to update and remove a TOC:

- **Updating a TOC:** If you add, remove, or edit a heading in your document, your TOC needs updating. To update it, go to the Document Elements tab and click the Update button. A dialog box asks how to update the TOC. Either update the page numbers only or update the entire table, including all TOC entries and page numbers.

- **Removing a TOC:** Drag in the left margin from the top to the bottom of the TOC to select it. Then press the Delete key.

Customizing a TOC

Want to tinker with your TOC? You can number the headings in different ways and tell Word to include or exclude certain headings.

To change around a TOC, go to the Document Elements tab and click the Options button. You see the Table of Contents dialog box shown in Figure 8-8. Choose options to declare which headings you want for your TOC and how you want to format it:

- **Showing page numbers:** Deselect the Show Page Numbers check box if you want your TOC to be a simple list that doesn't refer to headings by page.

- **Aligning the page numbers:** Select the Right Align Page Numbers check box if you want page numbers to line up along the right side of the TOC so that the ones and tens line up under each other.

- **Choosing a tab leader:** A *leader* is the punctuation mark that appears between the heading and the page number the heading is on. If you don't want periods as the leader, choose another leader or choose (None).

- **Choosing a format:** Choose a format from the Formats drop-down list if you don't care to use the one from the template. Just be sure to watch the Preview box to see the results of your choice.

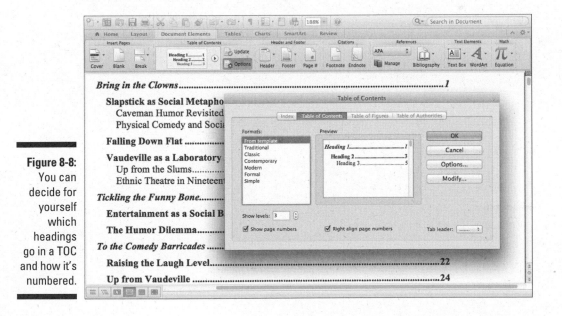

Figure 8-8: You can decide for yourself which headings go in a TOC and how it's numbered.

✔ **Choosing a TOC depth:** The Show Levels box determines how many heading levels are included in the TOC. Unless your document is a legal contract or other formal paper, enter a **2** or **3** here. A TOC is supposed to help readers find information quickly. Including lots of headings that take a long time to read through defeats the purpose of having a TOC.

Changing the structure of a TOC

Sometimes the conventional TOC that Word generates doesn't do the trick. Just because a heading has been given the Heading 1 style doesn't mean that it should receive first priority in the TOC. Suppose that you created another style called Chapter Title that should stand taller in the hierarchy than Heading 1. In that case, you need to rearrange the TOC so that Heading 1 headings rank second, not first, in the TOC hierarchy.

Follow these steps to change the structure of a TOC:

1. **On the Document Elements tab, click the Options button.**

   The Table of Contents dialog box opens.

2. **Click the Options button in the dialog box.**

   You see the Table of Contents Options dialog box, shown in Figure 8-9. This dialog box lists each paragraph style in the document you're working in.

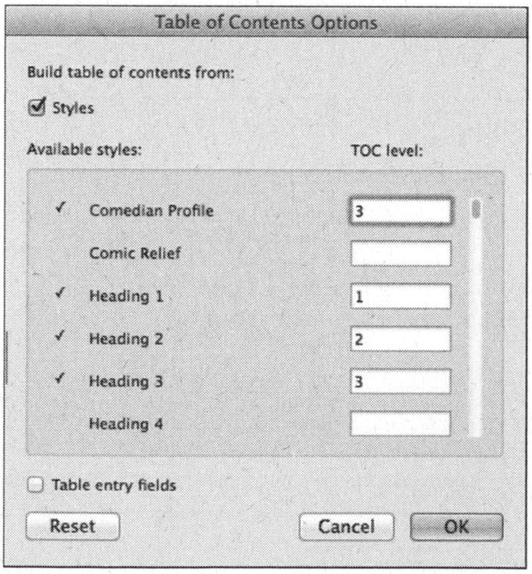

Figure 8-9: Changing a TOC's structure.

Table of Contents Options	
Build table of contents from:	
☑ Styles	
Available styles:	TOC level:
✓ Comedian Profile	3
Comic Relief	
✓ Heading 1	1
✓ Heading 2	2
✓ Heading 3	3
Heading 4	
☐ Table entry fields	
Reset	Cancel OK

3. **For headings you want to appear in the TOC, enter a number in the TOC Level text box to determine the headings' rank.**

   If headings assigned the Heading 1 style are to rank second in the TOC, for example, enter a 2 in Heading 1's TOC Level text box. You can exclude headings from a TOC by deleting a number in a TOC Level box.

4. **Click OK in the Table of Contents Options dialog box.**

5. **Click OK in the Table of Contents dialog box.**

Indexing a Document

A good index is a thing of beauty. User manuals, reference works of any length, and reports that readers will refer to all require indexes. Except for the table of contents, the only way to find information in a long document is to look in the index. An index at the end of a company report reflects well on the person who wrote the report. It gives the appearance that the author put in a fair amount of time to complete the work, even if he or she didn't really do that.

An index entry can be formatted in many ways. You can cross-reference index entries, list a page range in an index entry, and break out an index entry into subentries and sub-subentries. To help you with your index, Figure 8-10 explains indexing terminology.

Writing a good index entry is as hard as writing a good, descriptive heading. As you enter index entries in your document, ask yourself how you would look up information in the index, and enter your index entries accordingly.

Marking index items in the document

The first step in constructing an index is to mark index entries in your document. Marking index items yourself is easier than it seems. After you open the Mark Index Entry dialog box, it stays open so that you can scroll through your document and make entries.

1. **If you see a word or phrase in your document that you can use as a main, top-level entry, select it; otherwise, place the cursor in the paragraph or heading whose topic you want to include in the index.**

   You can save a little time by selecting a word, as I describe shortly.

2. **Press Shift+Option+Command+X.**

   The Mark Index Entry dialog box appears. If you selected a word or phrase, it appears in the Main Entry box.

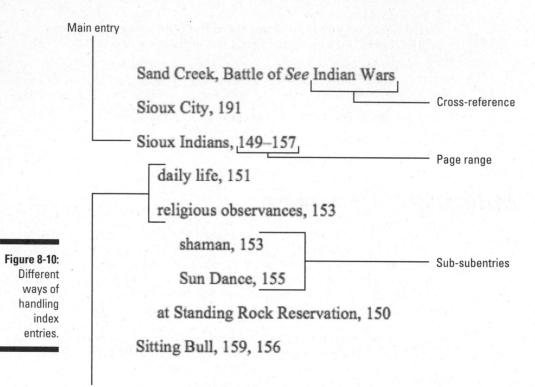

Main entry

Sand Creek, Battle of *See* Indian Wars

Cross-reference

Sioux City, 191

Sioux Indians, 149–157

Page range

daily life, 151

religious observances, 153

shaman, 153

Sub-subentries

Sun Dance, 155

at Standing Rock Reservation, 150

Sitting Bull, 159, 156

Figure 8-10: Different ways of handling index entries.

Subentries

3. **Choose how you want to handle this index entry (refer to Figure 8-10 to see the various ways to make index entries).**

When you enter the text, don't put a comma or period after it. Word does that when it generates the index. The text that you enter appears in your index.

- *Main Entry:* If you're entering a main, top-level entry, leave the text in the Main Entry box (if it's already there), type new text to describe this entry, or edit the text that's already there. Leave the Subentry box blank.

- *Subentry:* To create a subentry, enter text in the Subentry box. The subentry text will appear in the index below the main entry text, so make sure that some text is in the Main Entry box and that the subentry text fits under the main entry.

- *Sub-subentry:* A sub-subentry is the third level in the hierarchy. To create a sub-subentry, type the subentry in the Subentry box, enter a colon (:), and type the sub-subentry without entering a space, like so: **religious observances:shaman**.

4. Decide how to handle the page reference in the entry.

Again, your choices are many:

- *Cross-reference:* To go without a page reference and refer the reader to another index entry, click the Cross-Reference option button and type the other entry in the text box after the word *See.* What you type here appears in your index, so be sure that the topic you refer the reader to is really named in your index.

- *Current Page:* Choose this option to enter a single page number after the entry.

- *Page Range:* Choose this option if you're indexing a subject that covers several pages in your document. A page-range index entry looks something like this: "Sioux Indians, 149–157." To make a page-range entry, you must create a bookmark first. Leave the Mark Index Entry dialog box, select the text in the page range, and press Command+Shift+F5. In the Bookmark dialog box, enter a name in the Bookmark Name box and click the Add button. (Chapter 5 explains bookmarks.)

5. You can boldface or italicize a page number or page range by choosing a Page Number Format check box.

In some indexes, the page or page range where the topic is explained in the most depth is italicized or boldfaced so that readers can get to the juiciest parts first.

6. If you selected a single word or phrase in Step 1, you can click the Mark All button to have Word go through the document and mark all words that are identical to the one in the Main Entry box; click Mark to put this single entry in the index.

Click outside the Mark Index Entry dialog box and find the next topic or word that you want to mark for the index. Then press Command+Shift+F5 and make another entry.

 A bunch of ugly field codes appear in your document after you mark an index entry. You can render them invisible by clicking the Show All Nonprinting Characters button on the Standard toolbar.

Generating the index

After you mark all the index entries, it's time to generate the index:

1. Place the cursor where you want the index to go, most likely at the end of the document.

You might type the word **Index** at the top of the page and format the word in a decorative way.

2. **Choose Insert ⇨ Index and Tables.**

   The Index and Tables dialog box opens.

3. **Go to the Index tab of the dialog box.**

   You see the Index dialog box, shown in Figure 8-11.

4. **Choose options in the dialog box and click OK.**

   As you make your choices, watch the Preview box to see what happens.

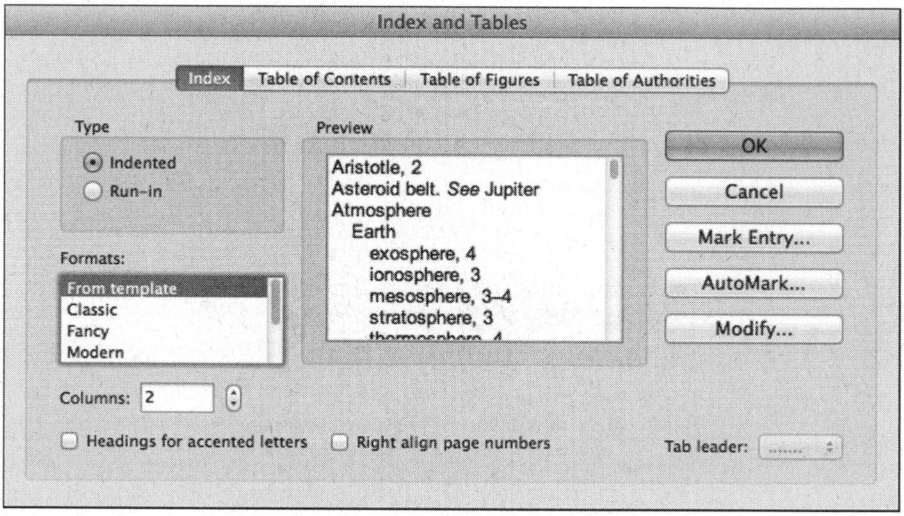

Figure 8-11: Generating an index.

Here are the options in the Index dialog box:

- **Type:** Choose Run-in if you want subentries and sub-subentries to run together; choose Indented to indent subentries and sub-subentries below main entries (refer to Figure 8-10).

- **Formats:** Word offers a number of attractive index layouts. You can choose one from the list.

- **Columns:** Stick with 2, unless you don't have subentries or sub-subentries and you can squeeze three columns on the page or you are working on a landscape document.

- **Headings for Accented Characters:** Index entries appear under letter headings. For example, entries that begin with the letter B appear under a heading called B. If you want accented letters to also appear as headings in the index, choose the Headings for Accented Characters check box.

✔ **Right Align Page Numbers:** Normally, page numbers appear right after entries and are separated from entries by a comma, but you can right-align the entries so that they line up under one another with this option.

✔ **Tab Leader:** Some index formats place a *leader* between the entry and the page number. A leader is a series of dots or dashes. If you're working with a format that has a leader, you can choose a leader from the drop-down list.

✔ **Modify:** Click this button if you're adventurous and want to create an index style of your own. (Chapter 6 explains styles.)

To update an index after you create or delete entries, click it and then click the Update Index button or right-click the index and then choose Update Field on the shortcut menu.

Editing an index

After you generate an index, read it carefully to make sure that all entries are useful to readers. Inevitably, something doesn't come out right, but you can edit index entries as you would the text in a document. Index field markers are enclosed in curly brackets with the letters *XE* and the text of the index entry in quotation marks, like so: { XE: "Wovoka: Ghost Dance" }. To edit an index marker, click the Show All Nonprinting Characters button on the Standard toolbar to see the field markers and find the one you need to edit. Then delete letters or type letters as you would do normal text.

Here's a quick way to find index field markers: After clicking the Show All Nonprinting Characters button, with the index fields showing, choose Edit➪Find➪Go To to open the Go To tab of the Find and Replace dialog box. In the Go to What menu, choose Field; then type **XE** in the Enter Field Name box and click the Next button until you find the marker you want to edit. You can also use the Find command to look for index entries. Word finds index entries as well as text as long as you click the Show All Nonprinting Characters button to display index fields in your document.

Putting Cross-References in a Document

Cross-references are very handy indeed. They tell readers where to go to find more information about a topic. The problem with cross-references, however, is that the thing being cross-referenced really has to be there. If you tell readers to go to a heading called "The Cat's Pajamas" on page 93, and neither the heading nor the page is really there, readers curse and tell you where to go, instead of the other way around.

Fortunately for you, Word lets you know when you make errant cross-references. You can refer readers to headings, page numbers, footnotes, endnotes, and plain-old paragraphs. If you delete the thing that a cross-reference refers to and render the cross-reference invalid, Word tells you about it the next time you update your cross-references. Best of all, if the page number, numbered item, or text that a cross-reference refers to changes, so does the cross-reference.

Follow these steps to create a cross-reference:

1. **Write the first part of the cross-reference text.**

   For example, you could write **To learn more about these cowboys of the pampas, see page** and then type a blank space. The blank space separates the word *page* from the page number in the cross-reference. If you are referring to a heading, write something like **For more information, see** ". Don't type a blank space this time because the cross-reference heading text will appear right after the double quotation mark.

2. **Choose Insert ⇨ Cross-reference.**

   The Cross-Reference dialog box appears, as shown in Figure 8-12.

3. **Choose what type of item you're referring to in the Reference Type drop-down list.**

   If you're referring to a plain old paragraph, choose Bookmark. Then click outside the dialog box, scroll to the paragraph you're referring to, and place a bookmark there. (Chapter 5 explains bookmarks.)

4. **Make a choice in the Insert Reference To box to refer to text, a page number, or a numbered item.**

   The options in this box are different, depending on what you chose in Step 3.

   • *Text:* Choose this option (Heading Text, Entire Caption, and so on) to include text in the cross-reference. For example, choose Heading Text if your cross-reference is to a heading.

   • *Number:* Choose this option to insert a page number or other kind of number, such as a table number, in the cross-reference.

   • *Include Above/Below:* Select this box to include the word *above* or *below* to tell readers where, in relation to the cross-reference, the thing being referred to is located in your document.

5. **If you wish, leave the check mark in the Insert as Hyperlink check box to create a hyperlink as well as a cross-reference.**

   With a hyperlink, someone reading the document onscreen can click the cross-reference and go directly to what it refers to.

6. **In the For Which box, tell Word where the thing you're referring to is located.**

   To do so, select a heading, bookmark, footnote, endnote, equation, figure, graph, or whatnot. In long documents, you almost certainly have to click the scroll bar to find the one you want.

7. **Click the Insert button and then click the Close button.**

8. **Back in your document, enter the rest of the cross-reference text, if necessary.**

When you finish creating your document, update all the cross-references. To do that, triple-click to select the entire document. Then right-click in the document and choose Update Field on the shortcut menu.

If the thing referred to in a cross-reference is no longer in your document, you see ~~Error! Reference source not found~~ where the cross-reference should be. To find cross-reference errors in long documents, look for the word *Error!* with the Find command. Investigate what went wrong, and repair or delete errant cross-references.

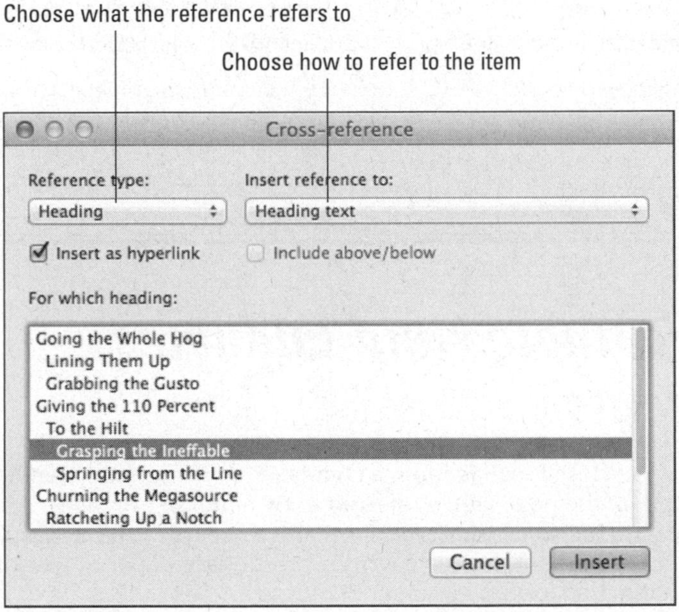

Choose what the reference refers to

Choose how to refer to the item

Figure 8-12:
Entering
a cross-
reference.

Creating a hyperlink to another place in your document

Create a hyperlink to a place in your document so that readers can click the link and travel immediately to a heading or other location in your document that you have bookmarked. (Chapter 5 explains bookmarks.) Follow these steps to create a hyperlink to another place in your document:

1. **Select the text or object that will form the hyperlink.**

2. **Choose Insert ⇨ Hyperlink (or press Command+K).**

   You see the Insert Hyperlink dialog box. Another way to open this dialog box is to right-click and choose Hyperlink on the shortcut menu.

3. **Click the Document tab in the dialog box.**

4. **Click the Locate button.**

   The Select Place in Document dialog box appears. This dialog box lists headings to which you've assigned a heading style and

bookmarks in your document. To see the names of headings and bookmarks, click the triangle next to Headings or Bookmarks to expand the list.

5. **Select the target of the hyperlink and click OK.**

   You return to the Insert Hyperlink dialog box.

6. **Click the ScreenTip button to open the Set Hyperlink ScreenTip dialog box.**

   When readers move their pointers over the link, they see the words you enter in the ScreenTip text box.

7. **Enter a ScreenTip that describes where the hyperlink goes and click OK.**

8. **Click OK in the Insert Hyperlink dialog box.**

   To test your hyperlink, move the pointer over it. You should see the ScreenTip description you wrote. Click the link to see whether it takes you to the right place.

Putting Footnotes and Endnotes in Documents

A *footnote* is a bit of explanation, a comment, or a reference that appears at the bottom of the page and is referred to by a number or symbol in the text. An *endnote* is the same thing, except that it appears at the end of the section, chapter, or document. If you've written a scholarly paper of any kind, you know what a drag footnotes and endnotes are.

You will be glad to know that Word takes some of the drudgery out of footnotes and endnotes. For example, if you delete or add a note, all notes after the one you added or deleted are renumbered. And you don't have to worry about long footnotes because Word adjusts the page layout to make room for them. You can change the numbering scheme of footnotes and endnotes at will. When you are reviewing a document, all you have to do is move the pointer over a footnote or endnote citation. The note icon appears, as does a pop-up box with the text of the note.

Entering a footnote or endnote

To enter a footnote or endnote in a document:

1. **Place the cursor in the text where you want the note's number or symbol to appear.**

2. **Choose Insert ⇨ Footnote.**

   The Insert Footnote and Endnote dialog appears, as shown in Figure 8-13.

3. **Choose the Footnotes or Endnotes option.**

4. **On the drop-down menu, choose where to place the footnote or endnote.**

   Later in this chapter, "Choosing the numbering scheme and position of notes" explains these options.

5. **Click the Insert button.**

   If you are in Print Layout view, Word scrolls to the bottom of the page or the end of the document or section so that you can enter the note, as shown in Figure 8-13. In Draft view, the Notes pane opens at the bottom of the screen with the cursor beside the number of the note you're about to enter.

6. **Enter your footnote or endnote.**

7. **Click the Close button in the Notes pane if you're in Draft view; in Print Layout view, scroll upward to return to the main text.**

To quickly return from writing a note to the place in your document where the footnote or endnote number citation is located, double-click the number citation at the bottom of the page (in Print Layout view) or the Notes pane (in Draft view). For example, if you just finished entering footnote 3, double-click the number *3*.

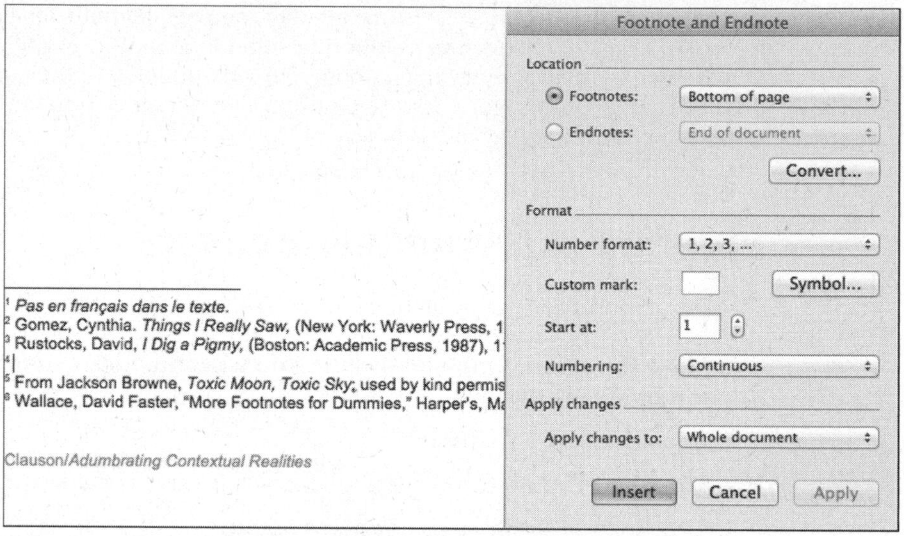

Figure 8-13:
Entering a
footnote in
Print Layout
view (left);
the Footnote
and Endnote
dialog box
(right).

¹ *Pas en français dans le texte.*
² Gomez, Cynthia. *Things I Really Saw,* (New York: Waverly Press, 1
³ Rustocks, David, *I Dig a Pigmy,* (Boston: Academic Press, 1987), 1
⁴|
⁵ From Jackson Browne, *Toxic Moon, Toxic Sky;* used by kind permis
⁸ Wallace, David Faster, "More Footnotes for Dummies," Harper's, Ma

Clauson/*Adumbrating Contextual Realities*

Choosing the numbering scheme and position of notes

Choosing the numbering scheme and positioning of endnotes and footnotes is quite easy. Choose Insert ➪ Footnote. The Footnote and Endnote dialog box appears (refer to Figure 8-13). Tell Word where to place your notes:

- **Footnotes:** Choose Bottom of Page to put footnotes at the bottom of the page no matter where the text ends; choose Beneath Text to put footnotes directly below the last line of text on the page.

- **Endnotes:** Choose End of Section if your document is divided into sections (such as chapters) and you want endnotes to appear at the back of sections; choose End of Document to put all endnotes at the very back of the document.

In the Format area, tell Word how to number the notes:

- **Number Format:** Choose A B C, i ii iii, or another numbering scheme, if you want. You can also enter symbols by choosing the last option on this drop-down list.

- **Custom Mark:** You can mark the note with a symbol by clicking the Symbol button and choosing a symbol in the Symbol dialog box. If you go this route, you have to enter a symbol each time you insert a note. Not only that, you may have to enter two or three symbols for the second and third notes on each page or document because Word can't renumber symbols.

✔ **Start At:** To start numbering the notes at a place other than 1, A, or i, enter **2**, **B**, **ii**, or whatever in this box.

✔ **Numbering:** To number the notes continuously from the start of your document to the end, choose Continuous. Choose Restart Each Section to begin anew at each section of your document. For footnotes, you can begin anew on each page by choosing Restart Each Page.

Deleting, moving, and editing notes

If a devious editor tells you that a footnote or endnote is in the wrong place, that you don't need a note, or that you need to change the text in a note, all is not lost:

✔ **Editing:** To edit a note, double-click its number or symbol in the text. You see the note onscreen. Edit the note at this point.

✔ **Moving:** To move a note, select its number or symbol in the text and drag it to a new location, or cut and paste it to a new location.

✔ **Deleting:** To delete a note, select its number or symbol and press the Delete key.

Footnotes and endnotes are renumbered when you move or delete one of them.

Part III
Excel

Visit www.dummies.com/extras/officeipadmac to see how the Goal Seek command in Excel can help you in financial analyses.

In this part . . .

✔ Find out how to touch up Excel worksheets with Excel for the iPad, including how to enter and format data, construct formulas, and change the look of worksheets.

✔ Get acquainted with Excel 2011 for the Mac as you discover speed techniques for entering data, formatting data, and establishing data-validation rules.

✔ See how to make the data in your worksheets easy to read and understand by using comments, crafting formulas, using functions in formulas, and detecting and correcting formula errors.

✔ Fashion a chart that enables others to take in and understand data in a single glance.

Chapter 9

Excel for the iPad

This chapter delves into Excel for the iPad, the spreadsheet application in the Office for the iPad suite. Use Excel to track and analyze numbers.

Like the other Office for the iPad applications, Excel isn't as sophisticated as its Office 2011 counterpart, but it's well designed and gives you the opportunity to do analyses on the fly. In this chapter, you discover how to enter and edit data in a worksheet, view a worksheet in different ways, format data, construct formulas, and put data in tables so that you can sort and filter it.

Finding Your Way Around the Excel Screen

When you arrive at a new place, you'd best get the lay of the land. Figure 9-1 shows what's what on the Excel for the iPad screen. If you're acquainted with other versions of Excel, this screen probably looks familiar. Only the Formula result indicator in the lower-right corner of the screen is new. Here's what's what on the Excel screen:

✔ **Formula bar:** The place to enter data and formulas to compute data.

✔ **Gridlines:** The lines on the worksheet that demarcate columns and rows. Each cell has an address where a column and row intersect: A1, A2, A3 and so on.

✔ **Active cell:** The cell that's selected in the worksheet. To enter data in a cell, select it first. To select a cell, double-tap it. (See "Entering data in a cell," later in this chapter.)

✔ **Worksheet tabs:** An Excel file is called a *workbook*. Each workbook can include more than one worksheet. To go from worksheet to worksheet, click tabs in the lower-left corner of the screen. (See "Adding and Deleting Worksheets," later in this chapter, for information about worksheets.)

✔ **Formula result indicator:** After you select cells with data, you can tap the Formula result indicator and choose a function on the pop-up list to see the results of applying the function to the cells you selected. (Later in this chapter, "Constructing a Formula" explains functions.)

Formula bar   Active cell

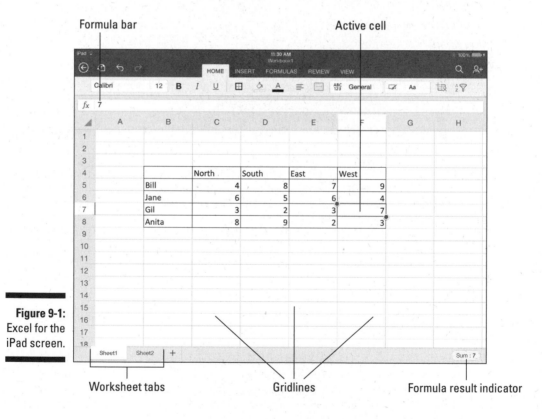

Figure 9-1:
Excel for the
iPad screen.

Worksheet tabs   Gridlines   Formula result indicator

Changing Your View of a Worksheet

The Excel for the iPad screen can seem mighty claustrophobic. When you start to suffer from claustrophobia, consider going to the View tab and taking advantage of these options for making the Excel screen easier to work in:

- ✔ **Formula Bar:** Hides or displays the Formula bar. The Formula bar is for entering data and formulas. Remove the Formula bar when you're reading a worksheet, not entering data in it.

- ✔ **Gridlines:** Hides or display gridlines. Gridlines show where worksheet cells are. Without the gridlines, a worksheet looks cleaner and is easier to read.

- ✔ **Headings:** Hides or displays the column letters and row numbers on the worksheet.

- ✔ **Sheet Tabs:** Hides or displays the worksheet tabs in the lower-left corner of the screen.

Entering and Editing Data

A worksheet wouldn't be worth very much without any data. You can't start analyzing, poking, and prodding data until you enter the numbers. These pages explain how to enter, select, and edit data. They also show how to delete, copy, and move data on a worksheet.

Chapter 10 explains what a workbook is and the basic concepts of entering data and setting up a worksheet. If you're completely new to Excel, I suggest reading the start of Chapter 10 before proceeding any further in this one.

Entering data in a cell

All data in worksheets is entered in cells, the places on the worksheet where columns and rows intersect. Each cell can hold text, a data value, a logical value (True or False), a formula, or nothing at all.

Follow these steps to enter data in a cell:

1. **Double-tap the cell where you want to enter data.**

   Excel activates the Formula bar, as shown in Figure 9-2. Meanwhile, the keyboard appears, as do the Letters button and the Numbers button so that you can switch between a lettered keyboard and a numbered keyboard.

2. Enter the data.

To enter numbers, tap the Numbers button to display the numbered keyboard, as shown in Figure 9-2. To enter text — for example, to enter a descriptive data label — tap the Letters button, if necessary.

3. Tap the Return key to enter your data in the cell.

Tapping Return enters the data, selects the cell below, and makes that cell the active cell so that you can enter data there. As well as tapping the Return key to enter data, you can tap an arrow key. Tapping an arrow key makes the cell above, the cell below, the cell to the left, or the cell to the right the active cell.

4. Tap the Keyboard key to close the keyboard.

This key is located in the lower-right corner of the keyboard.

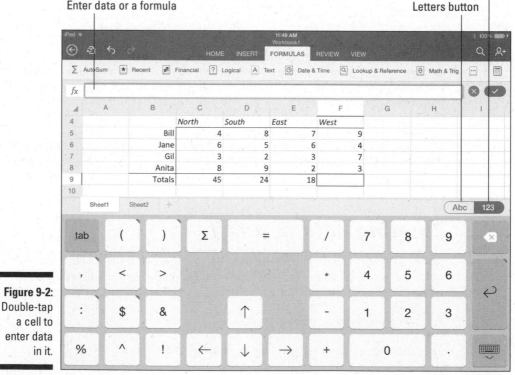

Enter data or a formula

Numbers button

Letters button

Figure 9-2:
Double-tap a cell to enter data in it.

Excel offers the Fill command for entering serial data such as number sequences and the days of the week. To enter serial data, start by selecting the first two items in the series. (Selecting cells is the next topic in this chapter.) For example, to enter the days of the week, enter **Monday** in one cell and **Tuesday** in the next, and select both cells. With the cells selected, tap Fill on the popover menu. Then drag a green arrow on the selected cell range to fill out the rest of the serial data.

Selecting cells

Before you can do much of anything with data — format it, delete it, move it, or copy it — you have to select the cells where it is stored. Here are techniques for selecting cells:

- **Selecting one cell:** Double-tap a cell to select it.

- **Selecting a range of cells:** Tap the first cell to make its selection handles appear, as shown in Figure 9-3. Then drag a selection handle to encompass all the cells you want to select (see Figure 9-3).

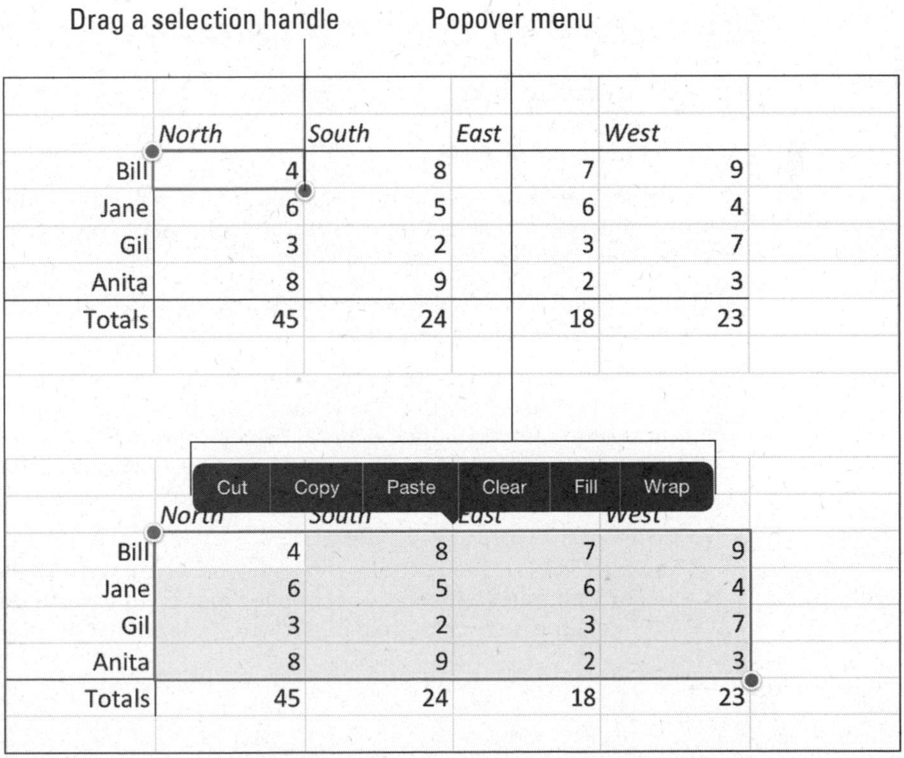

Drag a selection handle   Popover menu

	North	South	East	West
Bill	4	8	7	9
Jane	6	5	6	4
Gil	3	2	3	7
Anita	8	9	2	3
Totals	45	24	18	23

| Cut | Copy | Paste | Clear | Fill | Wrap |

	North	South	East	West
Bill	4	8	7	9
Jane	6	5	6	4
Gil	3	2	3	7
Anita	8	9	2	3
Totals	45	24	18	23

Figure 9-3: Selecting a range of cells.

Editing, deleting, moving, and copying data

Follow these instructions to manipulate data after you enter it:

- **Editing:** Double-tap to select the cell with data that needs editing. Then tap in the Formula bar where the data needs editing and edit to your heart's content.

- **Deleting:** Select the cells with the data you want to delete. Then, on the popover menu (refer to Figure 9-3), select Clear.

- **Moving and copying:** Select the cells with the data and choose Cut or Copy on the popover menu. Marquee lights appear around the data to show that it can be moved or copied. Select the cells where you want to move or copy the data and choose Paste on the popover menu.

  After you paste data, you see the Paste Options button. Click this button and choose an option from the drop-down list to keep the cells' formatting, paste values only, or paste formulas.

Inserting and deleting columns and rows

Follow these steps to insert or delete columns or rows:

1. **Select columns or rows.**

   To select a column or row, tap its column number or heading letter. At this point, you can select more than one column or row by dragging a green selection handle, as shown in Figure 9-4.

   Which columns or rows you select depends on whether you want to insert or delete columns or rows:

   - *Insert column(s).* Select the column to the right of where you want to insert columns. For example, to insert a column between what are now columns E and F, select column F. You can insert more than one column by selecting more than one. Excel inserts as many columns as the number you select before the Insert operation.

   - *Insert row(s).* Select the row below where you want to insert rows. For example, to insert a row above what is now row 8, select row 8. You can insert more than one row by selecting more than one.

Excel inserts as many rows as the number you select before the
Insert operation.

- *Delete columns or rows.* Select the row(s) or column(s) you want
  to delete.

2. Choose an option on the popover menu.

Which option you choose depends on what you want to do:

- *Insert columns.* Choose Insert Left on the popover menu.

- *Insert rows.* Choose Insert Above on the popover menu.

- *Delete columns or rows.* Choose Delete on the popover menu.

You can also insert and delete rows and columns with the Insert & Delete
Cells button on the Home tab. Select row(s) and column(s), click the
Insert & Delete Cells button, and choose an Insert or Delete option on the
drop-down menu.

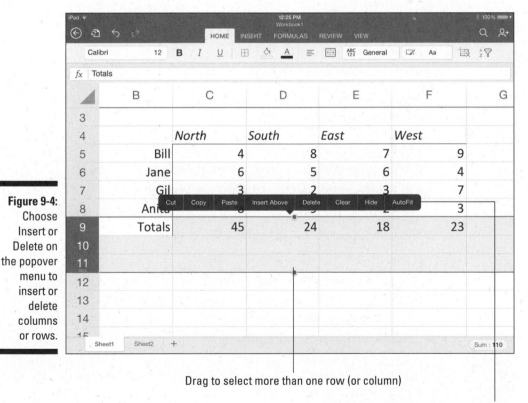

Figure 9-4:
Choose
Insert or
Delete on
the popover
menu to
insert or
delete
columns
or rows.

Drag to select more than one row (or column)

Choose an option on the popover menu

Putting the freeze on columns and rows

In a worksheet with many rows and columns, entering data in the correct row and column can be problematic. As columns and rows fill up, you lose sight of the labels in the first column and the labels in the top row that identify where to enter data.

To see the top row and first column no matter how far you stray down or to the right side of a worksheet, you can freeze columns and rows. Freezing makes the top row and first column visible no matter where you go in a worksheet.

Follow these steps to freeze columns and rows:

1. **Tap the cell below and to the right of the row and column you want to freeze.**

2. **On the View tab, tap the Freeze Panes button.**

   A drop-down menu appears.

3. **Choose a Freeze option.**

To "unfreeze" columns and rows, tap the Freeze Panes button and deselect the option you chose previously on the drop-down menu.

Choosing a Format for Data

As well as numbers, Excel can compute date and time values. When you enter data in a cell, tell Excel what type of data you propose to enter by choosing an option on the Data Format drop-down list. To wit, follow these instructions to choose a format for data:

1. **Select the cells.**

   Earlier in this chapter, "Selecting cells" explains this task.

2. **On the Home tab, tap the Data Format button.**

   A drop-down list with data formats appears, as shown in Figure 9-5.

3. **Select a format on the drop-down list.**

   Table 9-1 describes the data formats.

4. **Tap the Options button next to the name of the format you selected.**

   A submenu of options appears. Which options are on the submenu depends on the data format you chose.

5. **Choose an option on the submenu.**

   You can tell which data format was chosen for a cell by selecting the cell and looking at the Data Format button. It lists the format that is assigned to the cell.

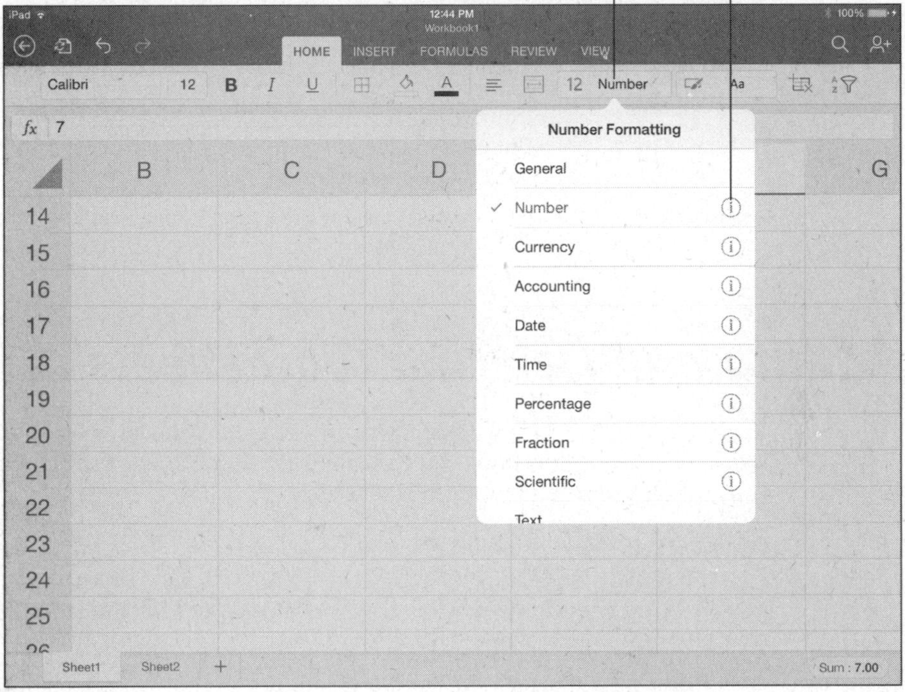

Data Format button   Tap for more options

Figure 9-5:
Choosing a
format for
data.

Table 9-1	**Excel for the iPad Data Formats**
Format	*What You Enter*
General	Text or numbers with no specific format
Number	Numbers with no specific format
Currency	Monetary values; choose among different currencies
Accounting	Monetary values (choose this option to line up currency symbols and decimal points in a column)
Date	Date values
Time	Time values
Percentage	Numbers as percentage values (to obtain the values, Excel multiplies the cell values by 100 and shows the result with a percent symbol)

(continued)

Table 9-1 *(continued)*

Format	What You Enter
Fraction	The value as a fraction (choose a fraction on the submenu)
Scientific	Numbers in scientific notation
Text	Numbers treated as text (choose this option when numbers are used as descriptive labels)
Special	Numbers that identify ZIP codes, phone numbers, or Social Security numbers

Adding and Deleting Worksheets

Each workbook comes with one worksheet called Sheet1, and you can add worksheets to a workbook. To go from worksheet to worksheet, click Sheet tabs in the lower-left corner of the screen.

Follow these instructions to handle worksheets:

- **Adding a worksheet:** Click the Add Worksheet button (the plus sign) to the right of the worksheet tab or tabs.

- **Deleting a worksheet:** Tap the Sheet tab of the worksheet you want to delete. Then choose Delete on the popover menu.

- **Renaming a worksheet:** Double-tap the tab of the worksheet you want to rename. The keyboard appears. Enter a name and tap Done.

Constructing a Formula

Construct formulas in a worksheet to compute the data you so carefully and painstakingly entered in cells. Constructing a formula is a matter of doing these tasks:

- Tell Excel which cells to use in the computation.
- Tell Excel how to compute the data in the cells by using operators or a function.

These pages describe how to construct formulas.

Chapter 11 explains the basics of entering a formula, how to use operators in formulas, and how functions work. Turn to that chapter if you are new to constructing formulas in Excel.

Constructing a simple formula

Follow these basic steps to construct a formula:

1. **Double-tap the cell where you want to enter the formula.**

   Double-tapping selects the cell and activates the Formula bar.

2. **If necessary because the numbered keyboard isn't displayed, click the Numbers button to display the numbered keyboard.**

3. **In the Formula bar, enter the equals sign (=).**

   Be sure to enter the equals sign to enter a formula. All formulas must begin with an equals sign.

4. **Enter the formula, including cell references and operators.**

   For example, enter **=C1*.04**. Make sure to enter all cell addresses correctly. To enter cell references:

   - Type a cell reference in the Formula bar.

   - Tap a cell to reference it. Excel enters the address of the cell you tapped on the Formula bar. You can also select cells on the screen to enter a cell range as a reference. For example, selecting cells D27, D28, and D29 enters the cell range D27:D29 in the Formula bar.

   Notice that Excel color-codes cell references as you enter them to help you identify which cells are used in a formula.

5. **Press Return or click the Enter button (the check mark on the right side of Formula bar).**

   The results of the formula appear in the cell you selected in Step 1.

Including functions in formulas

As Chapter 11 explains in detail, functions are ready-made formulas that Excel provides. A function works with one or more arguments to compute a result. For example, the SUM function totals the data in a cell range; the AVG function averages the data in a cell range.

Make sure the cursor is in the Formula bar where you want the function to appear and use one of these techniques to include a function in a formula:

- ✔ On the Formulas tab, tap a button that represents the function category you need, and choose a function on the drop-down list.

- ✔ Type the first couple letters of the function you want to enter. A drop-down menu of functions appears, as shown in Figure 9-6. Tap a function to select and enter it in the Formula bar.

After you select a function, Excel enters the function and placeholders for entering arguments on the Formula bar.

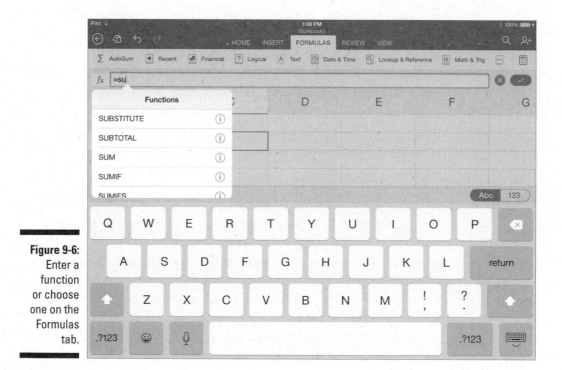

Figure 9-6:
Enter a
function
or choose
one on the
Formulas
tab.

Dressing Up a Worksheet

Excel for the iPad offers a handful of commands that you can use to dress up a worksheet and make it more presentable. You can apply colors to cells, draw borders around cells to call attention to data, and take advantage of cell styles to have Excel do the formatting work for you.

Select the cells you want to dress up, go to the Home tab, and follow these instructions to give your worksheet more pizazz:

- **Applying color:** Tap the Fill Color button and choose a color on the drop-down list. Choose No Fill (near the bottom of the list) to remove colors from cells.
- **Drawing borders:** Tap the Cell Borders button and choose a border on the drop-down list. The No Border option removes borders from cells.
- **Applying a cell style:** Tap the Cell Styles button and choose a style from the drop-down list. Choose the first option to remove a style.

You can copy cell formats from one cell range to another. To do so, select the cells with the formatting you want to copy and tap the Copy button on the popover menu. Then select the cells to which you will copy the formatting and choose Paste Format on the popover menu.

Another way to dress up a worksheet is to capture worksheet data in a table. Excel offers readymade table formats that you can apply to data. What's more, after you put data in a table, you can sort and filter data in the table. The next topic in this chapter describes tables.

Presenting Data in a Table

Although Excel is a spreadsheet program, many people use it to keep and maintain database tables, such as the table shown in Figure 9-7. Addresses, inventories, and employee data are examples of information that typically is kept in tables. These pages explain how to create a table, format the table, and sort and filter a table to make it yield more information. Sort a table to put it in alphabetical or numeric order; filter a table to isolate the information you need.

Creating and formatting a table

To create a table, start by entering the data. Make sure that the table has column headings to identify data. As well, consider entering row labels on the left side of the table to identify data in rows.

After you enter the data, follow these steps to turn it into a table:

1. **Tap anywhere in the data you want to use for the table.**
2. **Go to the Insert tab.**

3. Tap the Table button.

Excel creates the table. Notice the drop-down arrows on the column-heading cells. Tapping one of these arrows displays a drop-down menu with commands for sorting and filtering data (refer to Figure 9-7).

After you create or tap a table, the Table tab appears. It offers commands for handling tables.

4. On the Table tab, tap the Table Styles button.

A drop-down menu with table styles appears.

5. Select a table style.

The Table tab offers style options as well as table styles. Tap the Styles Options button and choose options on the drop-down list to format header rows, total rows, and the first and last column differently from the rest of the table.

To remove formats from a table, tap the Table Styles button and choose the first style on the drop-down menu. To remove a table but keep its data in the worksheet, tap the Convert To Range button on the Table tab.

Tap to see the Sort & Filter menu

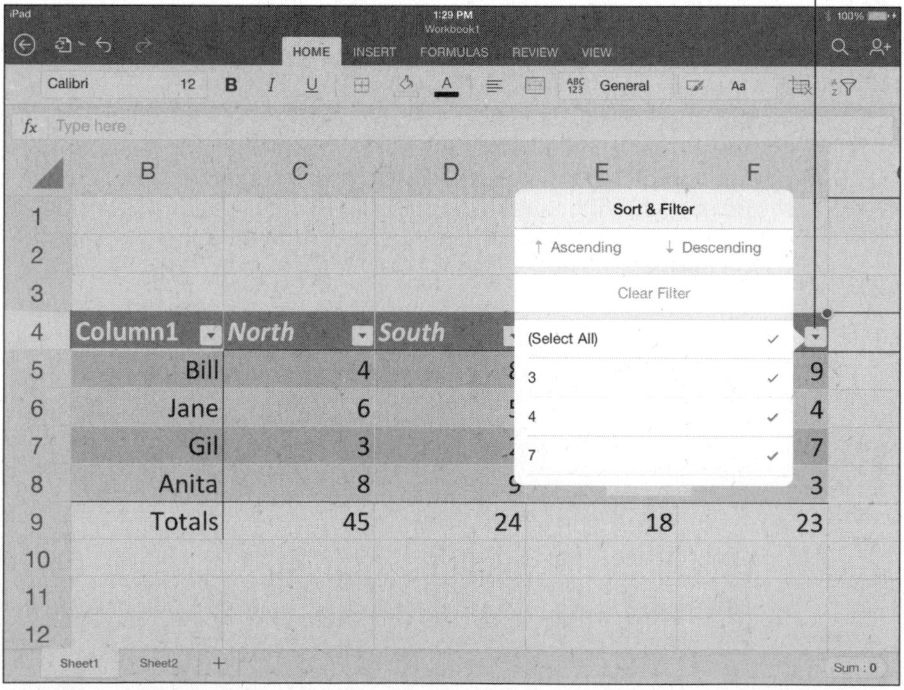

Figure 9-7: After you corral data into a table, you can sort and filter the information.

Sorting data in a table

Sorting means to rearrange the rows in a table on the basis of data in one or more columns. Sort a table on the Last Name column, for example, to arrange the table in alphabetical order by last name. Sort a table on the ZIP code column to arrange the rows in numerical order by ZIP code.

Follow these steps to sort data in a table:

1. **Decide which column to use for sorting.**

2. **At the top of the column you choose, tap the down-arrow.**

   The Sort & Filter drop-down menu appears (refer to Figure 9-7).

3. **Tap Ascending or Descending on the drop-down menu.**

   An *ascending sort* arranges data in alphabetical order, numerical order, or in order from the earliest in time to the latest in time.

   A *descending sort* arranges data from Z to A in alphabetical order; from the largest to the smallest number in numerical order; and from the latest to the earliest in time in the case of data that pertains to time.

You can tell how a table has been sorted because the Sort icon appears at the top of the column that was used for sorting. The arrow on the icon indicates whether the sort is descending or ascending.

Filtering for data in a table

Filtering means to scour a worksheet table for certain kinds of data. Excel for the iPad offers the ability to filter by exclusion. In this type of filter, you exclude data from the table. For example, to filter an address table for addresses in Boston, you designate Boston addresses as the ones you're filtering for and exclude all other cities from the table. The result is a table with Boston addresses only.

Follow these steps to filter a table:

1. **Decide which column to use for the filtering operation.**

2. **At the top of the column you choose, tap the down-arrow.**

   You see the Sort & Filter drop-down menu (refer to Figure 9-7). This menu lists all data in the table column you chose, with a check mark next to each data item.

3. **Tap Select All to remove the check mark next to this option and deselect all items in the menu.**

4. **On the Sort & Filter drop-down menu, tap each data item you want to include in the table.**

   For example, to include only the addresses of people from Boston in the table and exclude all other people, select Boston.

5. **Tap outside the table.**

   The table is filtered to present only the information you want.

To show that a table has been filtered, the filter icon appears at the top of the column used for filtering data.

To unfilter a table and make it display all its information, tap the filter icon and choose Select All on the Sort & Filter drop-down menu.

Chapter 10

Up and Running with Excel 2011

This chapter introduces *Excel,* the world's greatest number cruncher. The purpose of Excel is to track, analyze, and tabulate numbers. Use the program to project profits and losses, formulate a budget, or analyze Elvis sightings in North America. Doing the setup work takes time, but after you enter the numbers and tell Excel how to tabulate them, you're on Easy Street. Excel does the math for you. All you have to do is kick off your shoes, sit back, and see how the numbers stack up.

This chapter explains what a workbook and a worksheet is, and how rows and columns on a worksheet determine where cell addresses are. You also discover tips and tricks for entering data quickly in a worksheet, and how to construct data-validation rules to make sure that data is entered accurately.

Creating an Excel Workbook

When you start Excel, the program greets you with the Excel Workbook Gallery, as shown in Figure 10-1. *Workbook* is just the Excel term for the files you create with the program. You can track numbers with a generic workbook or you can take advantage of one of Excel's templates.

A *template* is a preformatted workbook designed for a specific purpose, such as budgeting, tracking inventories, or tracking purchase orders. Creating a workbook from a template is mighty convenient if you happen to find a template that suits your purposes, but in my experience, you almost always have to start from a generic, blank workbook because your data is your own. You need a workbook you create yourself, not one created from a template by someone else.

Follow these instructions to create a workbook:

- ✔ **Basic workbook:** Click the Close button in the Excel Workbook Gallery, click the New Workbook button on the Standard toolbar, press Command+N, or choose File➪New Workbook.

- ✔ **Template presentation:** Choose a template in the Excel Workbook Gallery (refer to Figure 10-1). To open this gallery, click the New from Template button on the Standard toolbar, press Shift+Command+P, or choose File➪New from Template.

    To choose a template in the Excel Workbook Gallery, select a templates category and then double-click a template. You can preview templates by clicking their names and looking in the Preview pane on the right side of the Excel Workbook Gallery.

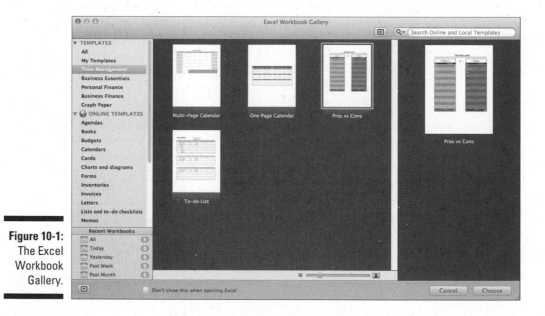

Figure 10-1:
The Excel Workbook Gallery.

Don't want to see the Excel Workbook Gallery when you start PowerPoint?

✔ Select the Don't Show This When Opening Excel check box at the bottom of the Excel Workbook Gallery.

✔ Choose Excel ⇨ Preferences. Then, in the Excel Preferences dialog box, choose General, and unselect the Open Excel Workbook Gallery When Application Opens check box.

Getting Acquainted with Excel

If you've spent any time in an Office program, much of the Excel screen may look familiar to you. The buttons on the Home tab — the Bold and the Align buttons, for example — work the same in Excel as they do in Word. The Font and Font Size drop-down lists work the same as well. Any command in Excel that has to do with formatting text and numbers works the same in Excel and Word.

As I mentioned earlier, an Excel file is a workbook. Each workbook comprises one or more worksheets. A *worksheet,* also known as a *spreadsheet,* is a table where you enter data and data labels. Figure 10-2 shows a worksheet with data about rainfall in different counties.

Active cell address

Formula bar

Active cell

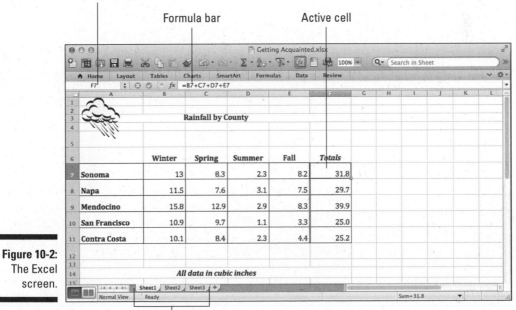

Figure 10-2:
The Excel
screen.

Worksheet tabs

A worksheet works like an accountant's ledger — only it's much easier to use. Notice how the worksheet is divided by gridlines into columns (A, B, C, and so on) and rows (1, 2, 3, and so on). The rectangles where columns and rows intersect are *cells,* and each cell can hold one data item, a formula for calculating data, or nothing at all. At the bottom of the worksheet are tabs — Sheet1, Sheet2, and Sheet3 — for visiting the other worksheets in the workbook.

Each cell has a different cell address. In Figure 10-2, cell B7 holds 13, the amount of rain that fell in Sonoma County in the winter. Meanwhile, as the Formula bar at the top of the screen shows, cell F7, the *active cell,* holds the formula =B7+C7+D7+E7, the sum of the numbers in cells — you guessed it — B7, C7, D7, and E7.

The beauty of Excel is that the program does all the calculations and recalculations for you after you enter the data. If I were to change the number in cell B7, Excel would instantly recalculate the total amount of rainfall in Sonoma County in cell F7. People like myself who struggled in math class will be glad to know that you don't have to worry about the math because Excel does it for you. All you have to do is make sure that the data and the formulas are entered correctly.

After you enter and label the data, enter the formulas, and turn your worksheet into a little masterpiece, you can start analyzing the data. For example, you can also generate charts like the one in Figure 10-3. Do you notice any similarities between the worksheet in Figure 10-2 and the chart in Figure 10-3? The chart is fashioned from data in the worksheet, and it took me about a half minute to create that chart. (Chapter 12 explains how to create charts in Excel.)

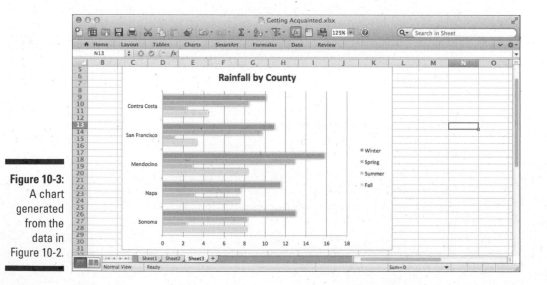

Figure 10-3:
A chart generated from the data in Figure 10-2.

Rows, columns, and cell addresses

Not that anyone needs all of them, but an Excel worksheet has numerous columns and over 1 million rows. The rows are numbered, and columns are labeled A to Z, then AA to AZ, then BA to BZ, and so on. The important thing to remember is that each cell has an address whose name comes from a column letter and a row number. The first cell in row 1 is A1, the second is B1, and so on. You need to enter cell addresses in formulas to tell Excel which numbers to compute.

To find a cell's address, either make note of which column and row it lies in, or click the cell and glance at the Formula bar (refer to Figure 10-2). The left side of the Formula bar lists the address of the *active cell,* the cell that is selected in the worksheet. In Figure 10-2, cell F7 is the active cell.

Workbooks and worksheets

When you create a new Excel file, you open a *workbook,* a file with one work-sheet in it. This worksheet is called Sheet1. (You can change its name and add more worksheets.) To get from worksheet to worksheet, click tabs along the bottom of the Excel window. You might need more than one worksheet for a single project. Think of a workbook as a stack of worksheets. Besides calculating the numbers in cells across the rows or down the columns of a worksheet, you can make calculations throughout a workbook by using numbers from different worksheets in a calculation.

Entering Data in a Worksheet

Entering data in a worksheet is an irksome activity. Fortunately, Excel offers a few shortcuts to take the sting out of it. These pages explain how to enter data in a worksheet, what the different types of data are, and how to enter text labels, numbers, dates, and times.

The basics of entering data

What you can enter in a worksheet cell falls into four categories:

- Text
- A value (numeric, date, or time)

✔ A logical value (True or False)

✔ A formula that returns a value, logical value, or text

Still, no matter what type of data you're entering, the basic steps are the same:

1. **Click the cell where you want to enter the data or text label.**

   As shown in Figure 10-4, a square appears around the cell to tell you that the cell you clicked is now the active cell. Glance at the left side of the Formula bar if you're not sure of the address of the cell you're about to enter data in. The Formula bar lists the cell address.

2. **Type the data in the cell.**

   If you find typing in the Formula bar easier, click and start typing there.

3. **Press the Return key to enter the number or label.**

   Notice the Cancel button (an *X*) and Enter button (a check mark) beside the Insert Function button (labeled *fx*) on the Formula bar. Besides pressing the Return key to enter a number or label, you can also press Tab or click the Enter button (the check mark) on the Formula bar.

   If you change your mind about entering data, click the Cancel button on the Formula bar or press Esc to delete what you entered and start over.

Chapter 11 explains how to enter logical values and formulas. The next several pages describe how to enter text labels, numeric values, date values, and time values.

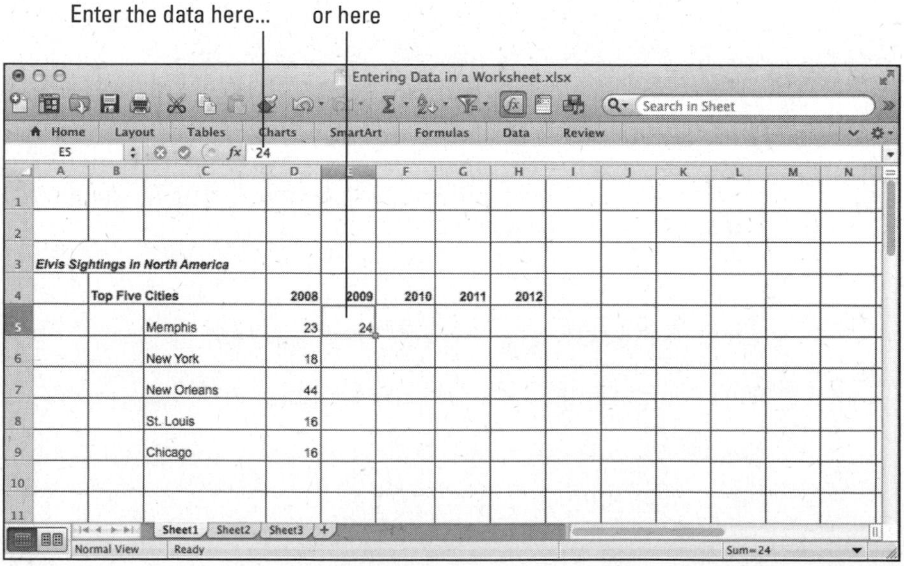

Enter the data here...   or here

Figure 10-4: Entering data.

Entering text labels

Sometimes a text entry is too long to fit in a cell. How Excel accommodates text entries that are too wide depends on whether data is in the cell to the right of the one you entered the text in:

- ✔ If the cell to the right is empty, Excel lets the text spill into the next cell.

- ✔ If the cell to the right contains data, the entry gets cut off. Nevertheless, the text you entered is in the cell. Nothing gets lost when it can't be displayed onscreen. You just can't see the text or numbers except by glancing at the Formula bar, where the contents of the active cell can be seen in their entirety.

To solve the problem of text that doesn't fit in a cell, widen the column, shorten the text entry, reorient the text (Chapter 11 explains aligning numbers and text in columns and rows), or wrap the contents of the cell. *Wrapping* means to run the text down to the next line, much the way the text in a paragraph runs to the next line when it reaches the right margin. Excel makes rows taller to accommodate wrapped text in a cell. To wrap text in cells, select the cells, go to the Home tab, click the Wrap Text button, and choose Wrap Text on the drop-down list.

Entering numeric values

When a number is too large to fit in a cell, Excel displays pound signs (###) instead of a number or displays the number in scientific notation. You can always glance at the Formula bar, however, to find out the number in the active cell. As well, you can always widen the column to display the entire number.

To enter a fraction in a cell, enter a 0 or a whole number, a blank space, and the fraction. For example, to enter $\frac{3}{8}$, type a **0**, press the spacebar, and type **3/8**. To enter $5\frac{3}{8}$, type the **5**, press the spacebar, and type **3/8**. For its purposes, Excel converts fractions to decimal numbers, as you can see by looking in the Formula bar after you enter a fraction. For example, $5\frac{3}{8}$ displays as 5.375 in the Formula bar.

Entering date and time values

Dates and times can be used in calculations, but entering a date or time value in a cell can be problematic because these values must be entered in such a way that Excel can recognize them as dates or times, not text.

Not that you need to know it especially, but Excel converts dates and times to serial values for the purpose of being able to use dates and times in calculations. For example, July 31, 2004, is the number 38199. July 31, 2004, at noon is 38199.5. These serial values represent the number of whole days since January 1, 1900. The portion of the serial value to the right of the decimal point is the time, represented as a portion of a full day.

Entering date values

You can enter a date value in a cell in just about any format you choose, and Excel understands that you're entering a date. For example, enter a date in any of the following formats and you'll be all right:

m/d/yy	7/31/10
m-d-yyyy	7-31-2010
d-mmm-yy	31-Jul-10

Here are some basic things to remember about entering dates:

- **Date formats:** You can quickly apply a format to dates by selecting cells and using one of these techniques:

  - On the Home tab, open the Number Format drop-down list and choose Date to render dates in this format: *m/d/yy*; 7/31/14, as shown in Figure 10-5.

  - On the Home tab, open the Number Format drop-down list and choose Custom (or press Command+1). The Number tab of the Format Cells dialog box, opens, as shown in Figure 10-5. Choose the Date category and then choose a date format.

- **Current date:** Press Control+; (semicolon) and press Return to enter the current date.

- **Current year's date:** If you don't enter the year as part of the date, Excel assumes that the date you entered is in the current year. For example, if you enter a date in the *m/d* (7/31) format during the year 2015, Excel enters the date as 7/31/15. As long as the date you want to enter is the current year, you can save a little time when entering dates by not entering the year, because Excel enters it for you.

- **Dates on the Formula bar:** No matter which format you use for dates, dates are displayed in the Formula bar in the format that Excel prefers for dates: *m/d/yyyy* (7/31/2010). How dates are displayed in the worksheet is up to you.

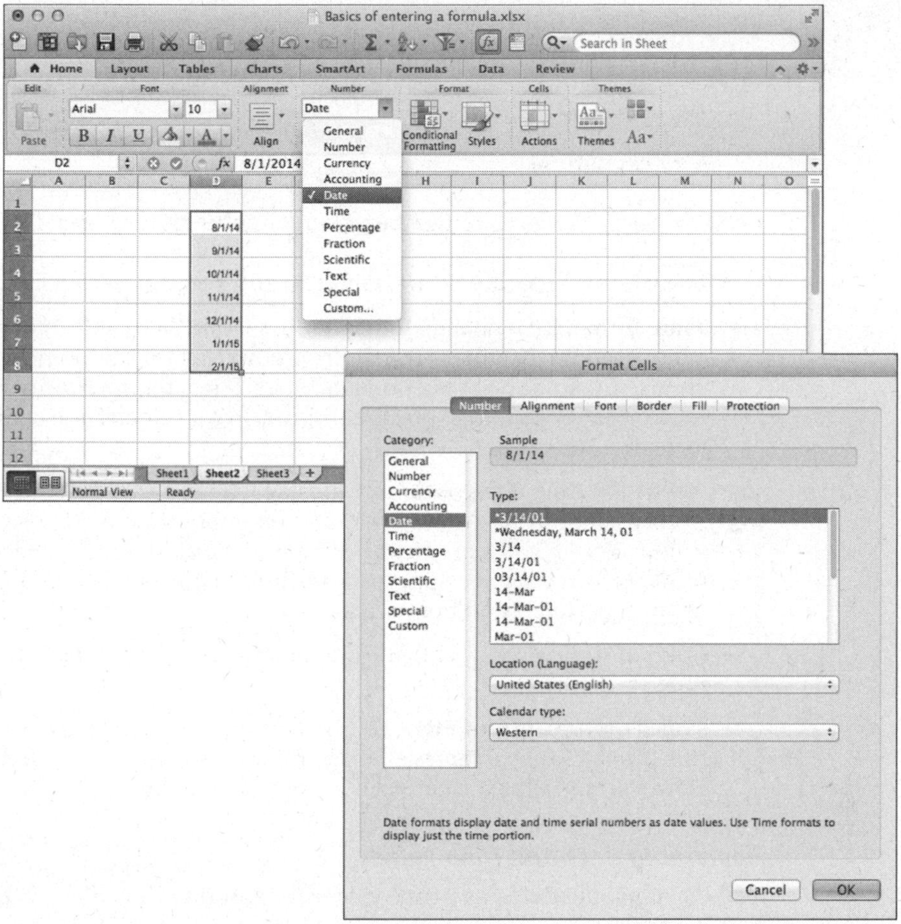

Figure 10-5:
Format
dates and
numbers on
the Number
Format
drop-down
list or
Format Cells
dialog box.

✔ **Twentieth and twenty-first century two-digit years:** When it comes to entering two-digit years in dates, the digits 30 through 99 belong to the 20th century (1930–1999), but the digits 00 through 29 belong to the 21st century (2000–2029). For example, 7/31/10 refers to July 31, 2010, not July 31, 1910. To enter a date in 1929 or earlier, enter four digits instead of two to describe the year: **7-31-1929**. To enter a date in 2030 or later, enter four digits instead of two: **7-31-2030**.

✔ **Dates in formulas:** To enter a date directly in a formula, enclose the date in quotation marks. (Make sure that the cell where the formula is entered has been given the Number format, not the Date format.) For example, the formula =TODAY()-"1/1/2010" calculates the number of days that have elapsed since January 1, 2010. Formulas are a subject of Chapter 11.

Entering time values

Excel recognizes time values that you enter in the following ways:

h:mm AM/PM	3:31 AM
h:mm:ss AM/PM	3:31:45 PM

Here are some things to remember when entering time values:

- **Use colons:** Separate hours, minutes, and seconds with a colon (:).
- **Time formats:** To change to the *h:mm:ss* AM/PM time format, select the cells, open the Number Format drop-down list on the Home tab, and choose Custom (or press Command+1). Then, on the Number tab of the Format Cells dialog box (see Figure 10-5), select Time and choose a format.
- **AM or PM time designations:** Unless you enter AM or PM with the time, Excel assumes that you're operating on military time. For example, 3:30 is considered 3:30 a.m.; 15:30 is 3:30 p.m. You can enter the letters *AM* or *PM* in lowercase or uppercase letters. Just be sure to enter the letters without periods (don't enter a.m. or p.m.).
- **Current time:** Press Control+Shift+; (semicolon) to enter the current time.
- **Times on the Formula bar:** On the Formula bar, times are displayed in this format: *hours:minutes:seconds,* followed by the letters AM or PM. However, the time format used in cells is up to you.

Combining date and time values

You can combine dates and time values by entering the date, a blank space, and the time:

- 7/31/10 3:31 am
- 7-31-10 3:31:45 pm

Quickly Entering Lists and Serial Data with the AutoFill Command

Data that falls in the "serial" category — month names, days of the week, and consecutive numbers and dates, for example — can be entered quickly with the AutoFill command. Believe it or not, Excel recognizes certain kinds of serial data and enters it for you as part of the AutoFill feature. Instead of laboriously entering this data one piece at a time, you can enter it all at one time by dragging the mouse. Follow these steps to "autofill" cells:

1. **Click the cell that is to be first in the series.**

   For example, if you intend to list the days of the week in consecutive cells, click where the first day is to go.

2. **Enter the first number, date, or list item in the series.**

3. **Move to the adjacent cell and enter the second number, date, or list item in the series.**

   If you want to enter the same number or piece of text in adjacent cells, it isn't necessary to take this step, but Excel needs the first and second items in the case of serial dates and numbers so that it can tell how much to increase or decrease the given amount or time period in each cell. For example, entering **5** and **10** tells Excel to increase the number by 5 each time so that the next serial entry is 15.

4. **Select the cell or cells you just entered data in.**

   To select a single cell, click it; to select two, drag over the cells.

5. **Click the AutoFill handle and start dragging in the direction in which you want the data series to appear on your worksheet.**

   The *AutoFill handle* is the small square in the lower-right corner of the cell or block of cells you selected. Finding it can be difficult. Carefully move the mouse pointer over the lower-right corner of the cell, and when you see the mouse pointer change into a black cross, click and start dragging. As you drag, the serial data appears in a pop-up box, as shown in Figure 10-6.

The AutoFill Options button appears after you enter the serial data. Click it and choose an option if you want to copy cells or fill the cells without carrying along their formats.

To enter the same number or text in several empty cells, drag over the cells to select them or select each cell by holding down the Command key as you click. Then type a number or some text and press Control+Return.

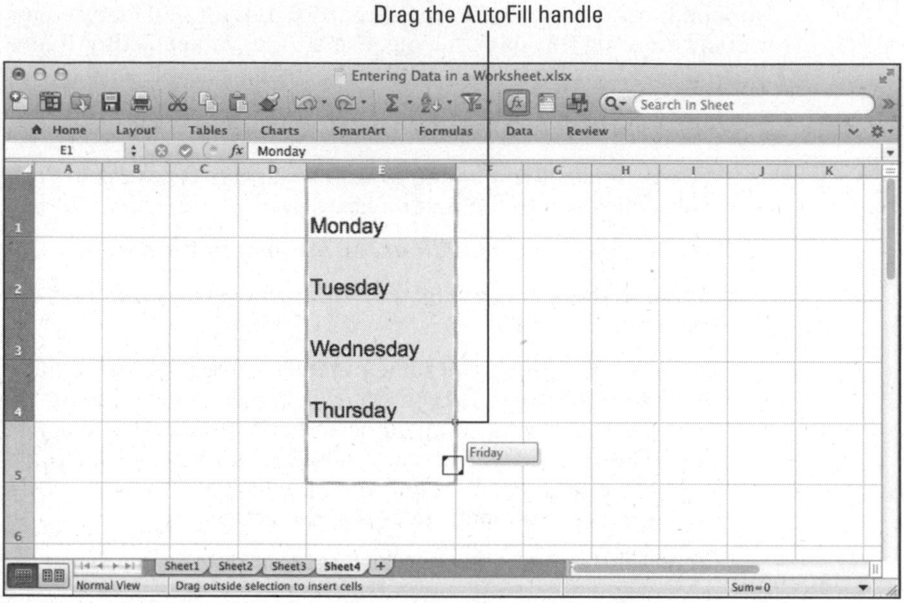

Drag the AutoFill handle

Figure 10-6:
Entering
serial
data —
days of the
week.

Creating your own AutoFill list

As you probably know, Excel is capable of completing lists on its own with the AutoFill feature. You can enter the days of the week or month names simply by entering one day or month and dragging the AutoFill handle to enter the others. Here's some good news: The AutoFill command can also reproduce the names of your co-workers, the roster of a softball team, street names, or any other list that you care to enter quickly and repeatedly in a worksheet.

Follow these steps to enter items for a list so that you can enter them in the future by dragging the AutoFill handle:

1. **If you've already entered items for the list on your worksheet, select the items.**

    If you haven't entered the items yet, skip to Step 2.

2. **Choose Excel ➪ Preferences.**

3. **Choose Custom Lists.**

    You see the Custom Lists dialog box shown here.

4. **In the List Entries box, do one of the following:**

    If you selected the items in Step 1, click the Import button. The items you selected appear in the List Entries box.

    If you need to enter items for the list, enter them in the List Entries box, with one item on each line.

5. **Click the Add button.**

6. **Click OK.**

Custom lists:	List entries:	
NEW LIST	Groucho	
Sun, Mon,...hu, Fri, Sat	Chico	
Sunday, M...y, Saturday	Harpo	
Jan, Feb,...ct, Nov, Dec	Zeppo	
January, F..., December		Add
Groucho,...arpo, Zeppo		Delete

Press RETURN to separate list entries.

Import list from cells:

$G$2:$G$5   [   ]   Import

Description

Import

Creates a custom list from existing items in a data range. Click in the Import List From Cells box, select the range on the sheet, and then click Import.

Cancel   OK

Formatting Numbers, Dates, and Time Values

When you enter a number that Excel recognizes as belonging to one of its formats, Excel assigns the number format automatically. Enter **45%**, for example, and Excel assigns the Percentage Style format. Enter **$4.25**, and Excel assigns the Currency Style format. Besides assigning formats by hand, however, you can assign them to cells from the get-go and spare yourself the trouble of entering dollar signs, commas, percent signs, and other extraneous punctuation. All you have to do is enter the raw numbers. Excel does the window dressing for you.

Excel offers five number-formatting buttons on the Home tab — Accounting Number Format, Percent Style, Comma Style, Increase Decimal, and Decrease Decimal. Select cells with numbers in them and click one of these buttons to change how numbers are formatted:

- ✔ **Accounting Number Format:** Places a dollar sign before the number and gives it two decimal places. You can open the drop-down list on this button and choose a currency symbol apart from the dollar sign.

- ✔ **Percent Style:** Places a percent sign after the number and converts the number to a percentage.

- ✔ **Comma Style:** Places commas in the number.

- ✔ **Increase Decimal:** Increases the number of decimal places by one.

- ✔ **Decrease Decimal:** Decreases the number of decimal places by one.

To choose among many formats and to format dates and time values as well as numbers, choose Format ➪ Cells (or press Command+1) to open the Number tab of the Format Cells dialog box. Figure 10-7 shows this dialog box. Choose a category and select options to describe how you want numbers or text to appear.

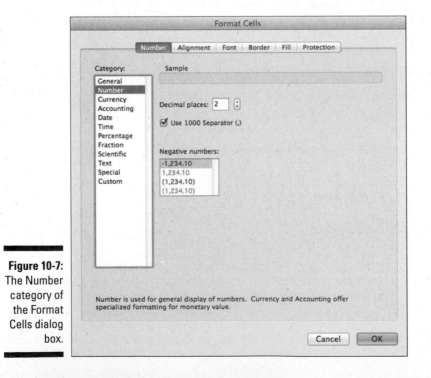

Figure 10-7: The Number category of the Format Cells dialog box.

To strip formats from the data in cells, select the cells and choose Edit ⇨ Clear ⇨ Formats.

 Entering ZIP codes can be problematic because Excel strips the initial zero from the number if it begins with a zero. To get around that problem, visit the Number tab of the Format Cells dialog box (see Figure 10-7), choose Special in the Category list, and select a ZIP Code option.

Conditional Formats for Calling Attention to Data

A *conditional format* is one that applies when data meets certain conditions. To call attention to numbers greater than 10,000, for example, you can tell Excel to highlight those numbers automatically. To highlight negative numbers, you can tell Excel to display them in bright red. Conditional formats help you analyze and understand data better.

Select the cells that are candidates for conditional formatting and follow these steps to tell Excel when and how to format the cells:

1. **On the Home tab, click the Conditional Formatting button (you may have to click the Styles button first, depending on the size of your screen).**

2. **Choose Highlight Cells Rules or Top/Bottom Rules on the drop-down list.**

   You see a submenu with choices about establishing the rule for whether values in the cells are highlighted or otherwise made more prominent:

   • *Highlight Cells Rules:* These rules are for calling attention to data if it falls in a numerical or date range, or it's greater or lesser than a specific value. For example, you can highlight cells that are greater than 400.

   • *Top/Bottom Rules:* These rules are for calling attention to data if it falls within a percentage range relative to all the cells you selected. For example, you can highlight cells with data that falls in the bottom ten-percent range.

3. **Choose an option on the submenu.**

   You see a dialog box similar to the ones in Figure 10-8.

4. **Enter criteria to establish the rule for flagging data.**

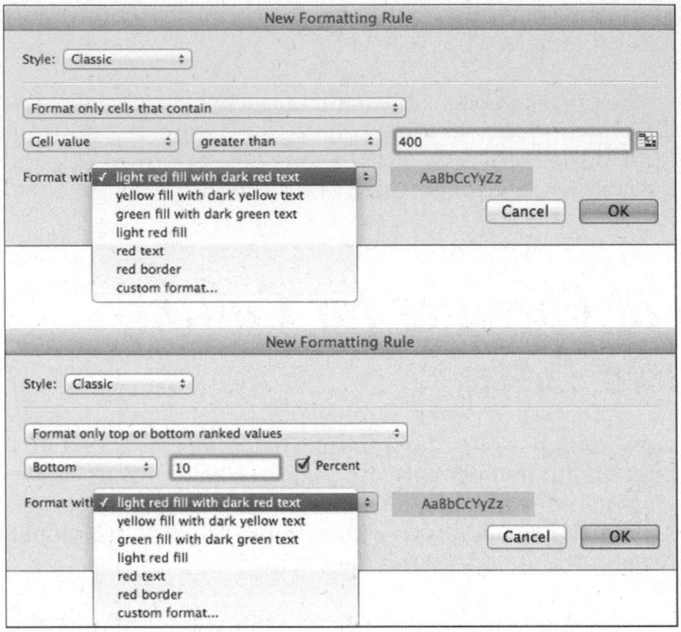

Figure 10-8:
Establishing
a condition
format for
data.

5. **On the Format With drop-down list, choose how you want to call attention to the data.**

   For example, you can display the data in red or yellow. You can choose Custom Format on the drop-down list to open the Format Cells dialog box and choose a font style or color for the text.

6. **Click OK.**

To remove conditional formats, select the cells with the formats, go to the Home tab, click the Conditional Formatting button, and choose Clear Rules ⇨ Clear Rules from Selected Cells.

Establishing Data-Validation Rules

By nature, people are prone to enter data incorrectly because the task of entering data is so dull. This is why data-validation rules are invaluable. A *data-validation rule* is a rule concerning what kind of data can be entered in a cell. When you select a cell that has been given a rule, an input message tells you what to enter, as shown in Figure 10-9. And if you enter the data incorrectly, an error alert tells you as much, also shown in Figure 10-9.

Input message   Error alert

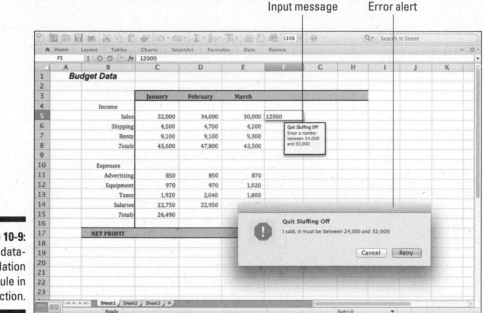

Figure 10-9:
A data-
validation
rule in
action.

Data-validation rules are an excellent defense against sloppy data entry and
that itchy feeling you get when you're in the middle of an irksome task. In a
cell that records date entries, you can require dates to fall in a certain time
frame. In a cell that records text entries, you can choose an item from a list
instead of typing it yourself. In a cell that records numeric entries, you can
require the number to fall within a certain range. Table 10-1 describes the
different categories of data-validation rules.

Table 10-1	Data-Validation Rule Categories
Rule	*What Can Be Entered*
Any Value	Anything whatsoever. This is the default setting.
Whole Number	Whole numbers (no decimal points allowed). Choose an operator from the Data drop-down list and values to describe the range of numbers that can be entered.
Decimal	Same as the Whole Number rule except that numbers with decimal points are permitted.

(continued)

Table 10-1 *(continued)*

Rule	What Can Be Entered
List	Items from a list. Enter the list items in cells on a worksheet, either the one you're working in or another. Then reopen the Data Validation dialog box, click the Range Selector button (you can find it on the right side of the Source text box), and select the cells that hold the list. The list items appear in a drop-down list on the worksheet.
Date	Date values. Choose an operator from the Data drop-down list and values to describe the date range. Earlier in this chapter, "Entering date and time values" describes the correct way to enter date values.
Time	Time values. Choose an operator from the Data drop-down list and values to describe the date and time range. Earlier in this chapter, "Entering date and time values" describes the correct way to enter a combination of date and time values.
Text Length	A certain number of characters. Choose an operator from the Data drop-down list and values to describe how many characters can be entered.
Custom	A logical value (True or False). Enter a formula that describes what constitutes a True or False data entry.

Follow these steps to establish a data-validation rule:

1. **Select the cell or cells that need a rule.**

2. **On the Data tab, click the Validate button.**

   As shown in Figure 10-10, you see the Settings tab of the Data Validation dialog box.

3. **On the Allow drop-down list, choose the category of rule you want.**

   Table 10-1, shown previously, describes these categories.

4. **Enter the criteria for the rule.**

   What the criteria is depends on what rule category you're working in. Table 10-1 describes how to enter the criteria for rules in each category. You can refer to cells in the worksheet by selecting them. To do that, either select them directly or click the Range Selector button and then select them.

Data Validation

Settings | Input Message | Error Alert

Validation criteria

Allow: ☑ Ignore blank
Whole number ⇕

Data:
between ⇕

Minimum:
24000

Maximum:
32000

☐ Apply the

Clear All

Data Validation

Settings | Input Message | Error Alert

☑ Show input message when cell is selected

When cell is selected, show this input message:

Title:
Quit Sluffing Off

Input message:
Enter a number between 24,000 and 32,000.

Clear All

Data Validation

Settings | Input Message | Error Alert

☑ Show error alert after invalid data is entered

When user enters invalid data, show this error alert:

Style: Title:
Stop ⇕   Quit Sluffing Off

                                Error message:
                                I said, enter a number between 24,000
                                and 32,000.

Clear All   Cancel   OK

**Figure
10-10:**
Creating
a data-
validation
rule.

5. **On the Input Message tab, enter a title and input message.**

   You can see a title ("Quit Sluffing Off") and input message ("Enter a number between 24,000 and 32,000") in Figure 10-9. The title appears in boldface. Briefly describe what kind of data belongs in the cell or cells you selected.

6. **On the Error Alert tab, choose a style for the symbol in the Message Alert dialog box, enter a title for the dialog box, and enter a warning message.**

   In the error message in the bottom part of Figure 10-10, the Stop symbol was chosen. The title you enter appears across the top of the dialog box, and the message appears beside the symbol.

7. **Click OK.**

   To remove data-validation rules from cells, select the cells, go to the Data tab, click the Validate button, and on the Settings tab of the Data Validation dialog box, click the Clear All button; then click OK.

Chapter 11

Refining Your Worksheet

This chapter delves into the workaday world of worksheets (say that three times fast). It explains how to edit worksheet data and move quickly here and there in a worksheet. You also discover techniques for entering data quickly, selecting cells, and copying and moving data in cells. This chapter describes how to move, delete, and rename worksheets, as well as protect them from being edited or altered.

Formulas are where it's at as far as Excel is concerned. After you know how to construct formulas — and constructing them is pretty easy — you can put Excel to work. You can make the numbers speak to you. You can turn a bunch of unruly numbers into meaningful figures and statistics. This chapter explains what a formula is, how to enter a formula, and how to make use of the hundred or so functions that Excel offers.

Editing Worksheet Data

Not everyone enters data correctly the first time. To edit data you entered in a cell, do one of the following:

- **Double-click the cell.** Doing so places the cursor squarely in the cell, where you can start deleting or entering numbers and text.

- **Click the cell you want to edit.** With this technique, you edit the data on the Formula bar.

Moving Around in a Worksheet

Use these techniques to get from place to place in a worksheet:

- **Scroll bars:** Use the vertical and horizontal scroll bars to move to different areas.

- **Scroll wheel on the mouse:** If your mouse is equipped with a scroll wheel, turn the wheel to quickly scroll up and down.

- **Name Box:** Enter a cell address in the Name Box and press Return to go to the cell. The Name Box is found to the left of the Formula bar.

- **The Go To command:** Choose Edit ⇨ Go To (or press Control+G). You see the Go To dialog box. Enter a cell address in the Reference box and click OK. Cell addresses you've already visited with the Go To command are already listed in the dialog box. Click the Special button to open the Go To Special dialog box and visit a formula, comment, or other esoteric item.

- **The Find command:** Choose Edit ⇨ Find (or press Ctrl+F). Enter the data you seek in the Find What box and click the Find Next button.

To scroll to the active cell if you no longer see it onscreen, press Control+Delete.

Getting a Better Look at the Worksheet

Especially when you're entering data, it pays to get a good look at the worksheet. You need to know which column and row you're entering data in. These pages explain techniques for changing your view of a worksheet so that you always know where you are. Read on to discover how to freeze, split, and hide columns and rows.

Freezing and splitting columns and rows

Sometimes your adventures in a worksheet take you to a faraway cell address, such as X31 or C39. Out there in the wilderness, it's hard to tell where to enter data because you can't see the data labels in the first column or first row that tell you where to enter data on the worksheet.

To see one part of a worksheet no matter how far you stray from it, you can *split* the worksheet or *freeze* columns and rows onscreen. In Figure 11-1, I split the worksheet so that column A (Property) always appears onscreen no matter how far I scroll to the right; similarly, row 1 (Property, Rent, Management Fees, and so on) also appears at the top of the worksheet no matter how far I scroll down. Notice how the row numbers and column letters are interrupted in Figure 11-1. Because I split the screen, I always know what data to enter in a cell because I can clearly see property names in the first column and the column headings along the top of the worksheet.

Freezing columns or rows on a worksheet works much like splitting except that lines instead of gray bars appear onscreen to show which columns and rows are frozen, and you can't adjust where the split occurs by dragging the boundary where the worksheet is split.

Splitting the worksheet is superior to freezing columns or rows because, for one, you can drag the split lines to new locations when you split the worksheet, and moreover, you can remove a horizontal or vertical split simply by double-clicking it. However, if your goal is simply to freeze the topmost row or leftmost column in your worksheet, use a Freeze Panes command because all you have to do is go to the View tab, click the Freeze Panes button, and choose Freeze Top Row or Freeze First Column.

Double-click to remove a split

Drag to adjust the split   Split bar

	A	D	E	F	G	H	I	J	K	L	M	N
1	Property	Rent	Management Fee	Utilities	Trash							
2	4127 Darius St.	450.00	67.50	45.19	13.48							
10	28 Chula Vista	450.00	67.50	56.13	22.45							
11	999 Cortland Ave.											
12	Apt. A	400.00	60.00	210.12	198.12							
13	Apt. B	350.00	52.50									
14	Apt. C	785.00	117.75									
15	Apt. D	650.00	97.50									
16	93 Churnwell Terrac	490.00	73.50	87.12	37.32							
17	127 Firth St.	900.00	135.00	56.14	45.12							
18	239 Ferrow Dr.	450.00	67.50	23.29	22.45							
19	410 North Umbert St	685.00	102.75	47.14	16.8							
20		10,230.00	1,534.50	786.01	540.14							
21												

Getting a Better Look at the Worksheet.xlsx

G12 — 198.12

Home   Layout   Tables   Charts   SmartArt   Formulas   Data   Review

Normal View   Ready   Sum= 198.12

Figure 11-1:
Splitting a
worksheet.

Giving the Split or Freeze Panes command

Follow these steps to split or freeze columns and rows onscreen:

1. **Click the cell directly below the row you want to freeze or split, and click in the column to the right of the column that you want to freeze or split.**

   In other words, click where you want the split to occur.

2. **Split or freeze the columns and rows.**

   Use one of these techniques:

   - *Splitting:* Choose Window ⇨ Split and then click and drag the split bars to split the screen horizontally or vertically. The other way to split a worksheet is to grab hold of a *split bar,* the little division markers directly above the vertical scroll bar and directly to the right of the horizontal scroll bar (in the lower-right corner of your screen). You can tell where split bars are because the pointer turns into a double arrow when it's over a split bar.

   - *Freezing:* Choose Window ⇨ Freeze Panes. This freezes the column(s) to the left and the row(s) above the cell you selected in Step 1.

   Bars or lines appear onscreen to show which row(s) and column(s) have been frozen or split. Move where you will in the worksheet. The column(s) and row(s) you froze or split stay onscreen.

Unsplitting and unfreezing

Use one of these techniques to keep your worksheet from splitting or freezing to death:

- **Unsplitting:** Double-click one of the split bars to remove it, drag a split bar into the top or left side of the worksheet window, or choose Window ⇨ Remove Split.

- **Unfreezing:** Choose Window ⇨ Unfreeze Panes.

Hiding columns and rows

Another way to take the clutter out of a worksheet is to temporarily hide columns and rows:

- **Hiding columns or rows:** Drag over the column letters or row numbers of the columns or rows that you want to hide. Dragging this way selects entire columns or rows. Then right-click the columns or rows you selected and choose Hide on the shortcut menu.

✔ **Unhiding columns and rows:** Select columns to the right and left of the hidden columns, or select rows above and below the hidden rows. To select columns or rows, drag over their letters or numbers. Then right-click and choose Unhide.

Your own customized views

After you go to the trouble of freezing the screen or zooming in to a position you're comfortable with, you may as well save your view of the screen as a customized view. That way, you can call upon the customized view whenever you need it. View settings, the window size, the position of the grid onscreen, and cells that are selected can all be saved in a customized view.

Follow these steps to create a customized view:

1. **Choose View⇨Custom Views.**

You see the Custom Views dialog box. It lists views you've already created, if you've created any.

2. **Click the Add button.**

The Add View dialog box appears.

3. **Enter a name for the view and click OK.**

To switch to a customized view, click the Custom Views button, select a view in the Custom Views dialog box, and click the Show button.

Custom Views

Views:

Freezer
Zoomer

Show

Close

Add...

Delete

Add View

Name: Entry

Include in view

☑ Print settings
☑ Hidden rows, columns and filter settings

Cancel   OK

Comments for Documenting Your Worksheet

It may happen that you return to your worksheet days or months from now and discover to your dismay that you don't know why certain numbers or formulas are there. For that matter, someone else may inherit your worksheet and be mystified as to what the heck is going on. To take the mystery out of a worksheet, you can document it by entering comments here and there.

A *comment* is a note that describes part of a worksheet. Each comment is connected to a cell. You can tell where a comment is because a small red triangle appears in the upper-right corner of cells that have been commented on. Move the pointer over one of these triangles and you see the pop-up box, a comment, and the name of the person who entered the comment, as shown in Figure 11-2. Click the Show All button on the Review tab to see every comment in a worksheet.

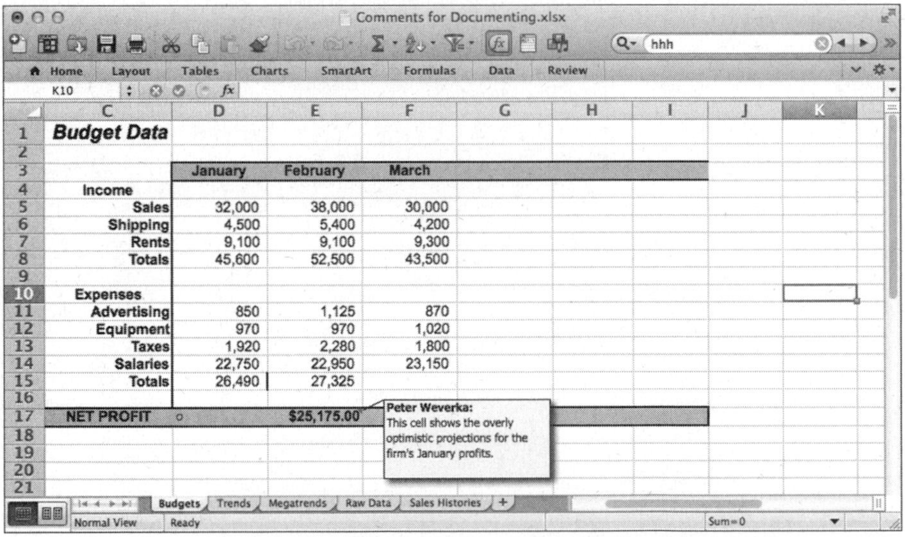

Figure 11-2: Comments explain what's what in a worksheet.

Here's everything a mere mortal needs to know about comments:

- ✔ **Entering a comment:** Click the cell that deserves the comment, go to the Review tab, and click the New button. Enter your comment in the pop-up box. Click in a different cell when you finish entering your comment.

✔ **Reading a comment:** Move the pointer over the small red triangle and read the comment in the pop-up box (refer to Figure 11-2).

✔ **Finding comments:** On the Review tab, click the Previous or Next button to go from comment to comment.

✔ **Editing a comment:** Select the cell with the comment and then right-click the cell and choose Edit Comment.

✔ **Deleting comments:** On the Review tab, click a cell with a comment and then click the Delete button, or right-click the cell and choose Delete Comment. To delete several comments, select them by Command+clicking and then click the Delete button.

If your name doesn't appear in the pop-up box after you enter a comment, and you want it to appear there, choose Excel⇨Preferences, select the General category in the Excel Preferences dialog box, and enter your name in the User Name text box.

Selecting Cells in a Worksheet

To copy, move, delete, and format numbers and words in a worksheet, you have to select the cells in which the numbers and words are found. Here are ways to select cells and the data inside them:

✔ **A block of cells:** Drag diagonally across the worksheet from one corner of the block of cells to the opposite corner. You can also click in one corner and Shift+click the opposite corner.

✔ **Adjacent cells in a row or column:** Drag across the cells.

✔ **Cells in various places:** While holding down the Command key, click different cells.

✔ **A row or rows:** Click a row number to select an entire row. Click and drag down the row numbers to select several adjacent rows.

✔ **A column or columns:** Click a column letter to select an entire column. Click and drag across letters to select adjacent columns.

✔ **Entire worksheet:** Click the Select All button, the square to the left of the column letters and above the row numbers; or press Command+A.

Press Ctrl+spacebar to select the column that the active cell is in; press Shift+spacebar to select the row where the active cell is.

Deleting, Copying, and Moving Data

In the course of putting together a worksheet, it is sometimes necessary to delete, copy, and move cell contents. Here are instructions for doing these chores:

- **Deleting cell contents:** Choose Edit ⇨ Clear ⇨ Contents or right-click and choose Clear Contents.

- **Copying and moving cell contents:** Select the cells and use one of these techniques:

  - *Cut or Copy and Paste commands:* Use the Cut or Copy command (choose Edit ⇨ Cut or Edit ⇨ Copy, or click the Cut or Copy button on the Standard toolbar). Then, to paste the data, click where you want the first cell of the block of cells you're copying or moving to go and choose Edit ⇨ Paste or click the Paste button on the Standard toolbar. After you paste data, you see the Paste Options button. Click this button and choose an option from the drop-down list to format the data in different ways.

  - *Drag and drop:* Move the pointer to the edge of the cell block, click when you see the hand pointer, and start dragging.

Handling the Worksheets in a Workbook

As a glance at the bottom of the worksheet tells you, each workbook comes with one worksheet named (not very creatively) Sheet1. Follow these instructions to add, move among, delete, rename, and change the order of worksheets:

- **Inserting a new worksheet:** Click the Insert Sheet button or press Insert ⇨ Sheet ⇨ Blank Sheet.

- **Moving among worksheets:** To go from one worksheet to another, click a worksheet tab along the bottom of the screen. If you can't see a tab, click one of the scroll arrows to the left of the worksheet tabs.

- **Renaming a worksheet:** Double-click the worksheet tab, type a new name, and press Return. You can also choose Format ⇨ Sheet ⇨ Rename and enter a new name. Spaces are allowed in names, and names can be 31 characters long.

- **Selecting worksheets:** Click the worksheet's tab to select it. To select several worksheets, Command+click their tabs or click the first tab and then Shift+click the last tab in the set. To select all the worksheets, right-click a tab and choose Select All Sheets on the shortcut menu.

✔ **Rearranging worksheets:** Drag the worksheet tab to a new location. As you drag, a tiny black triangle appears to show you where the worksheet will land after you release the mouse button. You can also right-click a worksheet and choose Move or Copy Sheet on the drop-down list. The Move or Copy dialog box appears, as shown in Figure 11-3. Select the sheet in the Before Sheet list where you want the worksheet to go and click OK.

✔ **Deleting a worksheet:** Right-click a worksheet tab and choose Delete. Be careful, because you can't restore your deleted worksheet by pressing the Undo button.

✔ **Color-coding a worksheet:** Right-click a worksheet tab and choose Tab Color. Then select a color in the Tab Color dialog box, or choose More Colors and select a color in the Colors dialog box. Click the dialog box's Close button (in the upper-right corner) to close the dialog box.

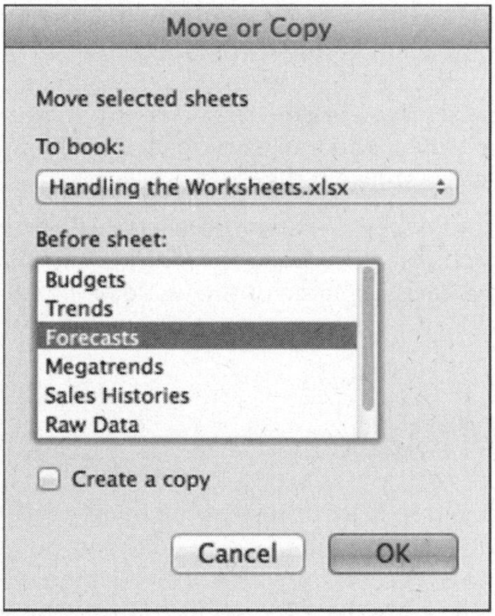

Figure 11-3:
Besides dragging it, you can move a worksheet in this dialog box.

> **Move or Copy**
>
> Move selected sheets
> **To book:**
> Handling the Worksheets.xlsx ⬍
> **Before sheet:**
> Budgets
> Trends
> Forecasts
> Megatrends
> Sales Histories
> Raw Data
>
> ☐ Create a copy
>
> Cancel   OK

TIP You can change the size of columns or apply numeric formats to the same addresses in different worksheets by selecting all the sheets first and then formatting one worksheet. The formats apply to all the worksheets that you select. Being able to format several different worksheets simultaneously comes in handy, for example, when your workbook tracks monthly data and each worksheet pertains to one month. Another way to handle worksheets with similar data is to create the first worksheet and copy it to the second, third, and fourth worksheets with the Copy and Paste commands.

Keeping Others from Tampering with Worksheets

People with savvy and foresight sometimes set up workbooks so that one worksheet holds raw data and the other worksheets hold formulas that calculate the raw data. This technique prevents others from tampering with the raw data. Furthermore, if the worksheet with raw data is hidden, the chance that it will be tampered with is lower; and if the worksheet is protected, no one can tamper with it unless he or she has a password. These pages explain how to hide a worksheet so that others are less likely to find it, as well as how to protect a worksheet from being edited.

Hiding a worksheet

Follow these instructions to hide and unhide worksheets:

- **Hiding a worksheet:** Select the worksheet you want to hide; then choose Format ⇨ Sheet ⇨ Hide. You can also right-click the worksheet's tab and choose Hide on the shortcut menu.

- **Unhiding a worksheet:** Choose Format ⇨ Sheet ⇨ Unhide or right-click any worksheet tab and choose Unhide on the shortcut menu. You see the Unhide dialog box. Select the name of the worksheet you want to unhide and click OK.

Protecting a worksheet

Protecting a worksheet means to restrict others from changing it — from formatting it, inserting new rows and columns, or deleting rows and columns, among other tasks. You can also prevent any editorial changes whatsoever from being made to a worksheet. Follow these steps to protect a worksheet from tampering by others:

1. **Open the worksheet that needs protection.**

2. **On the Review tab, click the Sheet button.**

   You see the Protect Sheet dialog box shown in Figure 11-4. You can also open this dialog box by right-clicking a worksheet tab and choosing Protect Sheet.

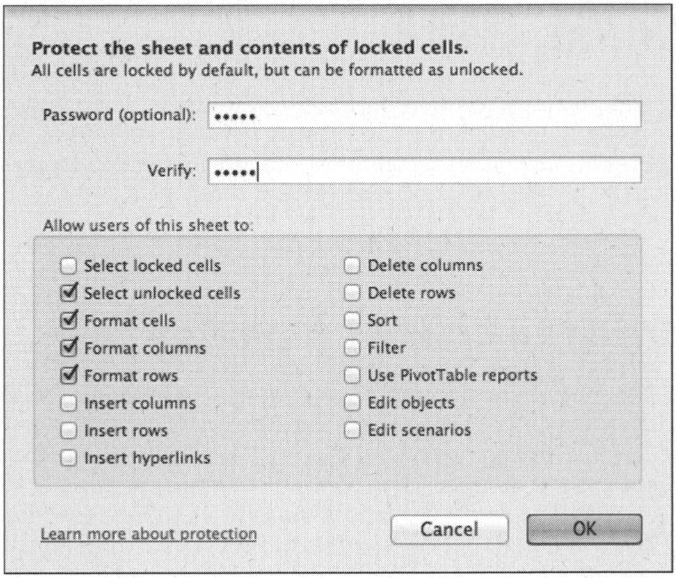

Protect the sheet and contents of locked cells.
All cells are locked by default, but can be formatted as unlocked.

Password (optional): •••••

Verify: •••••

Allow users of this sheet to:

☐ Select locked cells   ☐ Delete columns
☑ Select unlocked cells   ☐ Delete rows
☑ Format cells   ☐ Sort
☑ Format columns   ☐ Filter
☑ Format rows   ☐ Use PivotTable reports
☐ Insert columns   ☐ Edit objects
☐ Insert rows   ☐ Edit scenarios
☐ Insert hyperlinks

Learn more about protection   [Cancel] [OK]

Figure 11-4:
Select what
you want
others to be
able to do.

3. **Enter a password in the Password text box if you want only people with the password to be able to unprotect the worksheet after you protect it.**

   Enter the password in the Verify text box as well if you want to password-protect the sheet.

4. **On the Allow All Users of This Sheet To list, select the check box next to the name of each task that you want to permit others to do.**

   For example, click the Format Cells check box if you want others to be able to format cells.

   Deselect the Select Locked Cells check box to prevent any changes from being made to the worksheet. By default, all worksheet cells are locked, and by preventing others from selecting locked cells, you effectively prevent them from editing any cells.

5. **Click OK.**

   The Lock icon appears on worksheets that have been locked.

To unprotect a worksheet that you protected, choose
Tools ➪ Protection ➪ Unprotect Sheet. You must enter a password if you elected to require others to have a password before they can unprotect a worksheet.

How Formulas Work

A *formula,* as you may recall from the sleepy hours you spent in math class, is a way to calculate numbers. For example, 2+3=5 is a formula. When you enter a formula in a cell, Excel computes the formula and displays its results in the cell. Click in cell A3 and enter **=2+3**, for example, and Excel displays the number 5 in cell A3.

Referring to cells in formulas

As well as numbers, Excel formulas can refer to the contents of different cells. When a formula refers to a cell, the number in the cell is used to compute the formula. In Figure 11-5, for example, cell A1 contains the number 2; cell A2 contains the number 3; and cell A3 contains the formula =A1+A2. As shown in cell A3, the result of the formula is 5. If I change the number in cell A1 from 2 to 3, the result of the formula in cell A3 (=A1+A2) becomes 6, not 5. When a formula refers to a cell and the number in the cell changes, the result of the formula changes as well.

Formula in the Formula bar

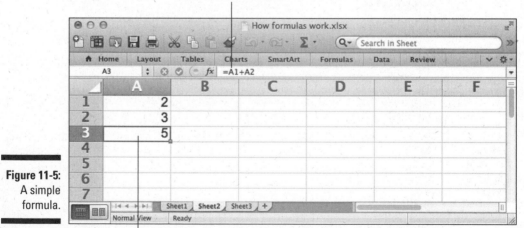

Figure 11-5:
A simple
formula.

Results of the formula

To see the value of using cell references in formulas, consider the worksheet shown in Figure 11-6. The purpose of this worksheet is to track the budget of a school's Parent Teacher Association (PTA):

- ✔ Column C, Actual Income, lists income from different sources.

- ✔ Column D, Projected Income, shows what the PTA members thought income from these sources would be.

- ✔ Column E, Over/Under Budget, shows how actual income compares to projected income from the different sources.

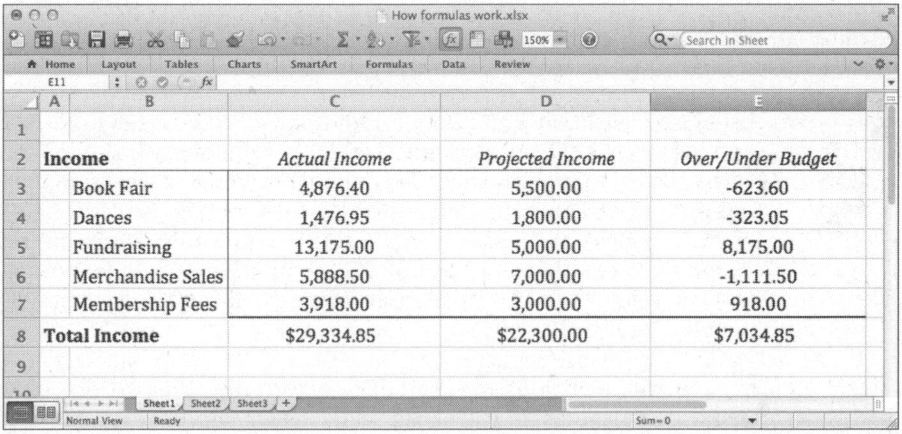

	Income	Actual Income	Projected Income	Over/Under Budget
3	Book Fair	4,876.40	5,500.00	-623.60
4	Dances	1,476.95	1,800.00	-323.05
5	Fundraising	13,175.00	5,000.00	8,175.00
6	Merchandise Sales	5,888.50	7,000.00	-1,111.50
7	Membership Fees	3,918.00	3,000.00	918.00
8	Total Income	$29,334.85	$22,300.00	$7,034.85

Figure 11-6: Using formulas in a worksheet.

As the figures in the Actual Income column (column C) are updated, figures in the Over/Under Budget column (column E) and the Total Income row (row 8) change instantaneously. These figures change instantaneously because the formulas refer to the numbers in cells, not to unchanging numbers (known as *constants*).

Figure 11-7 shows the formulas used to calculate the data in the worksheet in Figure 11-6. In column E, formulas deduct the numbers in column D from the numbers in column C to show where the PTA over- or underbudgeted for the different sources of income. In row 8, you can see how the SUM function is used to total cells in rows 3 through 7. The end of this chapter explains how to use functions in formulas.

	A	B	C	D	E
1					
2	**Income**		*Actual Income*	*Projected Income*	*Over/Under Budget*
3		Book Fair	4876.4	5500	=C3-D3
4		Dances	1476.95	1800	=C4-D4
5		Fundraising	13175	5000	=C5-D5
6		Merchandise Sales	5888.5	7000	=C6-D6
7		Membership Fees	3918	3000	=C7-D7
8	**Total Income**		=SUM(C3:C7)	=SUM(D3:D7)	=SUM(E3:E7)
9					

Figure 11-7:
The formulas used to generate the numbers in Figure 11-6.

Excel is remarkably good about updating cell references in formulas when you move cells. To see how good Excel is, consider what happens to cell addresses in formulas when you delete a row in a worksheet. If a formula refers to cell C1 but you delete row B, row C becomes row B, and the value in cell C1 changes addresses from C1 to B1. You would think that references in formulas to cell C1 would be out of date, but you would be wrong. Excel automatically adjusts all formulas that refer to cell C1. Those formulas now refer to cell B1 instead.

In case you're curious, you can display formulas themselves, instead of the results of formulas, in worksheet cells, as was done in Figure 11-7. To do so, go to the Formulas tab, click the Show button, and choose Show Formulas on the drop-down list.

Referring to formula results in formulas

Besides referring to cells with numbers in them, you can refer to formula results in a cell. Consider the worksheet shown in Figure 11-8. The purpose of this worksheet is to track scoring by the players on a basketball team over three games:

- The Totals column (column E) shows the total points each player scored in the three games.
- The Average column (column F), using the formula results in the Totals column, determines how much each player has scored on average. The Average column does that by dividing the results in column E by 3, the number of games played.

In this case, Excel uses the results of the total-calculation formulas in column E to compute average points per game in column F.

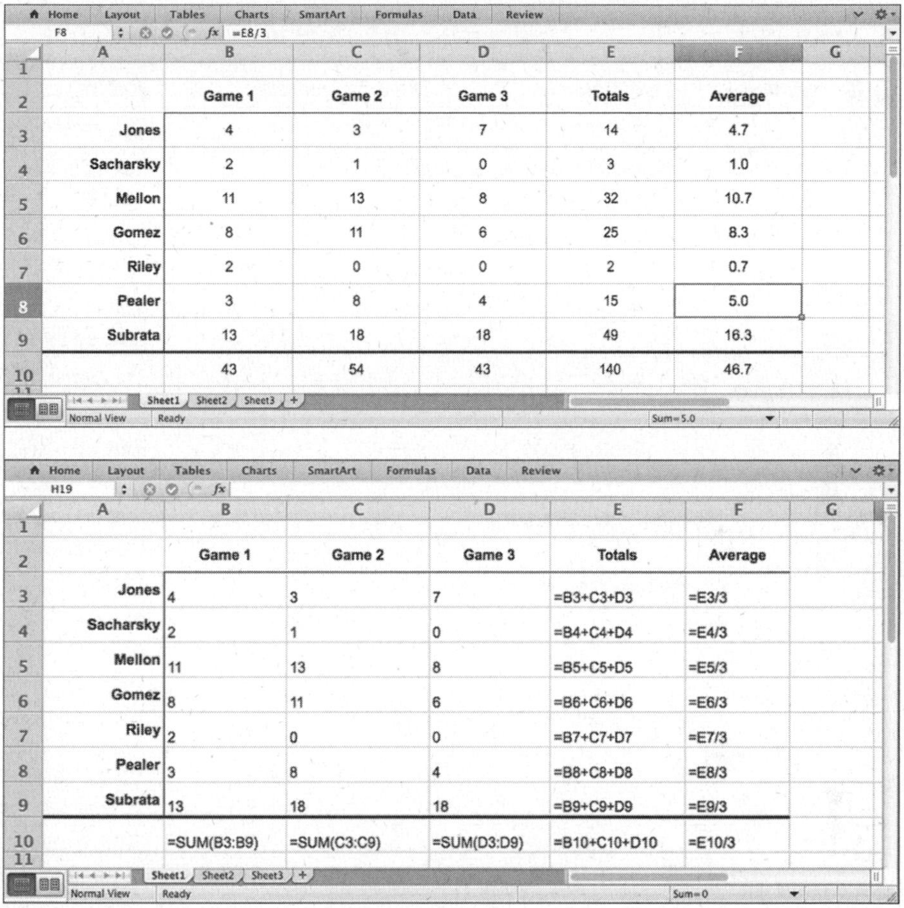

	A	B	C	D	E	F	G
F8		fx	=E8/3				
1							
2		Game 1	Game 2	Game 3	Totals	Average	
3	Jones	4	3	7	14	4.7	
4	Sacharsky	2	1	0	3	1.0	
5	Mellon	11	13	8	32	10.7	
6	Gomez	8	11	6	25	8.3	
7	Riley	2	0	0	2	0.7	
8	Pealer	3	8	4	15	5.0	
9	Subrata	13	18	18	49	16.3	
10		43	54	43	140	46.7	

Sheet1 Sheet2 Sheet3 +
Normal View Ready Sum = 5.0

	A	B	C	D	E	F	G
H19		fx					
1							
2		Game 1	Game 2	Game 3	Totals	Average	
3	Jones	4	3	7	=B3+C3+D3	=E3/3	
4	Sacharsky	2	1	0	=B4+C4+D4	=E4/3	
5	Mellon	11	13	8	=B5+C5+D5	=E5/3	
6	Gomez	8	11	6	=B6+C6+D6	=E6/3	
7	Riley	2	0	0	=B7+C7+D7	=E7/3	
8	Pealer	3	8	4	=B8+C8+D8	=E8/3	
9	Subrata	13	18	18	=B9+C9+D9	=E9/3	
10		=SUM(B3:B9)	=SUM(C3:C9)	=SUM(D3:D9)	=B10+C10+D10	=E10/3	

Sheet1 Sheet2 Sheet3 +
Normal View Ready Sum = 0

Figure 11-8:
Using for-
mula results
as other
formulas.

Operators in formulas

Addition, subtraction, and division aren't the only operators you can use in formulas. Table 11-1 explains the arithmetic operators you can use and the key you press to enter each operator. In the table, operators are listed in the order of precedence.

Another way to compute a formula is to make use of a function. As "Working with Functions" explains later in this chapter, a function is a built-in formula that comes with Excel. SUM, for example, adds the numbers in cells. AVG finds the average of different numbers.

Table 11-1   Arithmetic Operators for Use in Formulas

Precedence	Operator	Example Formula	Returns
1	% (Percent)	=50%	50 percent, or 0.5
2	^ (Exponentiation)	=50^2,	50 to the second power, or 2500
3	* (Multiplication)	=E2*4	The value in cell E2 multiplied by 4
3	/ (Division)	=E2/3	The value in cell E2 divided by 3
4	+ (Addition)	=F1+F2+F3,	The sum of the values in those cells
4	– (Subtraction)	=G5-8,	The value in cell G5 minus 8
5	& (Concatenation)	="Part No. "&D4	The text *Part No.* and the value in cell D4
6	= (Equal to)	=C5=4,	If the value in cell C5 is equal to 4, returns TRUE; returns FALSE otherwise
6	<> (Not equal to)	=F3<>9	If the value in cell F3 is *not* equal to 9, returns TRUE; returns FALSE otherwise
6	< (Less than)	=B9<E11	If the value in cell B9 is less than the value in cell E11; returns TRUE; returns FALSE otherwise
6	<= (Less than or equal to)	=A4<=9	If the value in cell A4 is less than or equal to 9, returns TRUE; returns FALSE otherwise
6	> (Greater than)	=E8>14	If the value in cell E8 is greater than 14, returns TRUE; returns FALSE otherwise
6	>= (Greater than or equal to)	=C3>=D3	If the value in cell C3 is less than or equal to the value in cell D3, returns TRUE; returns FALSE otherwise

The order of precedence

When a formula includes more than one operator, the order in which the operators appear in the formula matters a lot. Consider this formula:

=2+3*4

Does this formula result in 14 (2+[3*4]) or 20 ([2+3]*4)? The answer is 14 because Excel performs multiplication before addition in formulas. In other words, multiplication takes precedence over addition.

The order in which calculations are made in a formula that includes different operators is called the *order of precedence.* Be sure to remember the order of precedence when you construct complex formulas with more than one operator:

1. Percent (%)

2. Exponentiation (^)

3. Multiplication (*) and division (/); leftmost operations are calculated first

4. Addition (+) and subtraction (-); leftmost operations are calculated first

5. Concatenation (&)

6. Comparison (<, <=, >,>=, and <>)

To get around the order of precedence problem, enclose parts of formulas in parentheses. Operations in parentheses are calculated before all other parts of a formula. For example, the formula =2+3*4 equals 20 when it is written this way: =(2+3)*4.

The Basics of Entering a Formula

No matter what kind of formula you enter, no matter how complex the formula is, follow these basic steps to enter it:

1. **Click the cell in which you want to enter the formula.**

2. **Click in the Formula bar if you want to enter the data there rather than the cell.**

3. **Enter the equals sign (=).**

You must be sure to enter the equals sign before you enter a formula. Without it, Excel thinks you're entering text or a number, not a formula.

4. **Enter the formula.**

For example, enter **=B1*.06**. Make sure that you enter all cell addresses correctly. By the way, you can enter lowercase letters in cell references. Excel changes them to uppercase after you finish entering the formula. The next section in this chapter explains how to enter cell addresses quickly in formulas.

5. **Press Return or click the Enter button (the check mark on the Formula bar).**

   The result of the formula appears in the cell.

Speed Techniques for Entering Formulas

Entering formulas and making sure that all cell references are correct is a tedious activity, but fortunately for you, Excel offers a few techniques to make entering formulas easier. Read on to find out how ranges make entering cell references easier and how you can enter cell references in formulas by pointing and clicking. You also find instructions here for copying formulas.

Clicking cells to enter cell references

The hardest part about entering a formula is entering the cell references correctly. You have to squint to see which row and column the cell you want to refer to is in. You have to carefully type the right column letter and row number. However, instead of typing a cell reference, you can click the cell you want to refer to in a formula.

In the course of entering a formula, simply click the cell on your worksheet that you want to reference. As shown in Figure 11-9, shimmering marquee lights appear around the cell that you clicked so that you can clearly see which cell you're referring to. The cell's reference address, meanwhile, appears in the Formula bar. In Figure 11-9, I clicked cell F3 instead of entering its reference address on the Formula bar. The reference F3 appears on the Formula bar, and the marquee lights appear around cell F3.

Get in the habit of pointing and clicking cells to enter cell references in formulas. Clicking cells is easier than typing cell addresses, and the cell references are entered more accurately.

Entering a cell range

A *cell range* is a line or block of cells in a worksheet. Instead of typing cell reference addresses one at a time, you can simply select cells on your worksheet. In Figure 11-10, I selected cells C3, D3, E3, and F3 to form cell range C3:F3. This spares me the trouble of entering the cell addresses one at a time: C3, D3, E3, and F3. The formula in Figure 11-10 uses the SUM function to total the numeric values in cell range C3:F3. Notice that the range C3:F3 is highlighted. The highlights show precisely which range you're selecting. Cell ranges come in especially handy where functions are concerned (see "Working with Functions," later in this chapter).

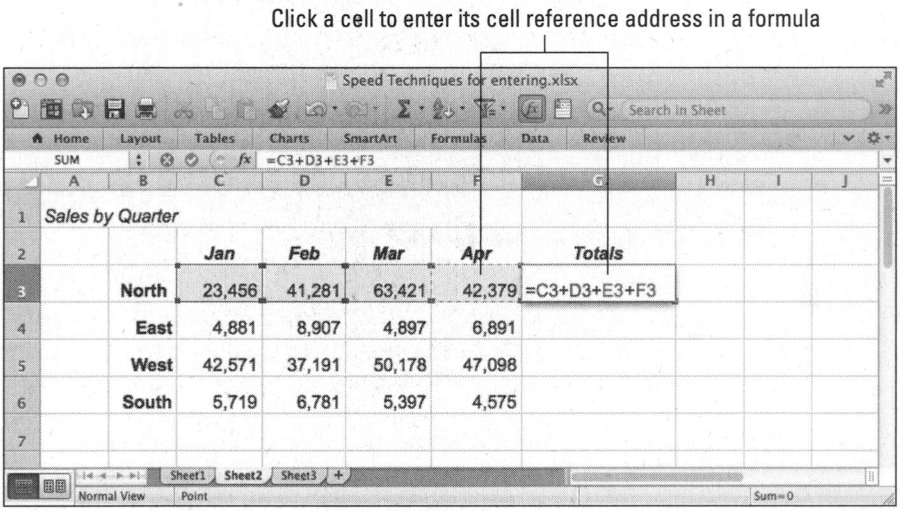

Click a cell to enter its cell reference address in a formula

Figure 11-9:
Clicking to enter a cell reference.

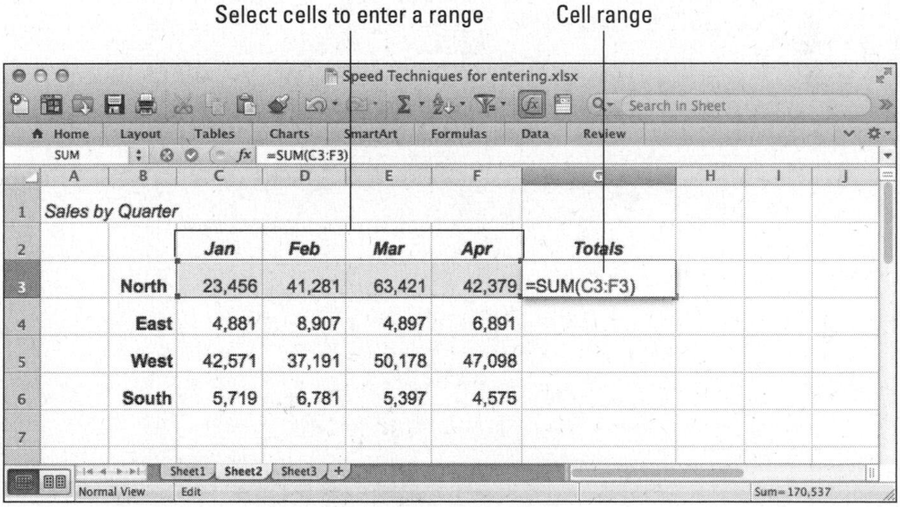

Select cells to enter a range   Cell range

Figure 11-10:
Using a cell range in a formula.

To identify a cell range, Excel lists the outermost cells in the range and places a colon (:) between cell addresses:

> ✔ A cell range comprising cells A1, A2, A3, and A4 is listed this way: A1:A4.

> ✔ A cell range comprising a block of cells from A1 to D4 is listed this way: A1:D4.

You can enter cell ranges on your own without selecting cells. To do so, type the first cell in the range, enter a colon (:), and type the last cell.

Naming cell ranges so that you can use them in formulas

Whether you type cell addresses yourself or drag across cells to enter a cell range, entering cell address references is a chore. Entering =C1+C2+C3+C4, for example, can cause a finger cramp; entering =SUM(C1:C4) is no piece of cake, either.

To take the tedium out of entering cell ranges in formulas, you can name cell ranges. Then, to enter a cell range in a formula, all you have to do is select a name in the Paste Name dialog box or click the Use in Formula button on the Formulas tab, as shown in Figure 11-11. Naming cell ranges has an added benefit: You can choose a name from the Name Box drop-down list and go directly to the cell range whose name you choose, as shown in Figure 11-11.

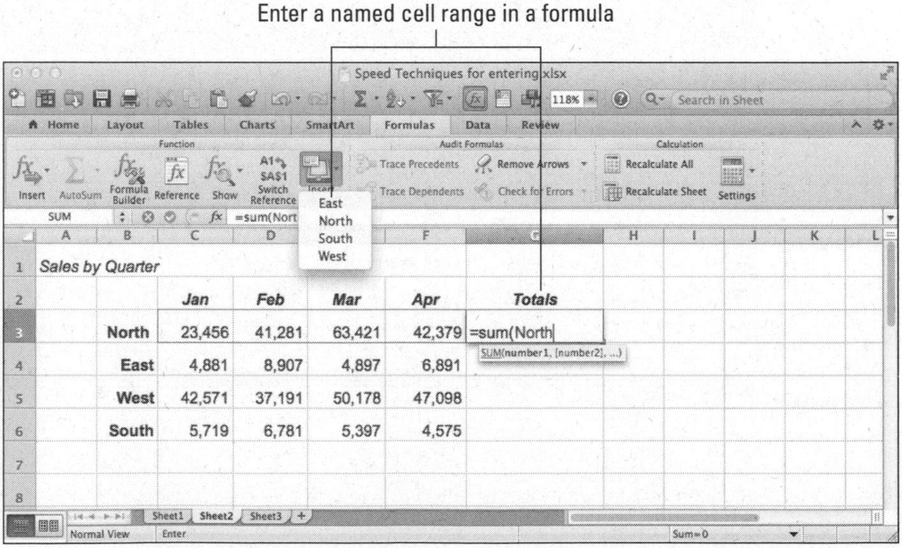

Enter a named cell range in a formula

Figure 11-11: Choosing a named cell range.

Naming cell ranges has one disadvantage, and it's a big one. Excel doesn't adjust cell references when you copy a formula with a range name from one cell to another. A range name always refers to the same set of cells. Later in this chapter, "Copying Formulas from Cell to Cell" explains how to copy formulas.

Creating a cell range name

Follow these steps to create a cell range name:

1. **Select the cells that you want to name.**

2. **Choose Insert ⇨ Name ⇨ Define.**

   You see the Define Name dialog box.

3. **Enter a descriptive name in the Name Box.**

   Names can't begin with a number or include blank spaces.

4. **Click OK.**

In case you're in a hurry, here's a fast way to enter a cell range name: Select the cells for the range, click in the Name Box (you can find it on the left side of the Formula bar, as shown in Figure 11-7), enter a name for the range, and press the Return key.

Entering a range name as part of a formula

Follow these steps to include a cell range name in a formula:

1. **Click in the Formula bar where you want to enter the range name.**

2. **On the Formulas tab, click the Insert Name button.**

   A drop-down list of range names appears (refer to Figure 11-11).

3. **Choose a range name on the drop-down list.**

   The range name appears in the formula.

Quickly traveling to a cell range that you named

To go quickly to a cell range that you named, open the drop-down list on the Name Box and choose a name. The Name Box drop-down list is located on the left side of the Formula bar.

To make this trick work, the cursor can't be in the Formula bar. The Name Box drop-down list isn't available when you're constructing a formula.

Deleting cell range names

To delete cell range names, choose Insert ⇨ Name ⇨ Define. You see the Define Name dialog box, as shown in Figure 11-12. This dialog box lists names and the worksheet on which the range name is found. To delete a cell range name, select it in the dialog box and click the Delete button.

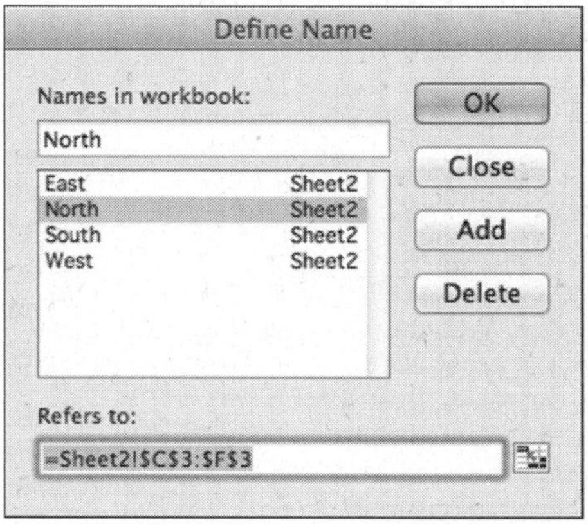

Define Name

Names in workbook:

North

East	Sheet2
North	Sheet2
South	Sheet2
West	Sheet2

OK
Close
Add
Delete

Refers to:
=Sheet2!$C$3:$F$3

Figure 11-12
The Define Name dialog box.

Referring to cells in different worksheets

Excel gives you the opportunity to use data from different worksheets in a formula. If one worksheet lists sales figures from January and the next lists sales figures from February, you can construct a "grand total" formula in either worksheet to tabulate sales in the two-month period. A reference to a cell on a different worksheet is called a *3D reference*.

Construct the formula as you normally would, but when you want to refer to a cell or cell range in a different worksheet, click a worksheet tab to move to the other worksheet and select the cell or range of cells there. Without returning to the original worksheet, complete your formula in the Formula bar and press Enter. Excel returns you to the original worksheet, where you can see the results of your formula.

The only thing odd about constructing formulas across worksheets are the cell references. As a glance at the Formula bar tells you, cell addresses in cross-worksheet formulas list the sheet name and an exclamation point (!) as well as the cell address itself. For example, this formula in Worksheet 1 adds the number in cell A4 to the numbers in cells D5 and E5 in Worksheet 2:

```
=A4+Sheet2!D5+Sheet2!E5
```

This formula in Sheet 2 multiplies the number in cell E18 by the number in cell C15 in Worksheet 1:

```
=E18*Sheet1!C15
```

This formula in Worksheet 2 finds the average of the numbers in the cell range C7:F7 in Worksheet 1:

```
=AVERAGE(Sheet1!C7:F7)
```

Copying Formulas from Cell to Cell

Often in worksheets, the same formula but with different cell references is used across a row or down a column. For example, in the worksheet shown in Figure 11-13, column F totals the rainfall figures in rows 7 through 11. To enter formulas for totaling the rainfall figures in column F, you could laboriously enter formulas in cells F7, F8, F9, F10, and F11. But a faster way is to enter the formula once in cell F7 and then copy the formula in F7 down the column to cells F8, F9, F10, and F11.

Drag the AutoFill handle

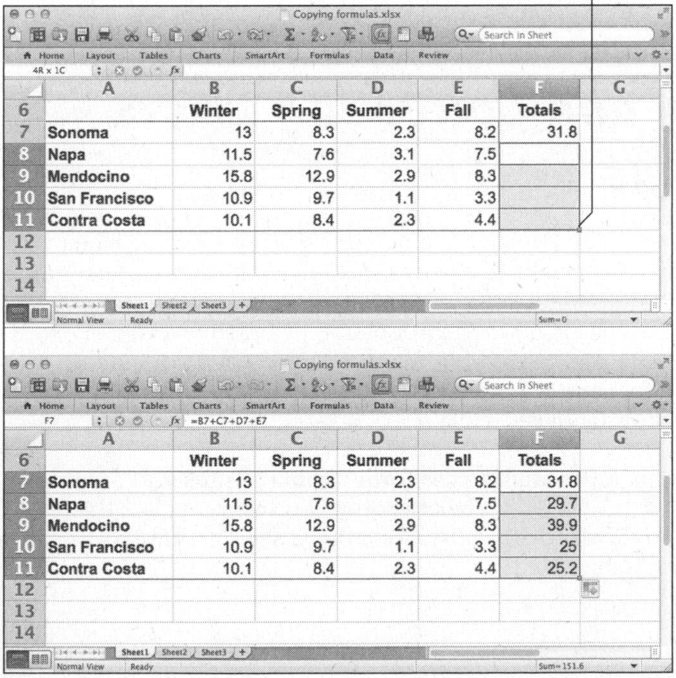

Figure 11-13: Copying a formula.

When you copy a formula to a new cell, Excel adjusts the cell references in the formula so that the formula works in the cells to which it has been copied. Astounding! Opportunities to copy formulas abound on most worksheets. And copying formulas is the fastest and safest (least error prone) way to enter formulas in a worksheet.

Follow these steps to copy a formula:

1. **Select the cell with the formula you want to copy down a column or across a row.**

2. **Drag the AutoFill handle across the cells to which you want to copy the formula.**

   This is the same AutoFill handle that you drag to enter serial data (see Chapter 10 about entering lists and serial data with the AutoFill command). The AutoFill handle is the small black square in the lower-right corner of the cell. Refer to Figure 11-13 to see a formula being copied.

3. **Release the mouse button.**

   If I were you, I would click in the cells to which you copied the formula and glance at the Formula bar to make sure that the formula was copied correctly. I'd bet you it was.

You can also copy formulas with the Copy and Paste commands. Just make sure that cell references refer correctly to the surrounding cells.

Detecting and Correcting Errors in Formulas

It happens. Everyone makes an error from time to time when entering formulas in cells. Especially in a worksheet in which formula results are calculated into other formulas, a single error in one formula can spread like a virus and cause miscalculations throughout a worksheet. To prevent that from happening, Excel offers several ways to correct errors in formulas. You can correct them one at a time, run the error checker, and trace cell references, as the following pages explain.

By the way, if you want to see formulas in cells instead of formula results, go to the Formulas tab, click the Show button, and click the Show Formulas button on the drop-down list. Sometimes seeing formulas this way helps to detect formula errors.

Correcting errors one at a time

When Excel detects what it thinks is a formula that has been entered incorrectly, a small green triangle appears in the upper-left corner of the cell where you entered the formula. And if the error is especially egregious, an *error message,* a cryptic three or four letters preceded by a pound sign (#), appears in the cell. Table 11-2 explains common error messages.

Table 11-2	Common Formula Error Messages
Message	*What Went Wrong*
#DIV/0!	You tried to divide a number by a zero (0) or an empty cell.
#NAME	You used a cell range name in the formula but the name isn't defined. Sometimes this error occurs because you type the name incorrectly. (Earlier in this chapter, "Naming cell ranges so that you can use them in formulas" explains how to name cell ranges.)
#N/A	The formula refers to an empty cell, so no data is available for computing the formula. Sometimes people enter N/A in a cell as a placeholder to signal the fact that data isn't entered yet. Revise the formula or enter a number or formula in the empty cells.
#NULL	The formula refers to a cell range that Excel can't understand. Make sure that the range is entered correctly.
#NUM	An argument that you use in your formula is invalid.
#REF	The cell or range of cells that the formula refers to aren't there.
#VALUE	The formula includes a function that was used incorrectly, takes an invalid argument, or is misspelled. Make sure that the function uses the right argument and is spelled correctly.

To find out more about a formula error and perhaps correct it, select the cell with the green triangle and click the Error button. This small button appears beside a cell with a formula error after you click the cell. The drop-down list on the Error button offers opportunities for correcting formula errors and finding out more about them.

Running the error checker

Another way to tackle formula errors is to run the error checker. When the checker encounters what it thinks is an error, the Error Checking dialog box tells you what the error is, as shown in Figure 11-14. To run the error checker, choose Tools ⇨ Error Checking.

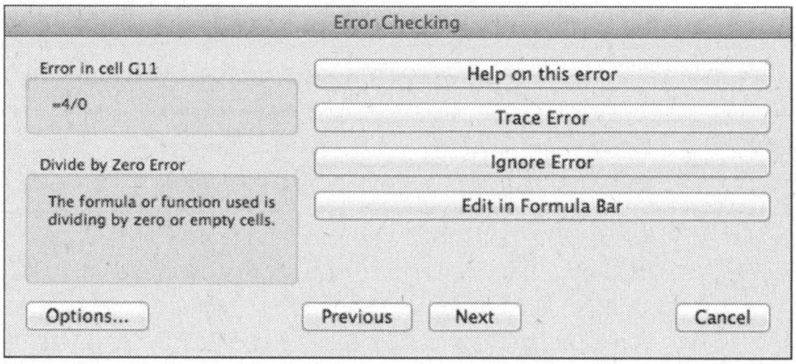

Figure 11-14:
Running
the error
checker.

If you see clearly what the error is, click the Edit in Formula Bar button and repair the error in the Formula bar. If the error isn't one that really needs correcting, either click the Ignore Error button or click the Next button to send the error checker in search of the next error in your worksheet.

Tracing cell references

In a complex worksheet in which formulas are piled on top of one another and the results of some formulas are computed into other formulas, it helps to be able to trace cell references. By tracing cell references, you can see how the data in a cell figures into a formula in another cell. Also, if the cell contains a formula, you can tell which cells the formula gathers its data from to make its computation. You can get a better idea of how your worksheet is constructed, and in so doing, find structural errors more easily.

Figure 11-15 shows how cell tracers describe the relationships between cells. A *cell tracer* is a blue arrow that shows the relationships between cells used in formulas. You can trace two types of relationships:

- ✔ **Tracing precedents:** Select a cell with a formula in it and trace the formula's *precedents* to find out which cells are computed to produce the results of the formula. Trace precedents when you want to find out where a formula gets its computation data. Cell tracer arrows point from the referenced cells to the cell with the formula results in it.

To trace precedents, go to the Formulas tab and click the Trace Precedents button.

✔ **Tracing dependents:** Select a cell and trace its *dependents* to find out which cells contain formulas that use data from the cell you selected. Cell tracer arrows point from the cell you selected to cells with formula results in them. Trace dependents when you want to find out how the data in a cell contributes to formulas elsewhere in the worksheet. The cell you select can contain a constant value or a formula in its own right (and contribute its results to another formula).

To trace dependents, go to the Formulas tab and click the Trace Dependents button.

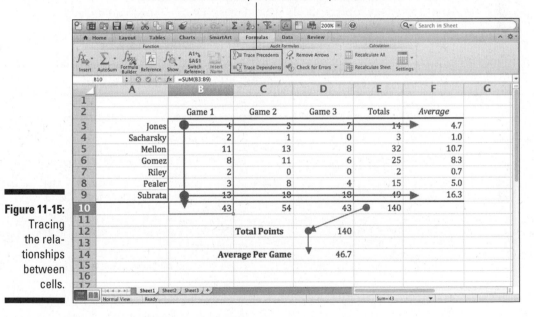

Figure 11-15: Tracing the relationships between cells.

To remove the cell tracer arrows from a worksheet, go to the Formulas tab and click the Remove Arrows button. You can open the drop-down list on this button and choose Remove Precedent Arrows or Remove Dependent Arrows to remove only cell-precedent or cell-dependent tracer arrows.

Working with Functions

A *function* is a canned formula that comes with Excel. Excel offers hundreds of functions, some of which are very obscure and fit only for use by rocket scientists or securities analysts. Other functions are very practical. For example, you can use the SUM function to quickly total the numbers in a range of cells. Instead of entering =C2+C3+C4+C5 on the Formula bar, you can enter =SUM(C2:C5), which tells Excel to total the numbers in cell C2, C3, C4, and C5. To obtain the product of the number in cell G4 and .06, you can use the PRODUCT function and enter =PRODUCT(G4,.06) on the Formula bar.

Table 11-3 lists the most common functions. (Chapter 19 describes my ten favorite functions.) To get an idea of the numerous functions that Excel offers, go to the Formulas tab and click the Reference button. The Help Center window opens, as shown in Figure 11-16. Choose a function category, choose a function name, and read the description.

Table 11-3	Common Functions and Their Use
Function	*Returns*
AVERAGE(*number1,number2,...*)	The average of the numbers in the cells listed in the arguments.
COUNT(*value1,value2,...*)	The number of cells that contain the numbers listed in the arguments.
MAX(*number1,number2,...*)	The largest value in the cells listed in the arguments.
MIN(*number1,number2,...*)	The smallest value in the cells listed in the arguments.
PRODUCT(*number1,number2,...*)	The product of multiplying the cells listed in the arguments.
STDEV(*number1,number2,...*)	An estimate of standard deviation based on the sample cells listed in the argument.
STDEVP(*number1,number2,...*)	An estimate of standard deviation based on the entire sample cells listed in the arguments.
SUM(*number1,number2,...*)	The total of the numbers in the arguments.
VAR(*number1,number2,...*)	An estimate of the variance based on the sample cells listed in the arguments.
VARP(*number1,number2,...*)	A variance calculation based on all cells listed in the arguments.

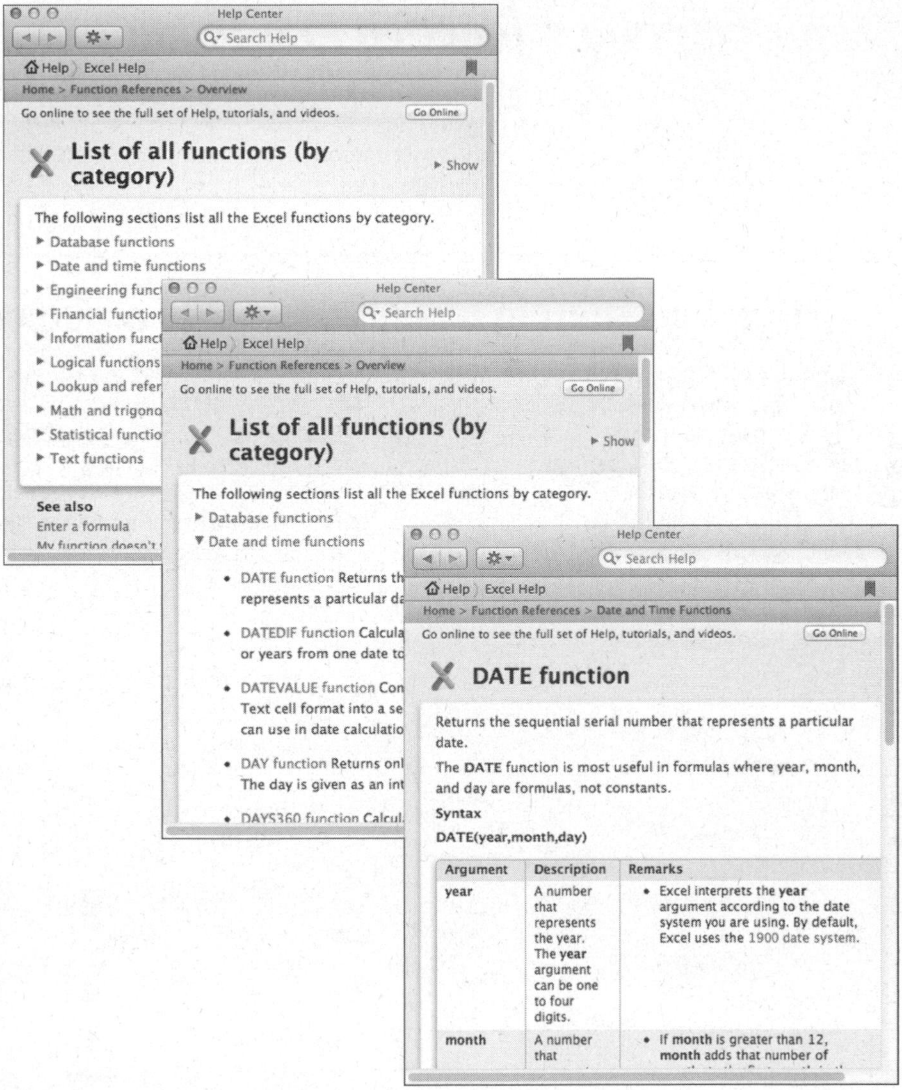

Figure 11-16:
Exploring
functions
in the Help
Center.

Using arguments in functions

Every function takes one or more *arguments*. Arguments are the cell references or numbers, enclosed in parentheses, that the function acts upon. For example, =AVERAGE(B1:B4) returns the average of the numbers in the cell range B1 through B4; =PRODUCT(6.5,C4) returns the product of multiplying the number 6.5 by the number in cell C4. When a function requires more than one argument, enter a comma between the arguments (enter a comma without a space).

Entering a function in a formula

To enter a function in a formula, you can enter the function name by typing it in the Formula bar, or you can rely on Excel to enter it for you. Enter function names yourself if you're well acquainted with a function and comfortable using it.

Quickly entering a function and its arguments

To quickly total the numbers in cells, click your worksheet where you want the total to appear, and then click the AutoSum button on Formulas tab. Excel takes an educated guess as to which cells need totaling, and the application highlights those cells. If Excel guesses correctly and highlights the cells you want to total, click the Enter button (or press Return) and be done with it. Otherwise, select the cells you want to add up and then press Return.

Similarly, as shown in the illustration here, you can use the drop-down list on the AutoSum button to quickly obtain the average, count of, maximum amount, or minimum amount of cells by clicking in a nearby cell, opening the drop-down list on the AutoSum button, and choosing Average, Count Numbers, Max, or Min.

No matter how you want to enter a function as part of a formula, start this way:

1. **Select the cell where you want to enter the formula.**

2. **In the Formula bar, type an equals sign (=).**

   Please, please, please be sure to start every formula by entering an equals sign (=). Without it, Excel thinks you're entering text or a number in the cell.

3. **Start constructing your formula, and when you come to the place where you want to enter the function, type the function's name or call upon Excel to help you enter the function and its arguments.**

   Later in this chapter, "Manually entering a function" shows you how to type in the function yourself; "Getting Excel's help to enter a function" shows you how to get Excel to do the work.

   If you enter the function on your own, it's up to you to type the arguments correctly; if you get Excel's help, you also get help with entering the cell references for the arguments.

Manually entering a function

Be sure to enclose the function's argument or arguments in parentheses. Don't enter a space between the function's name and the first parenthesis. Likewise, don't enter a comma and a space between arguments; enter a comma, nothing more:

```
=SUM(F11,F14,23)
```

You can enter function names in lowercase. Excel converts function names to uppercase after you click the Enter button or press Return to complete the formula. Entering function names in lowercase is recommended because doing so gives you a chance to find out whether you entered a function name correctly. If Excel doesn't convert your function name to uppercase, you made a typing error when you entered the function name.

Getting Excel's help to enter a function

Besides entering a function by typing it, you can do it by way of the Formula Builder, as shown in Figure 11-17. The beauty of using the Formula Builder is that it warns you if you enter arguments incorrectly, and it spares you the trouble of typing the function name without making an error. What's more, it shows you the results of the formula as you construct it so that you get an idea of whether you're using the function correctly.

Follow these steps to get Excel's help with entering a function as part of a formula:

1. **On the Formulas tab, click the Formula Builder.**

   You see the Formula Builder dialog box (refer to Figure 11-17).

2. **Find and double-click the name of a function.**

   You can search for a function or scroll through the list and select one. The functions are listed in alphabetical order by type. Functions you used most recently appear at the top of the list.

3. **Enter arguments in the spaces provided by the Formula Builder.**

   To enter cell references or ranges, you can click or select cells in your worksheet. To add space for another argument, click the Add an Argument button.

4. **Press the Return key or the Enter key on the Formula bar.**

   I hope you argued correctly with the Formula Builder and constructed a valid formula.

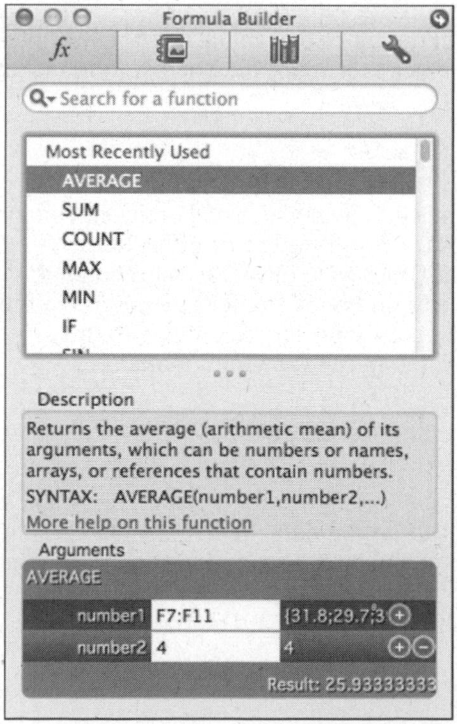

Figure 11-17
The Formula Builder.

Chapter 12

Creating a Chart

Nothing is more persuasive than a chart. The bars, pie slices, lines, or columns show immediately whether production is up or down, cats are better than dogs or dogs better than cats, or catsup tastes better than ketchup. Fans of charts and graphs will be glad to know that putting a chart in an Excel worksheet (or Word document or PowerPoint slide) is fairly easy.

This chapter explains how to create a chart. It looks at which charts are best for presenting different kinds of data, how to change a chart's appearance, and how to save charts in a template that you can use again. You discover some nice chart tricks, including how to make a picture the backdrop for a chart and how to draw trendlines on a chart.

The Basics: Creating a Chart

Throughout this chapter, I explain the whys, wherefores, and whatnots of creating a chart. Before going into details, here are the basic steps that everyone needs to know to create a chart:

1. **Go to the Charts tab.**

2. **Select the data you'll use to generate the chart.**

3. Open the drop-down list on one of the buttons in the Insert Chart group (Column, Line, Pie, Bar, or Other) and select a chart type, as shown in Figure 12-1.

The next portion of this chapter, "Choosing the Right Chart," describes all the charts types and advises you which to choose.

4. To modify your chart, start by selecting it.

Click the perimeter of a chart to select it (as you discover later in this chapter, you can select different parts of a chart — the plot area, the legend — to format them). Selecting a chart makes the Chart Layout and Format tabs appear on the Ribbon. You can use these tabs to make your chart just-so.

5. Visit the Chart Layout tab when you want to change the chart's layout, alter the data with which the chart is generated, or change the axis lines, among other things.

Later in this chapter, "Changing a Chart's Appearance" explains how to change the layout of a chart.

6. Select the Format tab when you want to change the appearance of your chart.

You can change colors and fills on your chart, as "Changing a chart element's color, font, or other particular" explains later in this chapter.

Click a chart button and choose a chart type

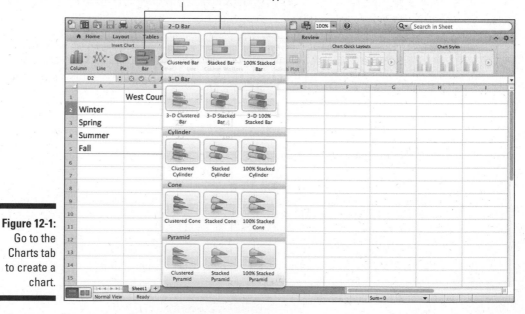

Figure 12-1:
Go to the
Charts tab
to create a
chart.

And if you decide to delete the chart you created? Click its perimeter to select it and then press the Delete key.

Choosing the Right Chart

If you're a fan of charts, the large selection of charts can make you feel like a kid in a candy store, but if charts aren't your *forté,* the wealth of charts you can choose from can be daunting. Which chart is best? The golden rule for choosing a chart type is to choose the one that presents information in the brightest possible light. The purpose of a chart is to compare information across different categories. Select a chart that draws out the comparison so that others can clearly make comparisons. Table 12-1 describes the 11 chart categories and explains in brief when to use each type of chart.

Table 12-1	Chart Types
Chart Type	*Best Use/Description*
Area	Examine how values in different categories fluctuate over time, and see the cumulative change in values. (Same as a line chart except that the area between trend lines is colored in.)
Bar	Compare values in different categories against one another, usually over time. Data is displayed in horizontal bars. (Same as a column chart except that the bars are horizontal.)
Bubble	Examine data relationships by studying the size and location of the bubbles that represent the relationships. Bubble charts are often used in financial analyses and market research. (Similar to scatter chart except that you can use three instead of two data series, and the data points appear as bubbles.)
Column	Compare values in different categories against one another, usually over time. Data is displayed in vertical columns. (Same as a bar chart except that the bars are vertical.)
Doughnut	See how values compare as percentages of a whole. (Similar to a pie chart except that you can use more than one data series and create concentric doughnut rings in the chart.)
Line	Examine how values fluctuate over time. Data is displayed in a set of points connected by a line.
Pie	See how values compare as percentages of a whole. Data from categories is displayed as a percentage of a whole. (Similar to a doughnut chart.)

(continued)

Table 12-1 *(continued)*

Chart Type	Best Use/Description
Radar	Examine data as it relates to one central point. Data is plotted on radial points from the central point. This kind of chart is used to make subjective performance analyses.
Scatter	Compare different numeric data point sets in space to reveal patterns and trends in data. (Similar to a bubble chart except that the data appears as points instead of bubbles.)
Stock	See how the value of an item fluctuates as well as its daily, weekly, or yearly high, low, and closing price. This chart is used to track stock prices, but it can also be used to track air temperature and other variable quantities.
Surface	Examine color-coded data on a 3D surface to explore relationships between data values.

Positioning Your Chart in a Workbook

To change the position of a chart, click its perimeter to select it, and use one of these repositioning techniques:

- *Moving on the worksheet.* Move the pointer over the perimeter of the chart, and when the pointer turns into a four-headed arrow, click and drag the chart to a different location.

- *Moving to a different worksheet.* Choose Edit ➪ Cut (or press Command+X) to move the chart to the scrapbook. Then go to the other worksheet and choose Edit ➪ Paste (or press Command+V) to paste the chart in the other worksheet.

Changing a Chart's Appearance

Charts are awfully nice already, but perhaps you want to redesign one. Perhaps you're an interior decorator type and you want to give charts your own personal touch.

These pages explain how to change a chart's appearance, starting with the biggest change you can make — exchanging one type of chart for another.

Changing the chart type

The biggest way to overhaul a chart is to ditch it in favor of a different chart type. Luckily for you, Office makes this task simple. I wish that changing jobs was this easy. Follow these steps to change a pumpkin into a carriage or an existing chart into a different kind of chart:

1. **Click your chart to select it.**

2. **Open the drop-down list on one of the buttons in the Change Chart Type group (Column, Line, Pie, Bar, or Other).**

3. **Select a new chart type on the drop-down list.**

Not all chart types can be converted successfully to other chart types. You may well have created a monster, in which case go back to Step 1 and start all over or click the Undo button.

Changing the size and shape of a chart

To make a chart taller or wider, follow these instructions:

✔ Click the perimeter of the chart to select it and then drag a handle on the side to make it wider, or a handle on the top or bottom to make it taller.

✔ Go to the Format tab and enter measurements in the Height and Width boxes. To keep the same proportions for your chart as you change its size, select the Lock Aspect Ratio check box before you change the size of the chart. This check box is located to the right of the Height and Width boxes.

Relying on a chart style to change appearances

The easiest way to change the look of a chart is to choose an option in the Chart Styles gallery in the Charts tab, as shown in Figure 12-2. These gallery options are quite sophisticated. You would have a hard time fashioning these charts on your own.

If your file includes more than one chart, make the charts consistent with one another. Give them a similar appearance so that your file doesn't turn into a chart fashion show. You can make charts consistent with one another by choosing similar options for charts in the Chart Styles gallery.

Select a chart style

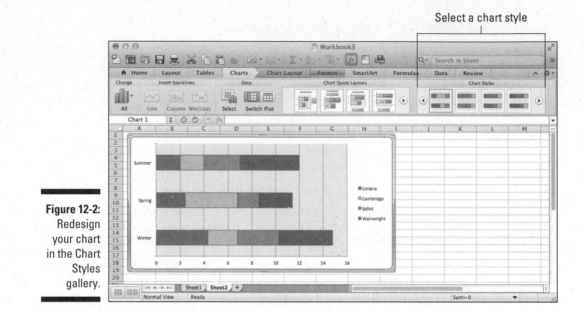

Figure 12-2:
Redesign
your chart
in the Chart
Styles
gallery.

Changing the layout of a chart

Figure 12-3 identifies the chart elements that you can lay out in different ways. Some of these elements can be removed as well as placed on different parts of a chart. For example, you can display the legend on any side of a chart or not display it at all. Some of the elements can be labeled in different ways. To decide on the layout of a chart, select it and visit the Chart Layout tab.

The following pages explain how to change the layout of a chart starting on the Chart Layout tab. However, before hurrying to the Chart Layout tab to change your chart's layout, you may consider taking a detour to the Charts tab. The Chart Quick Layouts gallery on the Charts tab offers ten ready-made layouts, one of which may meet your high expectations and spare you a trip to the Chart Layout tab.

Deciding where chart elements appear and how they are labeled

On the Chart Layout tab, open the drop-down list on these buttons and choose options to determine how and whether chart elements are labeled:

✔ **Chart Title:** The chart title appears above the chart and describes what the chart is about (refer to Figure 12-3).

✔ **Axis Titles:** Axis titles list the series name and category name of the data being plotted in the chart (refer to Figure 12-3).

✔ **Legend:** The legend is the box to the side, top, or bottom of the chart that describes what is being plotted (refer to Figure 12-3). Choose an option from the drop-down list to make the chart's legend overlap or appear above, below, or to the side of a chart.

✔ **Data Labels:** Data labels show the numeric values by which the data markers — the bars, columns, pie slices, or dots — in your chart are constructed (refer to Figure 12-3). For example, if a bar in your chart represents the number 28, the data label 28 appears in the bar. You can also label the series name or category name by choosing Data Label Options on the drop-down list and making selections in the Format Data Labels dialog box.

✔ **Axes:** The axis labels are the series names and scale markers that appear in the chart. Choose Horizontal Axis or Vertical Axis and then select No Axis to remove series names and scale markers from your chart. The other axis options are for deciding how to display axis labels (and are explained in the next section of this chapter).

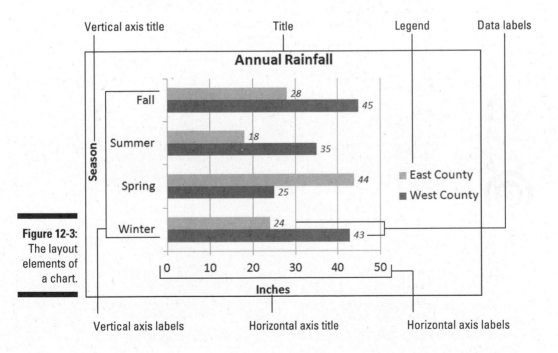

Figure 12-3:
The layout
elements of
a chart.

Handling the gridlines

Gridlines are lines that cross a chart and indicate value measurements. Most charts include major gridlines to show where bars or columns meet or surpass a major unit of measurement, and you can also include fainter, minor gridlines that mark less significant measurements. Figure 12-4 shows a chart with gridlines displayed in different ways.

Select your chart and follow these instructions to hide or display gridlines, change the lines' width, or change the lines' color:

- **Hiding and choosing the frequency of gridlines:** On the Chart Layout tab, click the Gridlines button, choose Horizontal Gridlines or Vertical Gridlines on the drop-down list, and choose an option on the submenu. You can hide gridlines (by choosing No Gridlines), display major gridlines, display minor gridlines, or display major and minor gridlines (refer to Figure 12-4).

- **Changing gridline width:** Double-click the gridlines to open the Format Gridlines dialog box. Then, in the Weights & Arrows tab of the Format Gridlines dialog box, enter a measurement in the Weight text box to make the gridlines heavier or thinner.

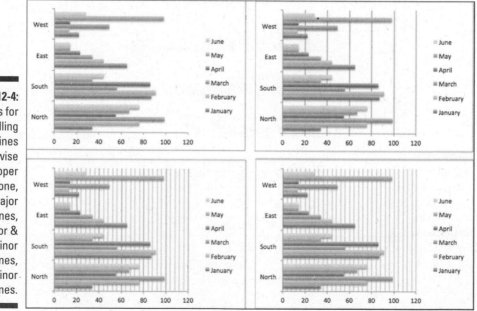

Figure 12-4: Options for handling gridlines (clockwise from upper left): None, Major Gridlines, Major & Minor Gridlines, and Minor Gridlines.

✔ **Changing gridline color:** Double-click the gridlines to open the Format Gridlines dialog box. Then, on the Solid tab of the Format Gridlines dialog box, open the Color drop-down menu and choose a color.

Gridlines are essential for helping read charts, but be very, very careful about displaying minor gridlines on charts. These lines can make your chart unreadable. They can turn a perfectly good chart into a gaudy pinstripe suit.

Changing a chart element's color, font, or other particular

The Format tab is the place to go to change the color, line width, font, or font size of a chart element. Follow these basic steps to change a color, line width, font, or font size in part of a chart:

1. **Go to the Format tab.**

2. **Select the chart element that needs a facelift.**

   To select a chart element, either click it or choose its name on the Current Selection drop-down list, as shown in Figure 12-5. You can find this list in the upper-left corner of the window.

Select a chart element so that you can reformat it

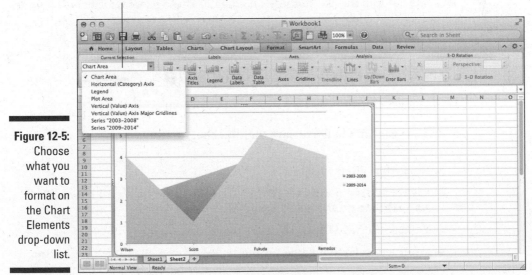

Figure 12-5: Choose what you want to format on the Chart Elements drop-down list.

3. Format the chart element you selected.

Use one of these techniques to format the chart element:

- *Open a Format dialog box.* Click the Format Selection button to open a Format dialog box. The dialog box offers commands for formatting the element you selected.

- *Do the work on your own.* Format the chart element as you would any object. For example, to change fonts in the chart element you selected, go to the Home tab to change font sizes. Or open the drop-down list on the Shape Fill button on the Format tab and select a new color.

Saving a Chart as a Template So That You Can Use It Again

If you go to the significant trouble of redecorating a chart and you expect to do it again the same way in the future, save your chart as a template. This way, you can call on the template in the future to create the same chart and not have to decorate it again. Perhaps you've created charts with your company's colors or you've created a chart that you're especially proud of. Save it as a template to spare yourself the work of reconstructing it.

A chart template holds data series colors, gridline settings, plot area colors, font settings, and the like. It doesn't hold data. These pages explain how to save a chart as a template and how to create a chart with a template you created.

Saving a chart as a template

Follow these steps to make a template out of a chart:

1. **Save your file to make sure that the chart settings are saved on your computer.**

2. **Click your chart to select it.**

3. **Right-click the perimeter of the chart (the blue box) and choose Save As Template on the shortcut menu.**

   You see the Save Chart Template dialog box.

4. **Enter a descriptive name for the template and click the Save button.**

   Include the type of chart you're dealing with in the name. This will help you understand which template you're selecting when the time comes to choose a chart template.

Creating a chart from a template

Follow these steps to create a chart from your own customized template:

1. **Select the data for the chart.**

2. **Go to the Charts tab.**

3. **Click the Other button.**

   A drop-down list opens.

4. **Scroll to the Templates category at the bottom of the drop-down list.**

5. **Select a template.**

   You can apply a self-made template to a chart you already created. See "Changing the chart type," earlier in this chapter.

Chart Tricks for the Daring and Heroic

This chapter wouldn't be complete without a handful of chart tricks to impress your friends and intimidate your enemies. In the pages that follow, you discover how to make charts roll over and play dead. You also find out how to decorate a chart with a picture, display worksheet data alongside a chart, and place a trendline on a chart.

Decorating a chart with a picture

As shown in Figure 12-6, a picture looks mighty nice on the plot area of a chart — especially a column chart. If you have a picture in your computer that would serve well to decorate a chart, you are hereby encouraged to start decorating. Follow these steps to place a picture in the plot area of a chart:

1. **Select your chart.**

2. **On the Format tab, open the Current Selection drop-down list and choose Plot Area.**

3. **Open the drop-down list on the Fill button and choose Fill Effects on the drop-down list.**

   You see the Format Plot Area dialog box.

4. **Go to the Picture of Texture Tab.**

5. **Click the Choose Picture button.**

   The Choose a Picture dialog box opens.

6. **Locate the picture you need and select it.**

   Try to select a light-colored picture that will serve as a background.

7. **Click the Insert button.**

   You return to the Format Plot area dialog box.

8. **Click the OK button.**

   The picture lands in your chart. While the picture is still selected, experiment by dragging the Transparency slider on the Format tab. Changing the transparency setting moves the picture nearer to the background of the chart.

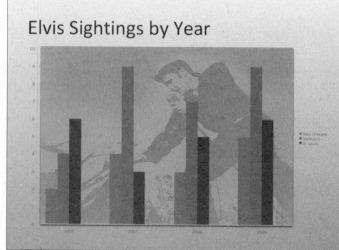

Figure 12-6:
Using a picture as the backdrop of a chart.

Displaying the raw data alongside the chart

Showing the worksheet data used to produce a chart is sort of like showing the cops your I.D. It proves you're the real thing. It makes your chart more authentic. If yours is a simple pie chart or other chart that wasn't generated with a large amount of raw data, you can display the data alongside your chart in a data table. Anyone who sees the table knows you're not kidding or fudging the numbers.

Select your chart and use of one of these techniques.

Follow these steps to place a table with the raw data below your chart:

1. **Select the chart.**

2. **Go to the Chart Layout tab.**

3. **Click the Data Table button and choose a Data Table option on the drop-down list.**

To format a data table, go to the Format tab and click the table data in the chart. You see the Format Data Table dialog box, where you can fill the table with color and choose colors for the lines in the table.

Placing a trendline on a chart

Especially on column charts, a *trendline* can help viewers more clearly see changes in data. Viewers can see, for example, that sales are going up or down, income is rising or falling, or annual rainfall is increasing or decreasing. Figure 12-7 shows an example of a trendline on a chart.

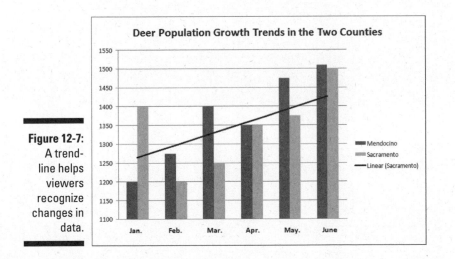

Figure 12-7:
A trend-line helps viewers recognize changes in data.

Follow these steps to put a trendline on a chart:

1. **On the Chart Layout tab, open the Chart Elements drop-down list and choose the data series that you want to highlight with a trendline.**

2. **Click the Trendline button and choose a trendline option on the drop-down list.**

   You can choose Trendline Options on the drop-down list to open the Format Trendline dialog box and choose additional types of trendlines.

   To change the look of a trendline, right-click it and choose Format Trendline. In the Format Trendline dialog box, choose a line color and line style.

To remove a trendline from a chart, go to the Chart Layout tab, click the Trendline button, and choose No Trendline on the drop-down list.

Part IV
PowerPoint

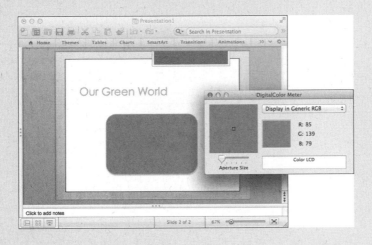

Go to www.dummies.com/extras/ipadatwork to see how to put a company logo or other image in the corner of all slides in a presentation.

In this part . . .

- ✔ Take advantage of commands for getting around, handling text, handling slides, and giving presentations in PowerPoint for the iPad.

- ✔ Create presentations from the ground up in PowerPoint 2011 for the Mac as you discover what makes a good presentation and how to manage slides, get a good look at your work, and hide slides.

- ✔ Make a presentation look just right by choosing themes, changing the slides' background, and using master slides for consistent presentations.

- ✔ See how to deliver a presentation in person, online, or in a kiosk, and how to make your presentations livelier.

Chapter 13

PowerPoint for the iPad

- -

- -

*T*his chapter looks into PowerPoint for the iPad, the slide presentation app in the Office for the iPad family. It explains how to get from slide to slide, add slides, and delete slides. You also discover how to handle the text, write and read speaker notes, put transitions between slides, and last but not least, give a presentation.

Finding Your Way Around the Screen

When you visit a place you haven't been before, take a look around and see what's what. Figure 13-1 shows the PowerPoint screen. Here's what you need to know about the PowerPoint screen:

- ✔ **Slides pane:** The place on the left side (or bottom) of the screen where you can see the slides in your presentation. Tap a slide to go from one slide to another.

- ✔ **Slide window:** Where the slide you're working on is displayed.

- ✔ **From Current button:** Tap this button to begin a slide show starting with the slide that is currently showing.

- ✔ **Notes button:** Tap this button to read and enter notes. You can refer to notes when giving a presentation.

Slides pane   Slide window   Tap to start the slide show

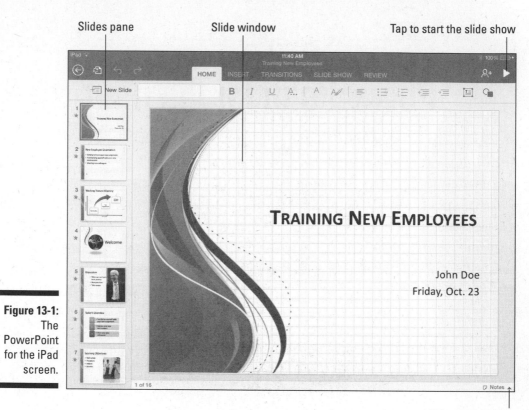

Figure 13-1:
The
PowerPoint
for the iPad
screen.

Tap to read notes

Chapter 3 explains how to create a new file in an Office for the iPad application, including how to create a file from a template.

Handling Text and Text Boxes

All text on PowerPoint slides is kept inside text boxes. Most slides come with preformatted text boxes to make entering text easier. Figure 13-2 shows what a text box looks like. When you tap text on a slide, its text box appears to show you've selected it. What's more, a popover menu for handling slide text appears as well.

These pages explain how to use the popover menu to edit text and how to use the text box to move and rotate text on a slide. You also find out how to create text boxes of your own.

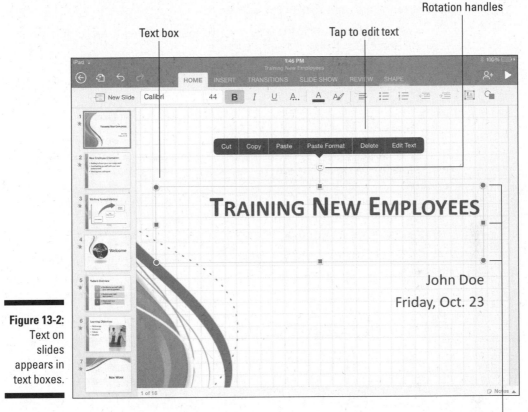

Figure 13-2:
Text on
slides
appears in
text boxes.

Entering and editing text on slides

Follow these steps to enter or edit text on a slide:

1. **Tap the text box where you want to enter or edit text.**

   Black lines and selection handles appear on the corners and sides of the
   text box to show it is selected (see Figure 13-2). Meanwhile, a popover
   menu appears.

2. **Choose Edit Text on the popover menu.**

   The keyboard appears so that you can enter or edit text.

3. **Enter or edit the text in the text box.**

   As you enter and edit text, you can use the text-formatting commands on the Home tab to make it look just so.

Choose Delete on the popover menu to delete all the text in a text box.

Creating a text box

Most slides come with text boxes for holding text. Enter a text box of your own to place text on a slide where you will. Follow these steps to create a text box:

1. **Go to the Insert tab or the Home tab.**
2. **Tap the Text Box button.**

   A text box appears. The next topic in this chapter explains how to move, resize, and rotate a text box.

Manipulating text boxes

Tap to select a text box and then follow these steps to move, resize, or rotate it:

- **Moving:** Drag the text box across the slide.
- **Resizing:** Drag a selection handle on the side or corner of the text box (refer to Figure 13-2).
- **Rotating:** Drag the rotation handle (refer to Figure 13-2).

Adding, Reordering, and Removing Slides

Tapping a slide in the Slides pane displays the slide in the Slide window. Tapping a second time opens a popover menu for reordering and removing slides, as shown in Figure 13-3. Use this popover menu and the New Slide command to manipulate slides. These pages explain how to add, reorder, and remove slides.

Tap to open the popover menu

Add a slide

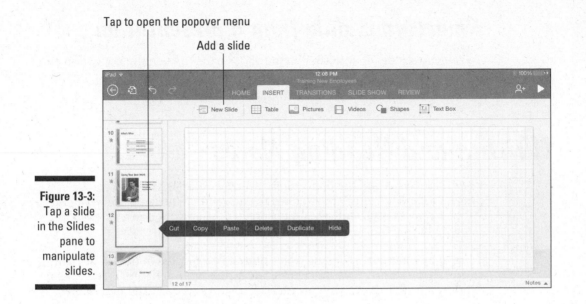

Figure 13-3:
Tap a slide
in the Slides
pane to
manipulate
slides.

Adding a new slide

1. **Select the slide that you want the new slide to go after.**

   To select a slide, tap it in the Slides pane.

2. **Go to the Insert tab if you aren't already there.**

3. **Tap the New Slide button.**

   The New Slide drop-down menu opens. It offers slide layouts for creating slides.

4. **Choose a slide layout.**

   Your new slide appears in the Slide window.

Reordering the slides in a presentation

Follow these steps to move a slide in a presentation:

1. **In the Slides pane, place your finger on the slide you want to move.**

2. **Leave your finger on the slide until the thumbnail changes size slightly.**

3. **Drag the slide to a new location in the Slides pane.**

Removing a slide from a presentation

To remove a slide, double-tap it in the Slides pane to open the popover menu for manipulating slides (refer to Figure 13-3). Then choose Delete on the popover menu.

Writing and Reading Notes

PowerPoint gives you the opportunity to write notes as you construct a presentation. The notes are attached to each slide. You can write what you intend to say as each slide comes onscreen or simply jot down notes to remind yourself how to design or lay out a slide.

To read or enter notes, tap the Notes button (it's located in the lower-right corner of the screen; refer to Figure 13-1, earlier in this chapter). The Notes window opens. Tap this window to bring up the keyboard and enter notes.

Tap the Notes button (located in the upper-right corner of the window) to close the Notes window and return to the Slide window.

Later in this chapter, "Presenter view for dual monitors," a sidebar, explains how, in Presenter view, you can read your notes as you give a presentation.

Applying Slide Transitions

In PowerPoint jargon, a *transition* is a little bit of drama that occurs between slides. Transitions include the wipe, fade, split, and flash. Rather than appear one after another, you can make slides fade or flash onto the screen, for example. PowerPoint for the iPad offers 47 transitions in all. After you choose a transition, you can decide which direction to make it come from.

Follow these steps to apply a transition to a single slide or all the slides in a presentation:

1. **Select a slide if you want the transition to apply to one slide only.**

   To apply a transition to all slides, it doesn't matter which slide is selected in the Slides pane.

2. **Go to the Transitions tab.**

3. **Tap the Transition Effect button to open the Transition to This Slide drop-down menu.**

   Figure 13-4 shows this menu.

4. **Tap a transition on the menu.**

   The Transition Effect button shows an image of the transition you chose.

5. **Tap the Effect Options button to open the Effect Options drop-down menu.**

   Figure 13-4 shows this menu.

6. **Tap an Effect Option.**

   Again, the Effect Options button shows an image representing the option you choose.

7. **Optionally, if you want the transition to apply to all the slides in your presentation, tap the Apply to All Slides button.**

   If I were you, I would start the slide show to see precisely what the transition you chose looks like.

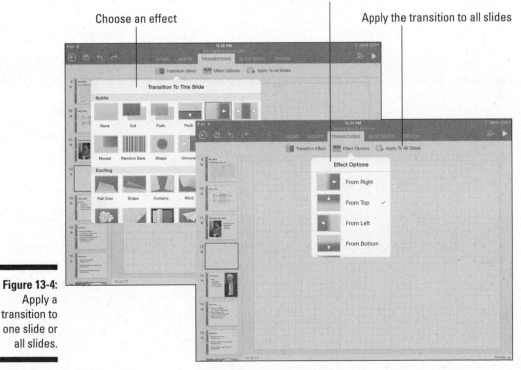

Choose an effect option

Choose an effect

Apply the transition to all slides

Figure 13-4:
Apply a
transition to
one slide or
all slides.

To remove the transition from a slide, select it, go to the Transitions tab, tap the Transition Effect button, and choose None on the drop-down menu. Tap Apply to All Slides as well to remove transitions from all the slides in the presentation.

Giving a Presentation

Finally! At last the day has arrived to give your presentation. I was getting impatient to see it.

PowerPoint for the iPad offers a bunch of ways to give a slide presentation. What's more, you can draw on slides and do one or two other things to make your presentation livelier.

 Display the Slide Show toolbar to end a presentation, draw on slides, and black out the screen. Figure 13-5 shows this toolbar. To display it, tap at the top of the screen while you're giving a presentation. The audience can't see the Slide Show toolbar.

Black out screen

Figure 13-5: The Slide Show toolbar.

End slide show   Draw on slides

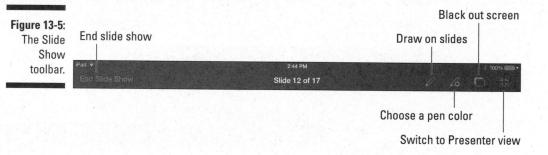

Choose a pen color

Switch to Presenter view

Starting and ending a presentation

Use one of these techniques to start giving a presentation:

- **From the first slide:** On the Slide Show tab, tap the From Start button.

- **From a particular slide:** Select a slide in the Slides pane (if necessary) and tap the From Current button. This button (a triangle) is located in the upper-right corner of the screen and on the Slide Show tab.

Use these techniques to end a presentation:

- **Prematurely in the middle:** Display the Slide Show toolbar and tap End Slide Show on this toolbar (see Figure 13-5). To display the Slide Show toolbar, tap at the top of the screen.
- **After the last slide:** Swipe to the left. A notice on the screen says, "End of slide show. Swipe forward to exit."

Going from slide to slide

Swipe to go from slide to slide:

- Swipe rightward to go to the previous slide.
- Swipe leftward to go to the next slide.

Putting some pizazz in a presentation

Thanks to the Slide Show toolbar (see Figure 13-5), you can do one or two things during a presentation to make it livelier:

- *Draw on the screen.* Tap the Pen button and drag onscreen to draw on a slide. For example, circle something of importance or draw a check mark to show you've finished covering a topic. Tap the Pen button a second time when you finish drawing.

   To choose a color for drawing, tap the Pen Settings button and choose a color on the drop-down menu.

   To erase all the lines you drew, tap the Pen Settings button and choose Clear Pen Markings on the drop-down menu. You can also choose an eraser on the menu and then drag over lines to erase them.

- *Black out the screen.* Tap the Black Out button to make the screen turn black. Black out the screen to get the audience's undivided attention. To display a slide again, tap the button a second time.

Presenter view for dual monitors

If your presentation is being shown on another display such as a projector, you have the option of using Presenter view to give presentations. In Presenter view, the full-screen slide appears on one monitor and a special screen for showing your presentation appears on the iPad, as shown in the illustration here. In this screen, speaker notes are easier to read and you tap thumbnail images to go from slide to slide.

Use one of these techniques to switch to Presenter view:

- ✔ On the Slide Show tab, tap the Presenter View button.
- ✔ On the Slide Show toolbar, tap the Presenter View button (the rightmost button on the toolbar).

To exit Presenter view, tap the Presenter View button in the upper-right corner of the screen.

Chapter 14

Getting Started in PowerPoint 2011

*I*t's impossible to sit through a conference, seminar, or trade show without seeing at least one PowerPoint presentation. PowerPoint has found its way into nearly every office and boardroom. I've heard of a man (a very unromantic man) who proposed to his wife by way of a PowerPoint presentation.

As nice as PowerPoint can be, it has its detractors. If the software isn't used properly, it can come between the speaker and the audience. In a *New Yorker* article titled "Absolute PowerPoint: Can a Software Package Edit Our Thoughts?" Ian Parker argued that PowerPoint may actually be more of a hindrance than a help in communicating. PowerPoint, Parker wrote, is "a social instrument, turning middle managers into bullet-point dandies." The software, he added, "has a private, interior influence. It edits ideas. . . . It helps you make a case, but also makes its own case about how to organize information, how to look at the world."

To make sure that you use PowerPoint wisely, this chapter shows what creating a PowerPoint presentation on a Mac entails. After a brief tour of PowerPoint, you find out how to create presentations, get a better view of your work, insert slides, and hide slides.

Getting Acquainted with PowerPoint

Figure 14-1 (top) shows the PowerPoint window. That thing in the middle is a *slide,* the PowerPoint word for an image that you show your audience. Surrounding the slide are many tools for entering text and decorating slides. When the time comes to show your slides to an audience, you dispense with the tools and make the slide fill the screen, as shown in Figure 14-1 (bottom).

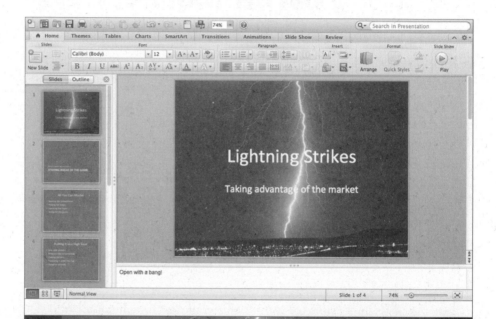

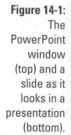

Figure 14-1:
The PowerPoint window (top) and a slide as it looks in a presentation (bottom).

To make PowerPoint do your bidding, you need to know a little jargon:

- **Presentation:** All the slides, from start to finish, that you show your audience. Sometimes presentations are called "slide shows." Presentations are saved in presentation files (.pptx files).

- **Slides:** The images you create with PowerPoint. During a presentation, slides appear onscreen one after the other. Don't be put off by the word *slide* and dreary memories of sitting through your uncle's slide show vacation memories. You don't need a slide projector to show these slides. At conferences you can plug a laptop or other computer into special monitors that display PowerPoint slides.

- **Notes:** Printed pages that you, the speaker, write and print so that you know what to say during a presentation. Only the speaker sees notes. Chapter 16 explains notes.

- **Handout:** Printed pages that you may give to the audience along with a presentation. A handout shows the slides in the presentation. Handouts are also known by the somewhat derogatory term *leave-behinds*. Chapter 16 explains handouts.

A Brief Geography Lesson

Figure 14-2 shows the different parts of the PowerPoint screen. I'd hate for you to get lost in PowerPoint Land. Fold down the corner of this page so that you can return here if screen terminology confuses you:

- **Slides pane:** In Normal view, the place on the left side of the screen where you can see the slides or the text on the slides in your presentation. Scroll in the Slides pane to move backward and forward in a presentation.

- **Slide window:** Where a slide (in Normal view) or slides (in Slide Sorter view) are displayed. Scroll to move backward or forward in your presentation.

- **Notes pane:** Where you type notes (in Normal view) that you can refer to when giving your presentation. The audience can't see these notes — they're for you and you alone. See Chapter 16 for details.

- **View buttons:** Buttons you can click to switch to (from left to right) Normal, Slide Sorter, and Slide Show view. See "Getting a Better View of Your Work," later in this chapter.

- **Zoom controls:** Tools for enlarging or shrinking a slide (in Normal and Slide Sorter view).

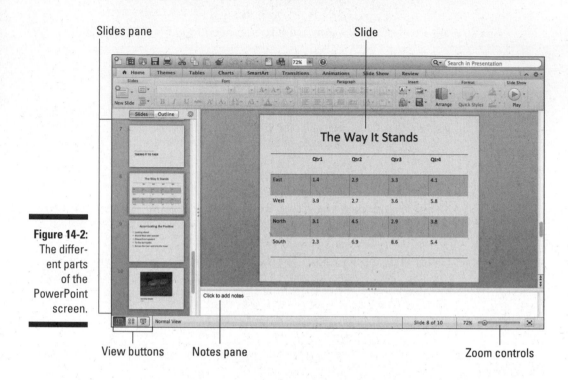

Figure 14-2:
The different parts of the PowerPoint screen.

Slides pane

Slide

View buttons   Notes pane   Zoom controls

Creating a New Presentation

The first thing you see when you start PowerPoint is the *PowerPoint Presentation Gallery,* as shown in Figure 14-3. Starting here, you can create a bare-bones presentation or you can get a more sophisticated, fully realized layout and design by starting with a *template.* Templates are a mixed blessing. They're designed by artists and they look very good. Some templates come with *boilerplate text* — already written material that you can recycle into your presentation. However, presentations made from templates are harder to modify. Sometimes the design gets in the way. As well, a loud or intricate background may overwhelm a diagram or chart you want to put on a slide.

Follow these instructions to create a presentation:

- ✔ **Basic presentation:** Click the Cancel button in the PowerPoint Presentation Gallery, click the New Presentation button on the Standard toolbar, press Command+N, or choose File➪New Presentation.

- ✔ **Template presentation:** Choose a template in the PowerPoint Presentation Gallery. To open this gallery, click the New from Template button on the Standard toolbar, press Shift+Command+P, or choose File➪New from Template.

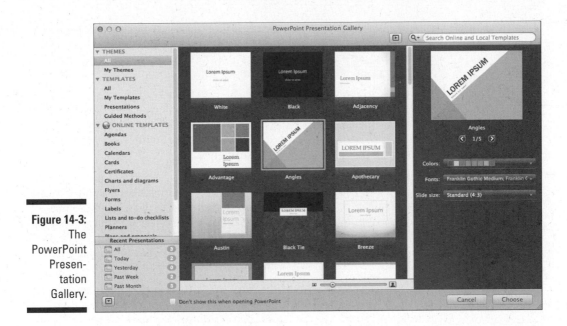

Figure 14-3:
The
PowerPoint
Presen-
tation
Gallery.

To choose a template in the PowerPoint Presentation Gallery, select a templates category, select a template, select a color scheme and font for your template in the Preview pane, and click the Choose button. (If you're in a hurry, you can double-click a template in the Gallery to create a presentation.)

If you don't care to see the PowerPoint Presentation Gallery when you start PowerPoint, choose PowerPoint ⇨ Preferences. Then, in the PowerPoint Preferences dialog box, choose General and deselect the Open PowerPoint Presentation Gallery When Application Opens check box.

Advice for Building Persuasive Presentations

Before you create any slides, think about what you want to communicate to your audience. Your goal isn't to dazzle the audience with your PowerPoint skills but rather to communicate something — a company policy, the merits of a product, the virtues of a strategic plan. Your goal is to bring the audience around to your side. To that end, here is some practical advice for building persuasive presentations:

✔ **Start by writing the text in Word.** Start in Microsoft Word, not PowerPoint, so that you can focus on the words. In Word, you can clearly see how a presentation develops. You can make sure that your presentation builds to its rightful conclusion. PowerPoint has a special command for getting headings from a Word file. (See "Conjuring slides from Word document headings," later in this chapter.)

✔ **When choosing a design, consider the audience.** A presentation to the American Casketmakers Association calls for a mute, quiet design; a presentation to the Cheerleaders of Tomorrow calls for something bright and splashy. Select a slide design that sets the tone for your presentation and wins the sympathy of the audience.

✔ **Keep it simple.** To make sure that PowerPoint doesn't upstage you, keep it simple. Make use of the PowerPoint features, but do so judiciously. An animation in the right place at the right time can serve a valuable purpose. It can highlight an important part of a presentation and grab the audience's attention. But stuffing a presentation with too many gizmos turns a presentation into a carnival sideshow and distracts from your message.

✔ **Follow the one-slide-per-minute rule.** At the very minimum, a slide should stay onscreen for at least one minute. If you have 15 minutes to speak, you're allotted no more than 15 slides for your presentation, according to the rule.

✔ **Beware the bullet point.** Terse bullet points have their place in a presentation, but if you put them there strictly to remind yourself what to say next, you're doing your audience a disfavor. Bullet points can cause drowsiness. They can be a distraction. The audience skims the bullets when it should be attending to your voice and the argument you're making.

✔ **Take control from the start.** Spend the first minute introducing yourself to the audience without running PowerPoint (or, if you do run PowerPoint, put a simple slide with your company name or logo onscreen). Make eye contact with the audience. This way, you establish your credibility. You give the audience a chance to get to know you.

✔ **Make clear what you're about.** In the early going, state very clearly what your presentation is about and what you intend to prove with your presentation. In other words, state the conclusion at the beginning as well as the end. This way, your audience knows exactly what you're driving at and can judge your presentation according to how well you build your case.

✔ **Personalize the presentation.** Make the presentation a personal one. Tell the audience what *your* personal reason for being there is or why *you* work for the company you work for. Knowing that you have a personal stake in the presentation, the audience is more likely to trust you. The audience understands that you're not a spokesperson, but a *speaker* — someone who has come before them to make a case for something that you believe in.

✔ **Tell a story.** Include an anecdote in the presentation. Everybody loves a pertinent and well-delivered story. This piece of advice is akin to the previous one about personalizing your presentation. Typically, a story illustrates a problem for *people* and how *people* solve the problem. Even if your presentation concerns technology or an abstract subject, make it about people. "The people in Shaker Heights needed faster Internet access," not "the data switches in Shaker Heights just weren't performing fast enough."

✔ **Rehearse and then rehearse some more.** The better you know your material, the less nervous you will be. To keep from getting nervous, rehearse your presentation until you know it backward and forward. Rehearse it out loud. Rehearse it while imagining you're in the presence of an audience.

✔ **Use visuals, not only words, to make your point.** You really owe it to your audience to take advantage of the table, chart, diagram, and picture capabilities of PowerPoint. People understand more from words and pictures than they do from words alone. It's up to you — not the slides — as the speaker to describe topics in detail with words.

Want to see how PowerPoint can suck the life and drama out of a dramatic presentation? Try visiting the Gettysburg PowerPoint Presentation, a rendering of Lincoln's Gettysburg Address in PowerPoint. Yikes! You can find it here: `http://norvig.com/Gettysburg/`.

Creating New Slides for Your Presentation

After you create a presentation, your next step on the path to glory is to start adding the slides. To create a new slide, you start by choosing a slide layout. *Slide layouts* are the preformatted slide designs that help you enter text, graphics, and other things. Some slide layouts have *text placeholder frames* for entering titles and text; some come with *content placeholder frames* designed especially for inserting a table, chart, diagram, picture, clip-art image, or media clip.

When you add a slide, select the slide layout that best approximates the slide you have in mind for your presentation. Figure 14-4 shows the slide layouts that are available when you create a basic presentation. These pages explain how to insert slides and harvest them from Word document headings.

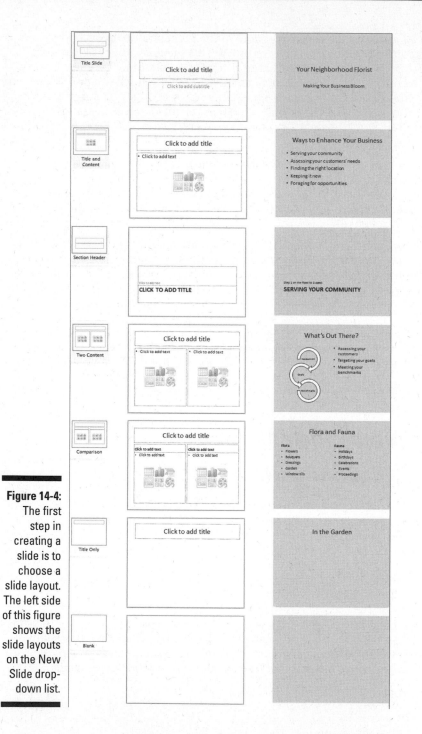

Figure 14-4:
The first step in creating a slide is to choose a slide layout. The left side of this figure shows the slide layouts on the New Slide drop-down list.

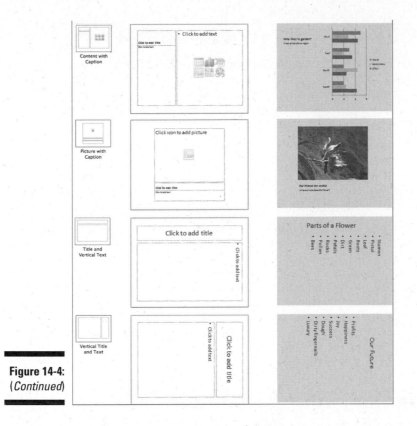

Figure 14-4:
(*Continued*)

Inserting a new slide

Follow these steps to insert a new slide in your presentation:

1. **Select the slide that you want the new slide to go after.**

   In Normal view, select the slide on the Slides pane. In Slide Sorter view, select the slide in the main window.

2. **On the Home tab, open the drop-down list on the New Slide button.**

   You see a drop-down list of slide layouts. (If you simply click the New Slide button, you insert a slide with the same layout as the one you selected in Step 1.) Figure 14-4 shows what the slide layouts look like (left), what a slide looks like right after you insert it (middle), and finished slides (right).

3. **Select the slide layout that best approximates the slide you want to create.**

   Don't worry too much about selecting the right layout. You can change slide layouts later on, as "Selecting a different layout for a slide" explains, later in this chapter.

Speed techniques for inserting slides

When you're in a hurry, use these techniques to insert a slide:

- ✔ **Creating a duplicate slide:** Select the slide or slides you want to duplicate, and on the Home tab, open the drop-down list on the New Slide button and choose Duplicate Selected Slides.

- ✔ **Copying and pasting slides:** Click the slide you want to copy (or Command+click to select more than one slide) and then click the Copy button on the Standard toolbar (or press Command+C). Next, click to select the slide that you want the copied slide (or slides) to appear after and click the Paste button (or press Command+V).

- ✔ **Recycling slides from other presentations:** Select the slide that you want the recycled slides to follow in your presentation, and on the Home tab, open the drop-down list on the New Slide button and choose Insert Slides from Other Presentation. The Choose a File dialog box opens. Find and select the presentation with the files you want to reuse, and click the Insert button. The Slide Finder dialog box opens. It shows thumbnail versions of slides in the presentation you selected. Either click Insert All to reuse all the slides or Shift+click the slides you want and then click the Insert button.

Conjuring slides from Word document headings

If you think about it, Word headings are similar to slide titles. Headings, like slide titles, introduce a new topic. If you know your way around Word and you want to get a head start creating a PowerPoint presentation, you can borrow the headings in a Word document for your PowerPoint slides. After you import the headings from Word, you get one slide for each level-1 heading (headings given the Heading 1 style). Level-1 headings form the title of the slides, level-2 headings form first-level bullets, level-3 headings form second-level bullets, and so on. Paragraph text isn't imported. Figure 14-5 shows what headings from a Word document look like after they land in a PowerPoint presentation.

Follow these steps to use headings in a Word document to create slides in a PowerPoint presentation:

1. **Open the Word file and save it as an RTF (rich text format) file.**

   To recycle headings from a Word document, the document must be saved as an RTF. In Word, choose File ➪ Save As, and in the Save As dialog box, open the Format drop-down list, choose Rich Text Format, and click the Save button.

Each level-1 heading in the Word document becomes a slide title in PowerPoint

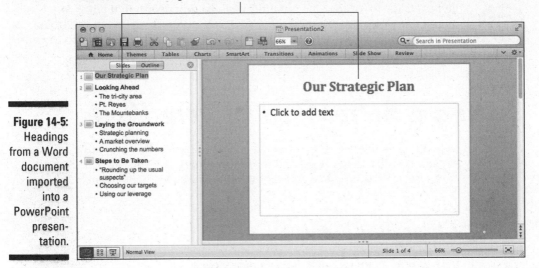

Figure 14-5:
Headings
from a Word
document
imported
into a
PowerPoint
presen-
tation.

2. **In PowerPoint, select the slide that the new slides from the Word document will follow.**

3. **Choose Insert ➪ Slides From ➪ Outline.**

   The Choose a File dialog box opens.

4. **Select the Word document with the headings you want for your presentation and click the Insert button.**

   Depending on how many first-level headings are in the Word document, you get a certain number of new slides. These slides probably need work. The Word text may need tweaking to make it suitable for a PowerPoint presentation.

Selecting a different layout for a slide

If you mistakenly choose the wrong layout for a slide, all is not lost. You can start all over. You can graft a new layout onto your slide by following these steps:

1. **On the Home tab, click the Change the Layout button.**

   A drop-down list with slide layouts appears.

2. **Select a layout.**

PowerPoint also offers the Reset Layout to Default Settings command for giving a slide its original layout after you've fiddled with it. If you push a slide all out of shape and you regret doing so, select your slide, go to the Home tab, click the Change the Layout button, and choose Reset Layout to Default Settings on the drop-down list.

Getting a Better View of Your Work

Depending on the task at hand, some views are better than others. These pages explain how to change views and the relative merits of Normal, Slide Sorter, Notes Page, Presenter, and Slide Show view, as well as the "slide master" views.

Changing views

PowerPoint offers two places to change views:

- ✔ **View buttons on the status bar:** Click a View button — Normal, Slide Sorter, or Slide Show — on the status bar to change views, as shown in Figure 14-6.

Open the View menu

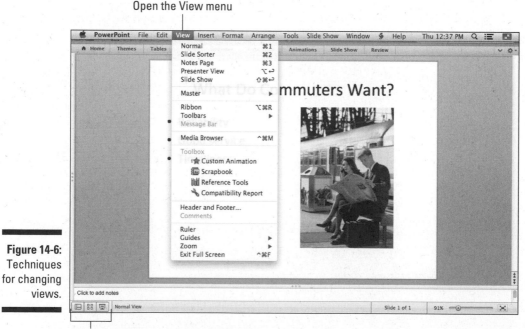

Figure 14-6: Techniques for changing views.

Click a View button on the status bar

✔ **View menu:** Open the View menu and choose a view, as shown in Figure 14-6.

Looking at the different views

Here is a survey of the different views with suggestions about using each one:

✔ **Normal/Slides view for examining slides:** Switch to Normal view, move the pointer to the Slides pane, and select the Slides tab when you want to examine a slide. In this view, thumbnail slides appear in the Slides pane, and you can see your slide in all its glory in the middle of the screen.

✔ **Normal/Outline view for fiddling with text:** Switch to Normal view, move the pointer to the Slides pane, and select the Outline tab to enter or read text. You can find the Outline tab at the top of the Slides pane. The words appear in outline form. Normal/Outline view is ideal for focusing on the words in a presentation.

✔ **Slide Sorter view for moving and deleting slides:** In Slide Sorter view, you see thumbnails of all the slides in the presentation (use the Zoom slider to change the size of thumbnails). From here, moving slides around is easy, and seeing many slides simultaneously gives you a sense of whether the different slides are consistent with one another and how the whole presentation is shaping up. The slides are numbered so that you can see where they appear in a presentation.

✔ **Slide Show view for giving a presentation:** In Slide Show view, you see a single slide. Not only that, but the slide fills the entire screen. This is what your presentation looks like when you show it to an audience.

✔ **Notes Page view for reading your speaker notes:** In Notes Page view, you see notes you've written to aid you in your presentation, if you've written any. You can write notes in this view as well as in the Notes pane in Normal view. Chapter 16 explains notes pages.

✔ **The Master views for a consistent presentation:** The master views — Slide Master, Handout Master, and Notes Master — are for handling *master styles,* the formatting commands that pertain to all the slides in a presentation, handouts, and notes. Chapter 15 looks into master slides and master styles.

PowerPoint offers a button called Fit Slide to Current Window that you can click while you're in Normal view to make the slide fill the window. This little button is located in the lower-right corner of the screen, to the right of the Zoom controls.

Hiding and Displaying the Slides Pane and Notes Pane

In Normal view, the Slides pane with its slide thumbnails appears on the left side of the screen, and the Notes pane appears on the bottom of the screen so that you can scribble notes about slides. Sometimes these panes just take up valuable space. They clutter the screen and occupy real estate that could be better used for formatting slides. Follow these instructions to temporarily close the Slides and Notes panes:

- **Closing and opening the Notes pane:** Move the pointer over the border between the pane and the rest of the screen, and after the pointer changes to a two-headed arrow, drag the border to the bottom of the screen. Drag the border upward to see the Notes pane again.

- **Closing the Slides pane:** Click the Close button on the Slides pane. This button is located to the right of the Outline tab. Clicking it closes the Notes pane as well as the Slides pane.

- **Restoring the Slides pane:** Click the Normal View button or choose View⇨Normal. You can also move the pointer to the left side or bottom of the screen and, when you see the double-headed arrow, click and start dragging toward the center of the screen.

You can change the size of either pane by moving the pointer over its border and then clicking and dragging.

Selecting, Moving, and Deleting Slides

As a presentation takes shape, you have to move slides forward and backward. Sometimes you have to delete a slide. And you can't move or delete slides until you select them first. Herewith are instructions for selecting, moving, and deleting slides.

Selecting slides

The best place to select slides is Slide Sorter view (if you want to select several at a time). Use one of these techniques to select slides:

- **Select one slide:** Click the slide.

- **Select several different slides**: Hold down the Command key and click each slide in the Slides pane or in Slide Sorter view.

- ✔ **Select several slides in succession:** Hold down the Shift key and click the first slide and then the last one.

- ✔ **Select a block of slides:** In Slide Sorter view, drag across the slides you want to select. Be sure when you click and start dragging that you don't click a slide.

- ✔ **Selecting all the slides:** Press Command+A (if you're in Normal view, click in the Slides pane before pressing Command+A).

Moving slides

To move or rearrange slides, you're advised to go to Slide Sorter view. Select the slide or slides that you want to move and use one of these techniques to move slides:

- ✔ **Dragging and dropping:** Click the slides you selected and drag them to a new location.

- ✔ **Cutting and pasting:** Cut the slide or slides to the Clipboard (click the Cut button on the Standard toolbar or press Command+X). Then select the slide that you want the slide or slides to appear after and give the Paste command (click the Paste button or press Command+V).

Deleting slides

Before you delete a slide, think twice about deleting. Short of using the Undo command, you can't resuscitate a deleted slide. Select the slide or slides you want to delete and use one of these techniques to delete slides:

- ✔ Press the Delete key.
- ✔ Right-click and choose Delete Slide on the shortcut menu.

Hidden Slides for All Contingencies

Hide a slide when you want to keep it on hand "just in case" during a presentation. Hidden slides don't appear in slide shows unless you shout *Ollie ollie oxen free!* and bring them out of hiding. Although you, the presenter, can see hidden slides in Normal view and Slide Sorter view, where they are grayed out, the audience doesn't see them in the course of a presentation unless you decide to show them. Create hidden slides if you anticipate having to steer your presentation in a different direction — to answer a question from the audience, prove your point more thoroughly, or revisit a topic in more depth. Merely by right-clicking and choosing a couple of commands, you can display a hidden slide in the course of a slide show.

Hiding a slide

The best place to put hidden slides is the end of a presentation where you know you can find them. Follow these steps to hide slides:

1. **Select the slide or slides that you want to hide.**

2. **On the Slide Show tab, click the Hide Slide button.**

   You can also right-click a slide in the Slides pane or Slide Sorter view and choose Hide Slide. Hidden slides are grayed out in the Slides pane and the Slide Sorter window.

To unhide a slide, click the Hide Slide button again or right-click the slide and choose Hide Slide.

Showing a hidden slide during a presentation

Hidden slides don't appear during the course of a presentation, but suppose that the need arises to show one. Before showing a hidden slide, take careful note of which slide you're viewing now. You have to return to this slide after viewing the hidden slide. Follow these steps to view a hidden slide during a presentation:

1. **Right-click the screen and choose Go to Slide.**

   You see a submenu with slide numbers and slide titles.

2. **Select a hidden slide so that the audience can view it.**

   You can tell which slides are hidden because their slide numbers are enclosed in parentheses.

How do you resume your presentation after viewing a hidden slide? If you look at only one hidden slide, you can right-click and choose Last Viewed on the shortcut menu to return to the slide you saw before the hidden slide. If you've viewed several hidden slides, right-click the screen, choose Go to Slide, and select a slide to pick up where you left off.

Chapter 15

Fashioning a Look for Your Presentation

*W*hat your presentation looks like — which theme and background style you select for the slides in your presentation — sets the tone. From the very first slide, the audience judges your presentation on its appearance. When you create a look for your presentation, what you're really doing is declaring what you want to communicate to your audience.

This chapter explains how to fashion a look for your presentation. It describes how to handle slide backgrounds and what to consider when you select colors and designs for backgrounds. You also discover how to select and customize a theme, and how to create your own slide backgrounds. This chapter looks into how to change the background of some but not all of the slides in a presentation. It also explains how to use master slides and master styles to make sure that slides throughout your presentation are consistent with one another. Finally, you find out how to put headers and footers on slides.

Looking at Themes and Background Styles

What a presentation looks like is mostly a matter of slide backgrounds, and when you select a background for slides, you start by selecting a theme.

A *theme* is a "canned" slide design. Themes are designed by graphic artists. Most themes include sophisticated background patterns and colors. For each theme, PowerPoint offers several alternative theme colors, fonts, and background styles. As well, you can create a background of your own from a single color, a gradient mixture of two colors, or a picture.

Figure 15-1 shows examples of themes. Themes range from the fairly simple to the quite complex. When you installed PowerPoint on your Mac, you also installed a dozen or more themes, and you can acquire more themes online from Office.com and other places. After you select a theme for your presentation, you can tweak it a little bit. You can do that by choosing a background style or by creating an entirely new background of your own.

Figure 15-1:
Examples of
themes.

Figure 15-2 shows examples of backgrounds that you can create yourself. Self-made backgrounds are not as intrusive as themes. The risk of having the background overwhelm the lists, tables, charts, and other items in the forefront of slides is less when you fashion a background style yourself.

More than any other design decision, what sets the tone for a presentation are the colors you select for slide backgrounds. If the purpose of your presentation is to show photographs that you took on a vacation to Arizona's Painted Desert, select light-tone, hot colors for the slide backgrounds. If your presentation is an aggressive sales pitch, consider a black background. There is no universal color theory for selecting the right colors in a design because everyone is different. Follow your intuition. It will guide you to the right background color choices.

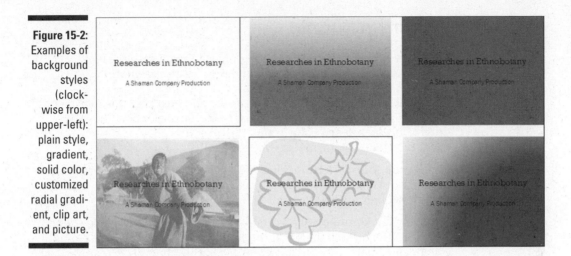

Figure 15-2:
Examples of background styles (clockwise from upper-left): plain style, gradient, solid color, customized radial gradient, clip art, and picture.

Choosing a Theme for Your Presentation

After you initially select a theme, you can do one or two things to customize it. These pages explain how to find and select a theme for your presentation and diddle with a theme after you select it.

Selecting a theme

Use one of these techniques to select a new theme for your presentation:

- ✔ **Selecting a theme in the Themes gallery:** On the Themes tab, open the Themes gallery and select a theme.

- ✔ **Borrowing a theme from another presentation:** On the Themes tab, open the Themes gallery, and choose Browse Themes. You see the Choose Themed Document or Slide Template dialog box. Locate and select a presentation with a theme that you can commandeer for your presentation and click the Apply button.

Tweaking a theme

Starting on the Themes tab, you can customize a theme with these techniques and in so doing alter all the slides in your presentation:

- ✓ **Choosing a new set of colors:** The easiest and best way to experiment with customizing a theme is to select a different color set. Click the Colors button, select a color set on the drop-down list, and see what effect that set's colors have on your slides.

- ✓ **Change the fonts:** Click the Fonts button and choose a font combination on the drop-down list. The first font in each pair applies to slide titles and the second to slide text.

- ✓ **Choosing background style variation:** Most themes offer background style variations. Click the Background button to open the Background gallery and select a style. The next topic in this chapter, "Creating Slide Backgrounds on Your Own," explains how you can create backgrounds similar to these, as well as how to create a single-color, gradient, clip-art, picture, and texture background.

Suppose you regret customizing a theme. To get the original theme back, select it again. Make like you were selecting a theme for the first time and select it in the Themes gallery.

Creating Slide Backgrounds on Your Own

Besides a theme or background style, your other option for creating slide backgrounds is to do it on your own. For a background, you can have a solid color, a transparent color, a gradient blend of colors, a picture, or a clip-art image.

- ✓ **Solid color:** A single, uniform color. You can adjust a color's transparency and in effect "bleach out" the color to push it farther into the background.

- ✓ **Gradient:** A mixture of different colors with the colors blending into one another.

- ✓ **Clip art:** A clip-art image from the Clipart folder.

✔ **Picture:** A photograph or graphic stored on your computer or network.

✔ **Texture:** A uniform pattern that gives the impression that the slide is displayed on a material such as cloth or stone.

How to create these kinds of slide backgrounds on your own is the subject of the next several pages.

Using a solid (or transparent) color for the slide background

Using a solid or transparent color for the background gives your slides a straightforward, honest look. Because all the slides are the same color or a transparent color, the audience can focus better on the presentation itself rather than the razzle-dazzle. Follow these steps to use a solid or transparent color as the background for slides:

1. **On the Themes tab, click the Background button and choose Format Background on the drop-down list.**

   You see the Fill category of the Format Background dialog box.

2. **Go to the Solid tab.**

3. **Click the Color button and choose a color on the drop-down list.**

   The theme colors are recommended because they look better in the background, but you can select a standard color or click the More Colors button and select a color in the Colors dialog box.

4. **Drag the Transparency slider if you want a "bleached out" color rather than a slide color.**

   At 0% transparency, you get a solid color; at 100%, you get no color at all.

5. **Click the Apply to All button and then the Close button.**

   I sincerely hope that you like your choice of colors, but if you don't, try, try, try again.

Creating a gradient color blend for slide backgrounds

Gradient refers to how and where two or more colors grade, or blend, into one another on a slide. As well as the standard linear gradient direction, you can opt for a radial, rectangular, or path gradient direction. Figure 15-3 shows examples of gradient fill backgrounds. These backgrounds look terribly elegant. Using a gradient is an excellent way to create an original background that looks different from all the other presenters' slide backgrounds.

Follow these steps to create a gradient background for slides:

1. **On the Themes tab, click the Background button and choose Format Background on the drop-down list.**

   You see the Format Background dialog box. You can drag this dialog box to the side of the screen if you want to get a better view of your slide.

2. **Go to the Gradient tab.**

3. **On the Style drop-down list, choose what type of gradient you want — Linear, Radial, Rectangular, Path, or From Title (refer to Figure 15-3).**

Figure 15-3:
Examples of gradient fill slide backgrounds (clockwise form upper-left): linear, radial, rectangular, and path.

If you choose Linear, you can enter a degree measurement in the Angle box to change the angle at which the colors blend. At 90 degrees, for example, colors blend horizontally across the slide; at 180 degrees, they blend vertically.

4. **Create a gradient stop for each color transition that you want on your slides.**

Gradient stops determine where colors are, how colors transition from one to the next, and which colors are used. You can create as many gradient stops as you want. Here are techniques for handling gradient stops:

- *Adding a gradient stop:* Click the Add Color button. A new gradient stop appears on the slider. Drag it to where you want the color blend to occur.

- *Removing a gradient stop:* Select a gradient stop on the slider and click the Delete Color button.

- *Choosing a color for a gradient stop:* Select a gradient stop on the slider, click the Color button, and choose a color on the drop-down list.

- *Positioning a gradient stop:* Drag a gradient stop on the slider or use the Position box to move it to a different location.

5. **Drag the Transparency slider to make the colors on the slides more or less transparent.**

   At 0% transparency, you get solid colors; at 100%, you get no color at all.

6. **Click the Apply to All button.**

   Very likely, you have to experiment with stop colors and stop positions until you blend the colors to your satisfaction. Good luck.

Using a picture or clip-art image for a slide background

As long as they're on the pale side or you've made them semitransparent, pictures and clip-art images do fine for slide backgrounds. They look especially good in title slides. PowerPoint comes with numerous clip-art images. You're invited to use a clip-art image or a photo of your own as the background of your slides. Figure 15-4 shows examples of photos and images in slide backgrounds.

Select a landscape-style picture or image that is wider than it is tall. PowerPoint expands pictures to make them fill the entire slide background. If you select a skinny, portrait-style picture, PowerPoint has to do a lot of expanding to make it fit on the slide, and you end up with a distorted background image.

Figure 15-4:
Examples
of pictures
used as
slide back-
grounds.

Follow these steps to use a picture or clip-art image as a slide background:

1. **On the Themes tab, click the Background button and choose Format Background on the drop-down list.**

   You see the Format Background dialog box.

2. **Go to the Picture or Texture tab.**

3. **Click the Choose a Picture button.**

   The Choose a Picture dialog box appears. The dialog box is open to the Clipart folder. Starting here, you can select a clip-art image or picture file of your own.

   Click the Preview button in the Choose a Picture dialog box so that you can preview images before you decide whether to put them on slides. The Preview button is one of three view buttons in the upper-left corner of the dialog box.

4. **Locate the picture you want, select it, and click the Insert button.**

   The picture or clip-art image you chose appears in the Format Background dialog box.

5. Enter a Transparency measurement to make the picture fade a bit into the background.

Drag the slider or enter a measurement in the Transparency box. The higher the percentage measurement you enter is, the more "bleached out" the picture is.

6. Click the Apply to All button.

How do you like your slide background? You may have to open the Format Background dialog box again and play with the transparency setting. Only the very lucky and the permanently blessed get it right the first time.

Using a texture for a slide background

Yet another option for slide backgrounds is to use a texture. As shown in Figure 15-5, a *texture* gives the impression that the slide is displayed on a material such as marble or parchment. A texture can make for a very elegant slide background. Follow these steps to use a texture as a slide background:

1. On the Themes tab, click the Background button and choose Format Background on the drop-down list.

The Format Background dialog box opens.

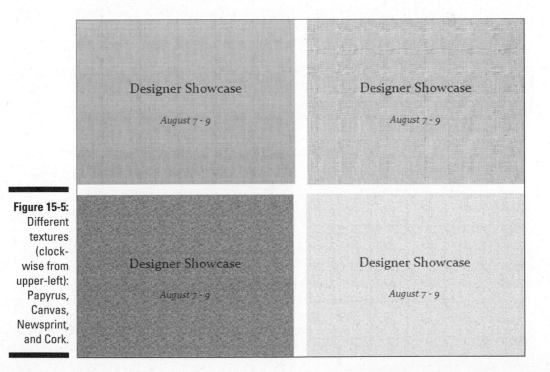

Figure 15-5: Different textures (clockwise from upper-left): Papyrus, Canvas, Newsprint, and Cork.

2. **Go to the Picture or Texture tab.**

3. **Click the Choose Texture button.**

   A pop-up list of texture options appears.

4. **Select a texture.**

5. **Enter a Transparency measurement to make the texture less imposing.**

   Drag the slider or enter a measurement in the Transparency box.

6. **Click the Apply to All button.**

Changing the Background of a Single Slide or Handful of Slides

To make a single slide (or a handful of slides) stand out in a presentation, change its background style or theme. A different background tells your audience that the slide being presented is a little different from the one before it. Maybe it imparts important information. Maybe it introduces another segment of the presentation. Use a different background style or theme to mark a transition, indicate that your presentation has shifted gears, or mark a milestone in your presentation.

Follow these steps to change the background of one or several slides in your presentation:

1. **In Slide Sorter view, select the slides that need a different look.**

   You can select more than one slide by Command+clicking slides.

2. **On the Themes tab, choose a different theme or background for the slides you selected.**

   How you do this depends on whether you're working with a theme or a slide background:

   • *Theme:* In the Themes Gallery, right-click a theme and choose Apply to Selected Slides.

   • *Slide background:* In Slide Sorter view, select the slides that need a different background. Then make like you're creating a background for all your slides (see "Creating Slide Backgrounds on Your Own," earlier in this chapter) but don't click the Apply to All button; click the Apply button instead.

When you assign a different theme to some of the slides in a presentation, PowerPoint creates another Slide Master. You may be surprised to discover that when you add a new slide to your presentation, a second, third, or fourth set of slide layouts appears on the New Slide drop-down list. These extra layouts appear because your presentation has more than one Slide Master. The next topic in this chapter, "Using Master Slides and Master Styles for a Consistent Design," explains what Slide Masters are.

Using Master Slides and Master Styles for a Consistent Design

Consistency is everything in a PowerPoint design. Consistency of design is a sign of professionalism and care. In a consistent design, the fonts and font sizes on slides are consistent from one slide to the next, the placeholder text frames are in the same positions, and the text is aligned the same way across different slides. In the bulleted lists, each entry is marked with the same bullet character. If the corner of each slide shows a company logo, the logo appears in the same position.

It would be torture to have to examine every slide to ensure its consistency with the others. To ease your way, PowerPoint offers master styles and master slides. A *master slide* is a model slide from which the slides in a presentation inherit their formats. A *master style* is a format that applies to many different slides. Starting from a master slide, you can change a master style and in so doing, reformat many slides the same way. These pages explain how master slides can help you quickly redesign a presentation.

Switching to Slide Master view

To work with master slides, switch to *Slide Master view,* as shown in Figure 15-6. From this view, you can start working with master slides.

To switch to Slide Master view, choose View ⇨ Master ⇨ Slide Master. The Slide Master tab opens. In Slide Master view, you can select a master slide in the Slides pane, format styles on a master slide, and in this way reformat many different slides. (Click the Close button or a view button such as Normal or Slide Sorter to leave Slide Master view.)

Understanding master slides and master styles

Master slides are special, high-powered slides. Use master slides to deliver the same formatting commands to many different slides. Whether the commands affect all the slides in your presentation or merely a handful of slides depends on whether you format the Slide Master (the topmost slide in Slide Master view) or a layout (one of the other slides):

✔ **The Slide Master:** The *Slide Master* is the first slide in the Slides pane in Slide Master view (refer to Figure 15-6). It's a little bigger than the layouts, as befits its status as Emperor of All Slides. Formatting changes you make to the Slide Master affect all the slides in your presentation. When you select a theme for your presentation, what you're really doing is assigning a theme to the Slide Master. Because formatting commands given to the Slide Master apply throughout a presentation, the theme design and colors are applied to all slides. If you want a company logo to appear on all your slides, place the logo on the Slide Master.

Select the Slide Master . . .

or a layout

Change a master style

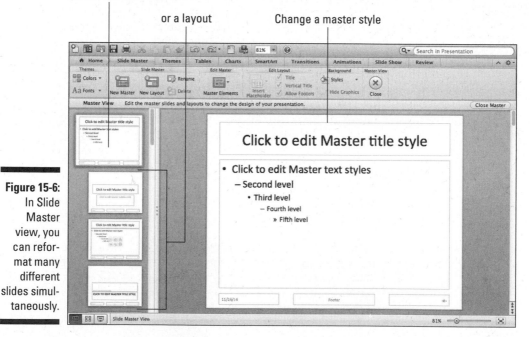

Figure 15-6: In Slide Master view, you can reformat many different slides simultaneously.

✔ **Layouts:** As you know, you choose a slide layout — Title and Content, for example — on the New Slide drop-down list to create a new slide. In Slide Master view, PowerPoint provides one *layout* for each type of slide layout in your presentation. By selecting and reformatting a layout in Slide Master view, you can reformat all slides in your presentation that were created with the same slide layout. For example, to change fonts, alignments, and other formats on all slides that you created with the Title Slide layout, select the Title Slide Layout in Slide Master view and change master styles on the Title Slide layout. Each layout controls its own little fiefdom in a PowerPoint presentation — a fiefdom comprised of slides created with the same slide layout.

✔ **Master styles:** Each master slide — the Slide Master and each layout — offers you the opportunity to click to edit master styles (refer to Figure 15-6). The master style governs how text is formatted on slides. By changing a master style on a master slide, you can change the look of slides throughout a presentation. For example, by changing the Master Title Style font, you can change fonts in all the slide titles in your presentation.

PowerPoint's system of Slide Master, layouts, and slides is designed on the "trickle down" theory. When you format a master style on the Slide Master, formats trickle down to layouts and then to slides. When you format a master style on a layout, the formats trickle down to slides you created using the same slide layout. This chain-of-command relationship is designed to work from the top down, with the master slide and layouts barking orders to the slides below. In the interest of design consistency, slides take orders from layouts, and layouts take orders from the Slide Master.

In Slide Master view, you can move the pointer over a layout thumbnail in the Slides pane to see a pop-up box that tells you the layout's name and which slides in your presentation "use" the layout. For example, a pop-up box that reads "Title and Content Layout: used by slide(s) 2-3, 8" tells you that slides 2 through 3 and 8 in your presentation are governed by the Title and Content layout.

Editing a master slide

Now that you know the relationship among the Slide Master, layouts, and slides, you're ready to start editing master slides. To edit a master slide, switch to Slide Master view, select a master slide, and change a master style.

Changing a master slide layout

Changing the layout of a master slide entails changing the position and size of text frames and content frames as well as removing those frames:

- ✔ **Changing size of frames:** Select the frame you want to change and then move the pointer over a frame handle on the corner, side, top or bottom of the frame; drag when you see the double-headed arrow.

- ✔ **Moving frames:** Move the pointer over the perimeter of a frame, click when you see the four-headed arrow, and drag.

- ✔ **Removing a frame from the Slide Master:** Click the perimeter of the frame to select it; then press Delete.

Putting Footers (and Headers) on Slides

A *footer* is a line of text that appears at the foot, or bottom, of a slide. Figure 15-7 shows a footer. Typically, a footer includes the date, a company name, and/or a slide number, and footers appear on every slide in a presentation if they appear at all. That doesn't mean that you can't exclude a footer from a slide or put footers on some slides, as I explain shortly. For that matter, you can move slide numbers, company names, and dates to the top of slides, in which case they become *headers*. When I was a kid, "header" meant crashing your bike and falling headfirst over the handlebars. How times change.

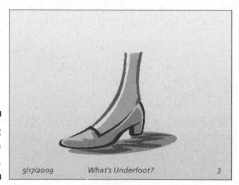

Figure 15-7:
An example
of a footer.

5/17/2009   *What's Underfoot?*   3

These pages explain everything a body needs to know about footers and headers — how to enter them, make them appear on all or some slides, and exclude them from slides.

Some background on footers and headers

PowerPoint provides the Header and Footer dialog box to enter the date, a word or two, and a slide number on the bottom of all slides in your presentation. This dialog box is really just a convenient way to enter a footer on the Slide Master without having to switch to Slide Master view. As "Using Master Slides and Master Styles for a Consistent Design" explains, earlier in this chapter, the Slide Master governs the formatting and layout of all slides in your presentation. The Slide Master includes text placeholder frames for a date, some text, and a slide number. Anything you enter on the Slide Master, including a footer, appears on all your slides.

If a date, some text, and a slide number along the bottom of all the slides in your presentation is precisely what you want, you've got it made. You can enter a footer on every slide in your presentation with no trouble at all by using the Header and Footer dialog box. However, if you're a maverick and you want your footers and headers to be a little different from the next guy's — if you want the date, for example, to be in the upper-right corner of slides or you want footers to appear on some slides but not others — you have some tweaking to do. You may have to create a nonstandard footer or remove the footer from some of the slides.

Putting a standard footer on all your slides

A standard footer includes the date, some text, and the page number. To put a standard footer on all the slides in your presentation, choose Insert ⇨ Header and Footer. You see the Header and Footer dialog box, shown in Figure 15-8. Choose some or all of these options and click the Apply to All button:

✔ **Date and Time:** Select this check box to make the date appear in the lower-right corner of all your slides. Then tell PowerPoint whether you want a current or fixed date:

- *Update Automatically:* Select this option button to make the day's date (or date and time) appear in the footer, and then open the drop-down list to choose a date (or date and time) format. With this option, the date you give your presentation always appears on slides.

- *Fixed:* Select this option button and enter a date in the text box. For example, enter the date you created the presentation. With this option, the date remains fixed no matter when or where you give the presentation.

- ✔ **Slide Number:** Select this check box to make slide numbers appear in the lower-left corner of all slides.

- ✔ **Footer:** Select this check box, and in the text box, enter the words that you want to appear in the bottom, middle of all the slides.

- ✔ **Don't Show on Title Slide:** Select this check box if you prefer that the footer not appear on the first slide in your presentation.

Creating a nonstandard footer

As "Some background on footers and headers" explains, earlier in this chapter, you have to look elsewhere than the Header and Footer dialog box if you want to create something besides the standard footer. Suppose you want to move the slide number from the lower-left corner of slides to another position? Or you want to fool with the fonts in headers and footers?

Follow these steps to create a nonstandard footer:

1. **Create a standard footer if you want your nonstandard footer to include today's date and/or a slide number.**

   If you want to move the slide number into the upper-right corner of slides, for example, create a standard footer first (see the preceding topic in this chapter). Later, you can move the slide number text frame into the upper-right corner of slides.

2. **Choose View ⇨ Master ⇨ Slide Master.**

   You switch to Slide Master view.

3. **Select the Slide Master, the topmost slide in the Slides pane.**

4. **Adjust and format the footer text boxes to taste (as they say in cookbooks).**

   For example, move the slide number text frame into the upper-right corner to put slide numbers there. Or change the font in the footer text boxes. Or place a company logo on the Slide Master to make the logo appear on all your slides.

5. **Click the Close button to leave Slide Master view.**

   You can always return to Slide Master view and adjust your footer.

Removing a footer from a single slide

On a crowded slide, the date, footer text, page number, and other items in the footer can get in the way or be a distraction. Fortunately, removing one or all of the footer text frames from a slide is easy:

1. **Switch to Normal view and display the slide with the footer that needs removing.**

2. **Choose Insert ⇨ Header and Footer.**

   The Header and Footer dialog box appears (refer to Figure 15-8).

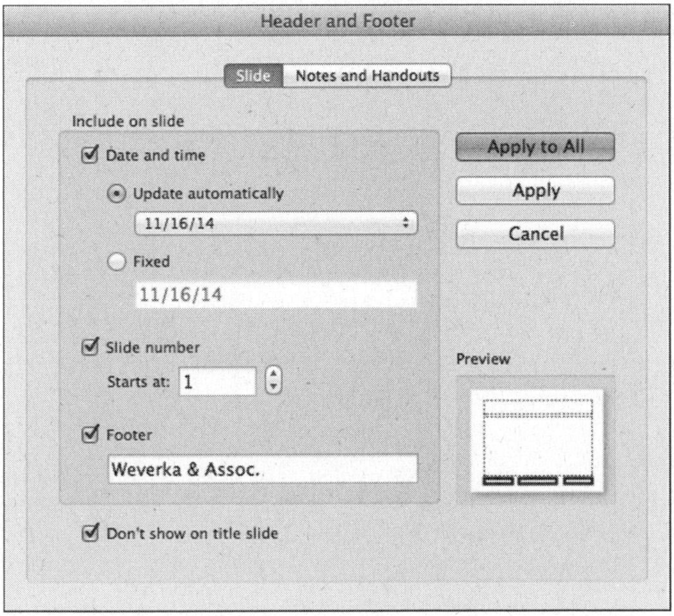

Figure 15-8:
Entering a
standard
footer.

3. **Deselect any appropriate check box — Date and Time, Slide Number, and Footer — to remove the footer or to tell PowerPoint which parts of the footer you want to remove.**

4. **Click the Apply button.**

   Be careful not to click the Apply to All button. Clicking this button removes footers throughout your slide presentation.

Chapter 16

Delivering a Presentation

At last, the big day has arrived. It's time to give the presentation. "Break a leg," as actors say before they go on stage. This chapter explains how to rehearse your presentation to find out how long it is and how to actually show your presentation. You discover some techniques to make your presentation livelier, including how to draw on slides with a pen or highlighter and how to blank out the screen to get the audience's full attention. The chapter describes handling the speaker notes and print handouts for your audience. In case you can't be there in person to deliver your presentation, this chapter shows you how to create a user-run presentation, a self-running presentation, and a video of a presentation.

All about Notes

Notes are strictly for the speaker. The unwashed masses can't see them. Don't hesitate to write notes to yourself when you put together your presentation. The notes will come in handy when you're rehearsing and giving your presentation. They give you ideas for what to say and help you communicate better. Here are instructions for entering, editing, and printing notes:

✔ **Entering a note:** To enter a note, start in Normal view, click in the Notes pane, and start typing. Treat the Notes pane like a page in a word processor. For example, press Return to start a new paragraph and press the Tab key to indent text. You can drag the border above the Notes pane up or down to make the pane larger or smaller.

✔ **Editing notes in Notes Page view:** After you've jotted down a bunch of notes, switch to Notes Page view and edit them. To switch to Notes Page view, choose View⇨Notes Page. Notes appear in a text frame below a picture of the slide to which they refer, as shown in Figure 16-1. You may have to zoom in to read them.

✔ **Printing your notes:** Choose File⇨Print (or press Command+P). You see the Print dialog box. On the Print What drop-down list, choose Notes. Then click the Print button.

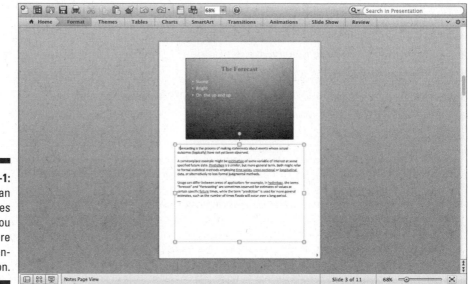

Figure 16-1:
You can write notes as you prepare a presentation.

Rehearsing and Timing Your Presentation

Slide presentations and theatrical presentations have this in common: They are as good as the number of times you rehearse them. Be sure to rehearse your presentation many times over. The more you rehearse, the more comfortable you are giving a presentation. Follow these steps to rehearse a presentation, record its length, and record how long each slide is displayed:

1. **Select the first slide in your presentation.**

2. **Go to the Slide Show tab.**

3. **Click the Rehearse button.**

   The Rehearse window opens, as shown in Figure 16-2.

Figure 16-2:
Timing a
rehearsal
in the
Rehearse
window.

4. Give your presentation one slide at a time and click the Next button to go from slide to slide.

The Next button is the right-pointing arrow below the slide image.

When each slide appears, imagine that you're presenting it to an audience. Say what you intend to say during the real presentation. If you anticipate audience members asking questions, allot time for questions.

The Rehearse window tells you how long each slide has been displayed and how long your presentation is so far. You can do the following tasks using the Rehearse toolbar:

- *Go to the next slide:* Click the Next button.

- *Pause recording:* Click the Pause button to temporarily stop the recording so that you can feed the dog or take a phone call. Click the Resume button to resume recording. These buttons are located next to the clock reading that tells you how long the current slide has been onscreen.

- *Repeat a slide:* Click the Repeat button if you get befuddled and want to start over with a slide. The slide timing returns to 0:00:00. The Repeat button is located below the Pause button. After you click Pause, click the Resume button to restart the rehearsal.

5. **Note how long your presentation is in the dialog box that tells you your presentation is complete and asks whether you want to save the slide timings.**

   Is your presentation too long or too short? I hope, like baby bear's porridge, your presentation is "just right." But if it's too long or short, you have some work to do. You have to figure out how to shorten or lengthen it.

6. **Click Yes if you want to see how long each slide stayed onscreen during the rehearsal.**

   By clicking Yes, you can go to Slide Sorter view and see how long each slide remained onscreen.

If you save the slide timings, PowerPoint assumes that, during a presentation, you want to advance to the next slide manually or after the recorded time, whichever comes first. For example, suppose the first slide in your presentation remained onscreen for a minute during the rehearsal. During your presentation, the first slide will remain onscreen for a minute and automatically yield to the second slide unless you click to advance to the second slide before the minute has elapsed. If you recorded slide timings strictly to find out how long your presentation is, you need to tell PowerPoint not to advance automatically to the next slide during a presentation after the recorded time period elapses. On the Slide Show tab, deselect the Use Timings check box.

Showing Your Presentation

Compared to the preliminary work, giving a presentation can seem kind of anticlimactic. All you have to do is go from slide to slide and woo your audience with your smooth-as-silk voice and powerful oratory skills. Well, at least the move-from-slide-to-slide part is pretty easy. These pages explain how to start and end a presentation, all the different ways to advance or retreat from slide to slide, and how to jump to different slides.

Starting and ending a presentation

Here are the different ways to start a presentation from the beginning:

- ✔ On the Slide Show tab, click the From Start button.
- ✔ Go to the first slide and then click the Slide Show view button.

You can start a presentation in the middle by selecting a slide in the middle and using one of these techniques:

 ✔ Click the Slide Show view button.

 ✔ Click the Play button on the Home tab.

 ✔ Click the From Current Slide button on the Slide Show tab.

Here are the different ways to end a presentation prematurely:

 ✔ Press Esc or – (the hyphen key).

 ✔ Click the Slide button and choose End Show on the pop-up menu. The Slide button is located in the lower-left corner of the screen.

 ✔ Right-click and choose End Show in the shortcut menu.

Going from slide to slide

In a nutshell, PowerPoint offers four ways to move from slide to slide in a presentation. Table 16-1 describes techniques for navigating a presentation using the four different ways:

 ✔ **Use the slide control buttons:** Click a slide control button — Previous, Next — in the lower-left corner of the screen, as shown in Figure 16-3. If you don't see the slide control buttons, jiggle the mouse.

 ✔ **Click the Slide button:** Click this button and make a choice on the pop-up menu (see Figure 16-3).

 ✔ **Right-click onscreen:** Right-click and choose a navigation option on the shortcut menu.

 ✔ **Press a keyboard shortcut:** Press one of the numerous keyboard shortcuts that PowerPoint offers for going from slide to slide (see Table 16-1).

Going forward (or backward) from slide to slide

To go forward from one slide to the following slide in a presentation, click onscreen. After you click, the next slide appears. If all goes well, clicking is the only technique you need to know when giving a presentation to go from slide to slide, but Table 16-1 lists other ways to go to the next slide in a presentation as well as techniques for going backward to the previous slide.

Figure 16-3: Besides using keyboard shortcuts, you can move from slide to slide by clicking onscreen.

Slide button

Slide controls

Table 16-1	Techniques for Getting from Slide to Slide		
To Go Here	**Button**	**Right-Click and Choose . . .**	**Keyboard Shortcut**
Next slide*	Next	Next	Return, spacebar, N, ↓, or →
Previous slide	Previous	Previous	Delete, P, ↑, or ←
Specific slide	Slide	Go to Slide	*Slide number*+Return; Ctrl+S
Last viewed slide	Slide	Last Viewed	

If animations are on a slide, commands for going to the next slide instead make animations play in sequence. To bypass animations and go to the next slide, use a command for going forward across several slides. (See "Jumping forward or backward to a specific slide.")

Jumping forward or backward to a specific slide

If you find it necessary to jump forward or backward across several slides in your presentation to get to the slide you want to show, use these techniques:

✔ Either click the Slide button or right-click, choose Go to Slide, and then choose a slide in your presentation on the submenu (refer to Figure 16-3).

✔ Press the slide number you want on your keyboard (if you can remember the slide's number) and then press the Return key. For example, to show the third slide in your presentation, press 3 and then press Return.

If you need to return to where you started after you make the jump to a different slide, you can do so by right-clicking and choosing Last Viewed on the shortcut menu. You can also click the Slide button and choose Last Viewed (refer to Figure 16-3). The Last Viewed command takes you to the last slide you showed, wherever it is in your presentation.

Tricks for Making Presentations a Little Livelier

To make presentations a little livelier, whip out a pen and draw on a slide or blank the screen. Draw to underline words or draw check marks as you hit the key points, as shown in Figure 16-4. Drawing on slides is an excellent way to add a little something to a presentation. Blank the screen when you want the audience's undivided attention.

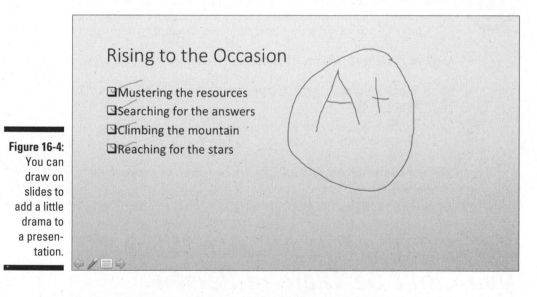

Figure 16-4: You can draw on slides to add a little drama to a presentation.

Wielding a pen or highlighter in a presentation

Follow these instructions so that you can draw on a slide during a slide presentation:

✓ **Selecting a pen:** PowerPoint offers the Pen for writing on slides. To select the Pen, click the Pen button (in the lower-left corner of the screen) and choose Pen (or press Command+P). You can also right-click, choose Pointer Options, and choose Pen.

✔ **Choosing a color for drawing:** After you select the Pen, click the Pen button, choose Pen Color, and select a color on the submenu.

Press Esc when you're finished using the pen. (Just be careful not to press Esc twice because the second press tells PowerPoint to end the presentation.)

Pen marks are erased when you go to the next slide. To erase them immediately, click the Slide button and choose Screen⇨Erase Pen (or right-click and choose Screen⇨Erase Pen).

Blanking the screen

Here's a technique for adding a little drama to a presentation: When you want the audience to focus on you, not the PowerPoint screen, blank the screen. Make an all-black or all-white screen appear where a PowerPoint slide used to be. Every head in the audience will turn your way and listen keenly to what you have to say next. I sure hope you have something important to say.

Follow these instructions to blank out the screen during a presentation:

✔ **Black screen:** Press B, the period key, or right-click and choose Screen⇨Black Screen.

✔ **White screen:** Press W, the comma key, or right-click and choose Screen⇨White Screen.

To see a PowerPoint slide again, click onscreen or press any key on the keyboard.

Delivering a Presentation When You Can't Be There in Person

PowerPoint offers numerous ways to deliver a presentation even when you're not there to do it. You can deliver your presentation in the form of a *handout,* a printed version of the presentation with thumbnail slides; create a self-running presentation; or create a user-run presentation with action buttons that others can click to get from slide to slide. The rest of this chapter explains how to do all that as well as make a video of your presentation so that people who don't have PowerPoint can view it.

Providing handouts for your audience

Handouts are thumbnail versions of slides that you print and distribute to the audience. Figure 16-4 shows examples of handouts. Handouts come in one, two, three, four, six, or nine slides per page. If you select three slides per page, the handout includes lines that your audience can take notes on (see Figure 16-5); the other sizes don't offer these lines.

Figure 16-5:
Examples
of handouts
(from left
to right) at
one, three,
six, and nine
slides per
page.

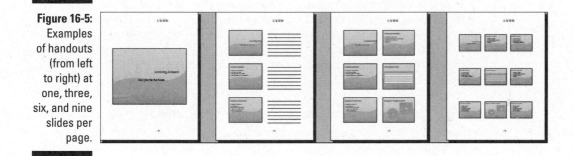

To tell PowerPoint how to construct handouts, choose View⇨Master⇨ Handout Master. In Handout Master view, on the Handout Master tab, you can do a number of things to make your handouts more useful and attractive. As you make your choices, keep your eye on the sample handout page; it shows what your choices mean in real terms.

- ✓ **Handout Orientation:** Select Portrait or Landscape. In landscape mode, the page is turned on its side and is longer than it is tall.

- ✓ **Slides Per Page:** Choose how many slides appear on each page. Figure 16-5 shows what some of the choices are.

- ✓ **Header:** Enter a header in the text frame to make a header appear in the upper-left corner of all handout pages. Candidates for headers include your name, your company name, and the location of a conference or seminar. The point is to help your audience identify the handout.

- ✓ **Footer:** Enter a footer in the text frame in the lower-left corner of handout pages. Candidates for footers are the same as candidates for headers.

- ✓ **Date:** The date you print the handout appears on handout pages automatically. Delete the date in the date text frame if you don't want the date to appear.

- ✓ **Page Number:** Page numbers appear by default on handout pages. Delete the page number text frame if you don't want them to appear.

To print handouts, choose File➪Print (or press Command+P). You see the Print dialog box. Open the Print What drop-down list and choose how many handouts to print on each page. Then click the Print button.

Creating a self-running, kiosk-style presentation

A self-running, kiosk-style presentation is one that plays on its own. You can make it play from a kiosk or simply send it to co-workers so that they can play it. In a self-running presentation, slides appear onscreen one after the other, and neither you nor anyone else has to advance the presentation from slide to slide. When the presentation finishes, it starts all over again from Slide 1.

Telling PowerPoint how long to keep slides onscreen

PowerPoint offers two ways to indicate how long you want each slide to stay onscreen:

- **Entering the time periods yourself:** Switch to Slide Sorter view and go to the Transitions tab. Then deselect the On Mouse Click check box and select the After check box, as shown in Figure 16-6. Next, tell PowerPoint to keep all slides onscreen the same amount of time or choose a different time period for each slide:

    - *All slides for the same amount of time:* Enter a time period in the After text box and click the All Slides button.

    - *Each slide for a different amount of time:* One by one, select each slide and enter a time period in the After text box.

- **Rehearsing the presentation:** Rehearse the presentation and save the timings. (See "Rehearsing and Timing Your Presentation," earlier in this chapter.) Be sure to save the slide timings after you're finished rehearsing. In Slide Sorter view, you can see how long each slide will stay onscreen (refer to Figure 16-6).

Telling PowerPoint that your presentation is self-running

Before you can "self-run" a presentation, you have to tell PowerPoint that you want it to do that. Self-running presentations don't have the control buttons in the lower-left corner. You can't click the screen or press a key to move forward or backward to the next or previous slide. The only control you have over a self-running presentation is to press the Esc key (pressing Esc ends the presentation).

Enter a time period

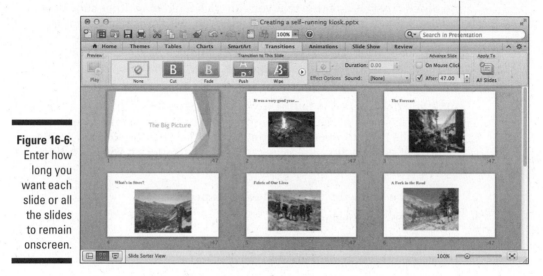

Figure 16-6:
Enter how
long you
want each
slide or all
the slides
to remain
onscreen.

Follow these steps to make yours a kiosk-style, self-running presentation:

1. **Go to the Slide Show tab.**

2. **Click the Set Up Show button.**

   You see the Set Up Show dialog box.

3. **Under Show Type, choose the Browsed at a Kiosk (Full Screen) option.**

   When you select this option, PowerPoint automatically selects the Loop
   Continuously Until 'Esc' check box.

4. **Make sure that the Using Timings, If Present option button is selected.**

5. **Click OK.**

   That's all there is to it.

Creating a user-run presentation

A *user-run,* or *interactive,* presentation is one that the viewer gets to control. The viewer decides which slide appears next and how long each slide remains onscreen. User-run presentations are similar to websites. Users can browse from slide to slide at their own speed. They can pick and choose what they want to investigate. They can backtrack and view slides that they saw previously or return to the first slide and start anew.

Another way to help users get from slide to slide is to create action buttons. An *action button* is a button that you can click to go to another slide in your presentation or the previous slide you viewed, whatever that slide was. PowerPoint provides 12 action buttons on the Shapes gallery. Figure 16-7 shows some action buttons and the dialog box you use to create them.

Drawing an action button

After you draw an action button from the Shapes gallery, the Action Settings dialog box, shown in Figure 16-7, appears so that you can tell PowerPoint which slide to go to when the button is clicked. Select the slide (or master slide) that needs action and follow these steps to adorn it with an action button:

1. **On the Home tab, click the Insert Shapes button.**

   A drop-down list appears.

2. **Select Action Buttons.**

   A submenu of action buttons appears.

3. **Click an action button to select it.**

   Choose the button that best illustrates which slide will appear when the button is clicked.

4. **Draw the button on the slide.**

   To do so, drag the pointer in a diagonal fashion. (As far as drawing them is concerned, action buttons work the same as all other shapes and other objects.) The Action Settings dialog box (refer to Figure 16-7) appears after you finish drawing your button.

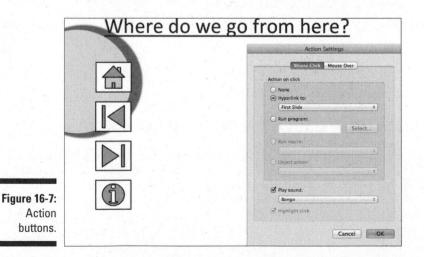

Figure 16-7:
Action
buttons.

5. **Go to the Mouse Over tab if you want users to activate the button by moving the mouse pointer over it, not clicking it.**

6. **Select the Hyperlink To option button.**

7. **On the Hyperlink To drop-down list, choose an action for the button.**

   For example, choose the next slide, the previous slide, the first or last slide in a presentation, the last slide you viewed, or a specific slide.

   To make clicking the action button take users to a specific slide, choose Slide on the list. You see the Hyperlink to Slide dialog box, which lists each slide in your presentation. Select a slide and click OK.

8. **To play a sound when your action button is activated, select the Play Sound check box and select a sound on the drop-down list.**

   "Mouse-over" hyperlinks, which are activated without the user's having to click them, work better with sound accompaniment because they help users understand when they've activated an action button.

9. **Click OK in the Actions Settings dialog box.**

   To test your button, you can right-click it and choose Hyperlink➪Open Hyperlink.

To change a button's action, select it and then right-click it and choose Hyperlink➪Edit Hyperlink. In the Action Settings dialog box, choose a new action and click OK.

Making yours a user-run presentation

Follow these steps to declare yours a user-run presentation:

1. **Go to the Slide Show tab.**

2. **Click the Set Up Show button.**

   You see the Set Up Show dialog box.

3. **Select the Browsed by an Individual (Window) option button.**

4. **Click OK.**

   Your presentation is no longer quite yours. It also belongs to all the people who view it in your absence.

Presenting a presentation online

Presenting online means to play a presentation on your computer for others to watch it over the Internet. As you go from slide to slide, audience members see the slides on their web browsers. Presenting online is an excellent way to show a presentation to others during a conference call or to others who don't have PowerPoint.

Presenting online is made possible by the PowerPoint Broadcast Service, a free service for everyone who has Office software and an Office 365 account. (What an Office 365 account is and how to obtain one are explained in detail in Chapter 1). The first time you attempt to show a presentation online, you are asked to provide your Office 365 username and password.

The PowerPoint Broadcast Service creates a temporary web address for you to show your presentation. Before showing it, you send audience members a link to this web address. Audience members, in turn, click the link to open and watch your presentation in their web browsers.

Before presenting online, make sure you know the email addresses of the people who will view your presentation. Make sure as well that they are available to view it. Online presentations are shown in real time. After you close a presentation, its link is broken and the audience can no longer watch it in their web browsers.

Follow these steps to show a presentation online:

1. **On the Slide Show tab, click the Broadcast the Slide Show button.**

   The Broadcast Slide Show dialog box appears. You can also open this dialog box by choosing File⇨Share⇨Broadcast Slide Show.

2. **Click the Connect button.**

3. **If you're not signed in to Office 365, provide your username and password in the Windows Live Sign In dialog box.**

   The PowerPoint Broadcast Service generates a URL link for you to send to the people who will view your presentation, as shown in Figure 16-8.

4. **Send the link to your audience.**

   You can send the link with Outlook or another email software.

   - *Copy and send the link by email:* Click Copy Link to copy the link to the Clipboard. Then, in your email software, paste the link into invitations you send to audience members.

   - *Send the link with Mail:* Click the Send in Email link. A Mail message window appears. Address and send the message.

5. **Make sure that audience members have received the email invitation and are ready to watch your presentation.**

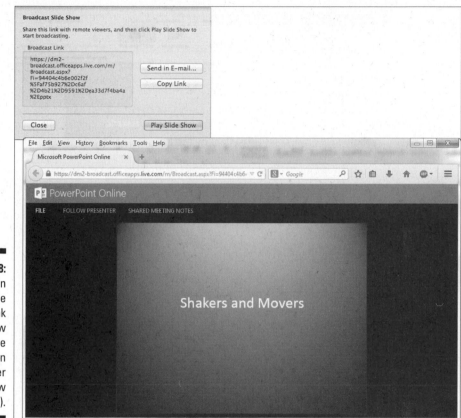

Figure 16-8:
Others can
click the
URL link
(top) to view
an online
presentation
in a browser
window
(bottom).

6. **Click the Play the Slide Show button in the Broadcast Slide Show dialog box.**

   Audience members see the presentation in their browsers, as shown in Figure 16-8.

7. **Give the presentation.**

   Use the same techniques to advance or retreat from slide to slide as you use in any presentation.

   When the presentation ends, you land on the Home (Broadcast) tab.

8. **On the Home (Broadcast) tab, click the End button; then click End Broadcast button in the confirmation dialog box.**

   Your audience sees this notice: "The presentation has ended."

Creating a presentation video

Yet another way to distribute a video is to record it in a QuickTime (MOV) file and distribute the file by email or post it on the Internet. PowerPoint offers a command for creating a QuickTime version of a presentation. Every aspect of a PowerPoint presentation, including transitions, animations, sound, video itself, and voice narrations, is recorded in the presentation video. Figure 16-9 shows a QuickTime version of a PowerPoint presentation being played in QuickTime Player.

To determine how long slides remain onscreen in the video, go to the Transitions tab and, in the Advance Slide area, enter a seconds measurement in the After text box. Earlier in this chapter, "Rehearsing and Timing Your Presentation" explains in detail how to tell PowerPoint how long to keep slides onscreen.

Follow these steps to create a QuickTime version of a PowerPoint presentation:

1. **Choose File⇨Save As Movie.**

   The Save As dialog box opens.

2. **Enter a name for the movie and choose which folder to store it in.**

   If you want, you can click the Movie Options button and choose options in the Movie Options dialog box. You'll find various options there for optimizing and presenting your presentation in movie form.

3. **Click the Save button.**

   Creating a video can take several minutes, depending on how large your PowerPoint presentation is and how many fancy gizmos, such as sound and animation, it contains.

Figure 16-9:
Viewing a QuickTime version of a PowerPoint presentation in QuickTime Player.

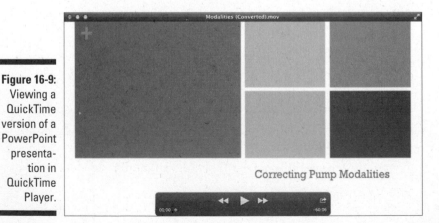

Part V
Sharing and Collaborating with Office 365

Go to www.dummies.com/extras/ipadatwork to see how to upload and store files on OneDrive.

In this part . . .

- ✔ Use OneDrive as a storage space for keeping archive files and as a launching pad for sharing files with others.

- ✔ Send invitations to others so that they can share and co-edit files you keep on OneDrive, and manage how files are shared.

Chapter 17

Managing Files and Folders on OneDrive

*T*his chapter introduces you to OneDrive, Microsoft's online facility for storing files, sharing files, and co-editing files with other people. It describes how to sign in and out of OneDrive so that you can get to your OneDrive folders. You also discover how to navigate on OneDrive, manage folders, and upload and download files from your desktop or laptop computer to OneDrive. Finally, this chapter shows how to make sure that files on your iPad or Mac are in sync with their counterparts on OneDrive.

To use OneDrive, you must be an Office 365 subscriber. Chapter 1 explains what Office 365 is and how to subscribe to it.

Because OneDrive is a Microsoft invention and the iPad was invented by Apple, sometimes the two don't work hand in hand. Nevertheless, I endeavor in this chapter to show you how iPad users and users of Office 2011 for Mac can get the most out of OneDrive, even if it means doing somersaults now and then.

Signing In to OneDrive

OneDrive is a component of Office 365, Microsoft's online suite of services. Before you can store, share, or co-edit files on OneDrive, you have to sign in to OneDrive. Read on to find out how to sign in from Office for the iPad and sign in from a web browser.

The OneDrive app

The App Store offers an application called OneDrive for managing files at OneDrive. You can get versions of the OneDrive app for the iPad, for Windows computers, and for Macintosh computers.

The OneDrive app that works with the iPad has a serious failing: You can't use it to upload files to OneDrive. However, one of the primary reasons for using Office for the iPad is to be able to take your work with you. You can upload Office files from your laptop or desktop computer to OneDrive and be able to work on these files on the iPad.

Because the OneDrive app made for the iPad doesn't allow uploading, I don't cover it in this book, but you are welcome to try the app. You can get it for free at the App Store. (Chapter 2 explains how to download and install apps from the App Store.)

This book *does* cover the version of the OneDrive app made for Mac computers because you need that app to sync files between the Mac and OneDrive. Later in this chapter, "Syncing Files between OneDrive and Your Machine" takes up the subject of syncing files between a Mac computer and file storage folders at OneDrive.

Signing in from Office for the iPad

Follow these instructions to sign in to OneDrive from an Office for the iPad application:

1. **Tap the Office button.**

   This button is located in the upper-left corner of the screen. The Office window appears, as shown at the top of Figure 17-1.

2. **Tap Sign In.**

   The Sign In window opens.

3. **Enter the email address you used to subscribe to Office 365 and tap Next.**

4. **Enter your password.**

5. **Tap Sign In.**

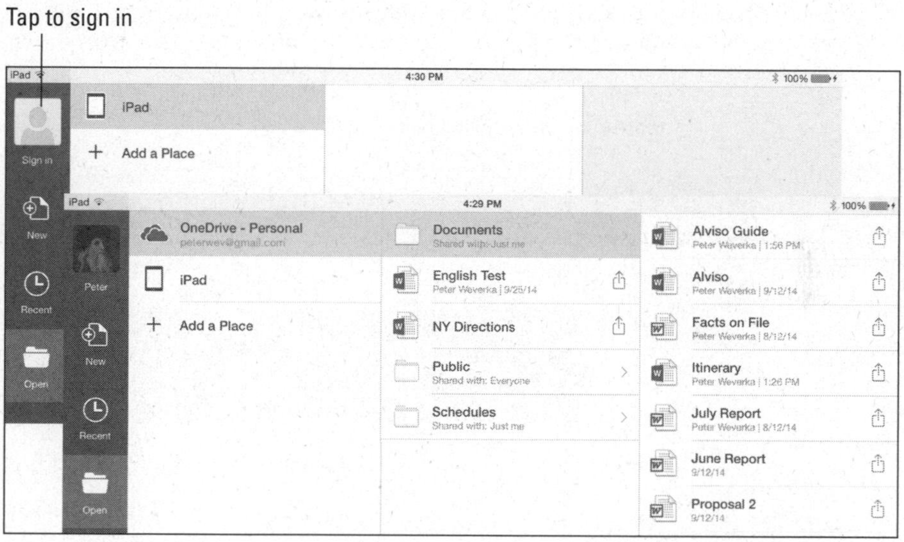

Tap to sign in

Figure 17-1:
When
you are
signed in to
OneDrive,
your name
appears in
the Office
window.

You can tell when you're signed in to Office 365 because your name and the name *OneDrive* appear in the upper-left corner of the Office window, as shown in Figure 17-1.

To sign out of Office 365, tap the Office button and tap your name in the Office window. You see the Account menu. On this menu, tap your log-in name and choose Sign Out on the submenu that appears.

Signing in from a web browser

Sign in to OneDrive from a web browser to move files between folders, create and delete folders, and create and delete files. Open a web browser and follow these steps to sign in to Office 365:

1. **Go to this web address: onedrive.live.com**

2. **Tap the Sign In button.**

   The Sign In window opens.

3. **Enter the email address of your Office 365 account and tap Next.**

   The OneDrive window opens.

4. **Enter your password and tap Sign In.**

   The OneDrive window opens in your browser, as shown in Figure 17-2.

To sign out of Office 365 in a web browser, tap your username in the upper-right corner of the screen and choose Sign Out on the drop-down menu.

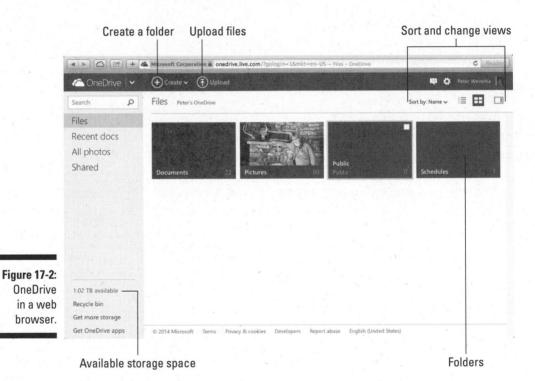

Figure 17-2: OneDrive in a web browser.

Create a folder   Upload files

Sort and change views

Available storage space

Folders

Exploring the OneDrive Window

OneDrive can store up to 15GB of files. To start with, OneDrive gives you two folders — Documents and Pictures — for storing files, and you can create additional folders as well. The lower-left corner of the browser window tells you how much storage space you have for files.

You can tell how many files are stored in each folder because folders list how many files they hold. To open a folder and view its contents, click a folder name.

Glance back at Figure 17-2 and take note of these tools in the OneDrive window for managing files:

✔ **Create folders:** Click the Create button to create a folder for storing files. See "Creating a folder," later in this chapter, for details.

✔ **Upload files:** Click the Upload button to upload files from your desktop or laptop computer to OneDrive. See "Uploading Files to a Folder on OneDrive," later in this chapter.

✔ **Arranging folders and files in the window:** Use the tools in the upper-right corner of the screen to arrange and locate folders and files. See "Viewing and locating folders in the OneDrive window," later in this chapter.

To return to the main OneDrive window, click OneDrive in the upper-left corner, or click Files, the first link on the left side of the screen.

Managing Your OneDrive Folders

All folders you create for storing files are kept on OneDrive. OneDrive gives you two folders — Documents and Pictures — for storing files, and you can create folders of your own, as well as subfolders. These pages explain how to create folders, get from folder to folder on OneDrive, and do folder-management tasks such as renaming, deleting, and moving folders.

Creating a folder

Create folders to store and organize your files on OneDrive. Sign in to OneDrive with your web browser and follow these steps to create a folder:

1. **If you want to create a subfolder (a folder inside another folder), open the folder that your new folder will go into.**

   To open a folder, tap or click its name.

2. **Tap or click the Create button and choose Folder on the drop-down list.**

   A new folder appears.

3. **Enter a name for the folder.**

   Later in this chapter, "Uploading Files to a Folder on OneDrive" explains how to upload files from your computer to a folder on OneDrive.

4. **Tap or click Create.**

   Later in this chapter, "Uploading Files to a Folder on OneDrive" explains how to upload files from your computer to a folder on OneDrive.

Viewing and locating folders in the OneDrive window

Use the OneDrive window to store and locate folders, subfolders, and files on OneDrive. The OneDrive window offers these tools for managing folders:

- **Searching:** Enter a search term in the Search box to search for a folder or file. The Search box is located in the upper-left corner of the window.

- **Sorting:** Tap or click the Sort By button and choose an option to rearrange folders and files in the OneDrive window. Sorting is helpful for finding a folder or file in a long list.

- **Viewing:** Tap or click the Details View or Thumbnails View button to see your folders and files in Details view or Thumbnails view, as shown in Figure 17-3:

  - *Details view* presents detailed information about folders and files — when they were last modified, whether they are shared, and file sizes.

  - *Thumbnails view* presents folders and files in thumbnail form.

- **Displaying the Details pane:** Select a folder or file and tap or click the Show or Hide Details Pane button to open the Details pane and get detailed information (see Figure 17-3). You can also display the Details pane by right-clicking a folder or file and choosing Properties.

Tap or click the check box on a folder or file to select it. Before you can rename, delete, or move a file, you have to select it.

Going from folder to folder on OneDrive

After you accumulate a few folders on OneDrive, getting to the folder you want to open can be an arduous, interminable journey. To help you on your way, OneDrive offers different techniques for going to a folder:

- **The drill-down method:** Starting in the OneDrive window, tap or click a top-level folder to display its subfolders. If necessary, keep drilling down this way until you reach the folder you want to open.

- **The OneDrive Navigation bar method:** The *OneDrive Navigation bar* — located beside the folder name — lists the path to the folder that is currently open. To backtrack, tap or click the name of a folder on the path, as shown in Figure 17-4.

- **The browser button method:** Tap or click the Back or Forward button in your browser to open a folder you previously opened.

Select a folder or file

Show or hide the Details pane

Change views

Figure 17-3:
The OneDrive window in Details view (top), Thumbnails view (middle), and Thumbnails view with the Details pane showing (bottom).

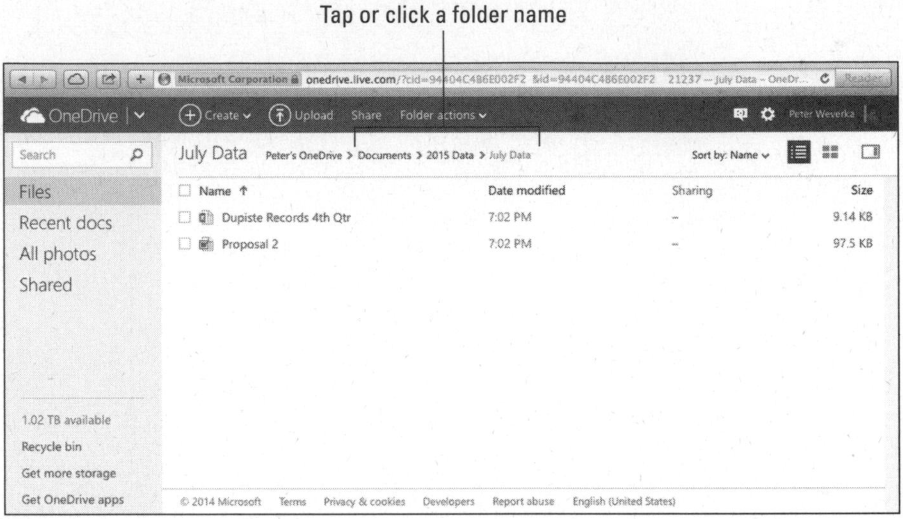

Tap or click a folder name

Figure 17-4:
Tap or click
a folder
name on the
Navigation
bar to open
a folder.

To return to the top-level OneDrive window, tap or click the OneDrive button, or tap or click Files in the OneDrive Navigation pane.

By bookmarking a folder in your browser, you can go straight to a folder without having to navigate to it on OneDrive. After you choose the bookmark (and enter your ID and password if you haven't signed in yet), the folder opens.

Deleting, moving, and renaming folders

To delete, move, or rename a folder, start by selecting it in the OneDrive window (select its check box). Then use these techniques:

- **Moving a folder:** Tap or click the Manage button and choose Move To on the drop-down list. A dialog box opens with a list of your folders on OneDrive. Select a folder in the list and tap or click the Move button. You can also right-click a folder and choose Move To.

- **Deleting a folder:** Tap or click the Manage button and choose Delete on the drop-down list. You can also right-click and choose Delete.

- **Renaming a folder:** Tap or click the Manage button and choose Rename on the drop-down list. Then enter a name. You can also right-click and choose Rename.

The Office Online applications

As an Office 365 subscriber, you are entitled to use the Office Online applications — Word, Excel, PowerPoint, and OneNote. These applications are available from the Office 365 toolbar. Click the Navigation button (the button to the left of the OneDrive button) to open this toolbar. Then choose Word Online, Excel Online, PowerPoint Online, or OneNote Online to test-drive an Office Online application.

Anyone can use these applications. You don't have to pay a fee of any kind or install Office.

All you need is an Internet connection and an Office 365 subscription. Moreover, users of Office Online apps can collaborate online with one another to create Word documents, Excel worksheets, PowerPoint presentations, and OneNote notebooks.

The Office Online applications, like Office for the iPad apps, are lightweight versions of Office software. You store the files you create with Office Online applications on OneDrive.

Uploading Files to a Folder on OneDrive

Upload a file from your computer to OneDrive so that you can share the file with others or be able to access it on your iPad or desktop computer. Sign in to OneDrive with your web browser and follow these steps to upload files from your computer to a folder you keep on OneDrive:

1. **On OneDrive, open the folder where you want to store the files.**
2. **Tap or click the Upload button.**

   A dialog box opens.
3. **Select the files.**
4. **Tap or click the Choose (or Open) button.**

   The file or files are uploaded to the folder you selected on OneDrive.

Another way to upload files is to drag them into the OneDrive window.

You can also upload an Excel, Word, or PowerPoint file by saving it to a OneDrive folder. See "Saving a File to OneDrive," the next topic in this chapter.

Saving a File to OneDrive

Sharing is caring, and you can save a Word, Excel, or PowerPoint file on your iPad or desktop computer directly to a OneDrive folder. After the file lands on OneDrive, others who have access to the folder on OneDrive can open the file. They can open it in an Office for the iPad application, Office Web App, or an Office 2010 program (if Office 2010 is installed on their computers).

Saving an Office for the iPad file to OneDrive

Sign in to OneDrive if necessary and follow these steps to save an Office for the iPad file that you store on the iPad to a OneDrive folder:

1. **In an Office for the iPad application, tap the Office button.**

2. **Locate the file you want to move.**

   To do so, tap Recent or Open and navigate in the Office window until you see the name of the file you want to move.

3. **Tap the Share icon next to the file's name.**

   A drop-down menu appears.

4. **Choose Move to Cloud.**

   The Choose Name and Location window appears.

5. **Choose a location on OneDrive to store your file.**

   Select a folder, for example.

6. **Tap Save.**

Saving a file to OneDrive in Office 2011 for the Mac

When saving a file to OneDrive in Office 2011 for the Mac, keep in mind that Office 365 used to be called Windows Live. Then follow these steps to save a file to OneDrive in an Office 2011 for the Mac program:

1. **In an Office 2011 program, choose File⇨Share⇨Save to OneDrive.**

   You see the Save As dialog box, as shown in Figure 17-5. It shows folders you keep on OneDrive.

If you aren't signed in to Office 365, you see the Windows Live Sign In dialog box. Enter your Office 365 user ID and password in this dialog box, and click Sign In.

2. **Select a folder in which to save the file.**

   A new folder appears.

3. **Click the Save button.**

   Earlier in this chapter, "Uploading Files to a Folder on OneDrive" explains how to upload files from your computer to a folder on OneDrive.

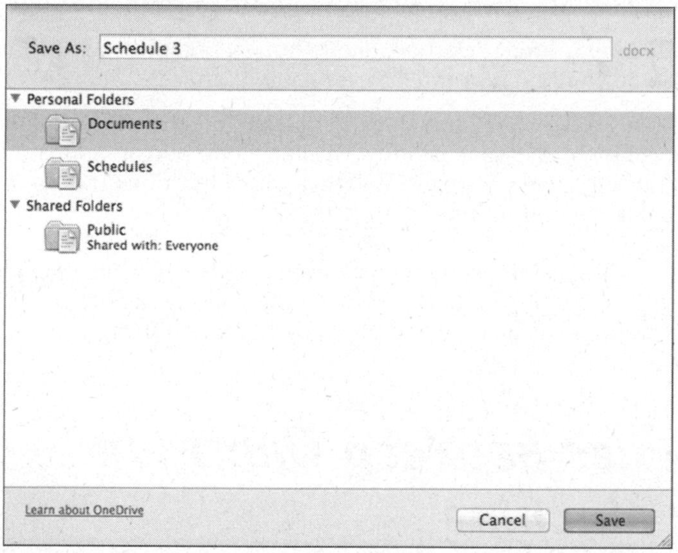

Figure 17-5:
On the Mac,
saving a file
to OneDrive.

Downloading Files from OneDrive to Your Computer

Follow these instructions to download files to a Macintosh computer:

- **Downloading a file:** Select the file you want to download and click the Download button. The file is downloaded. Look for it in the Downloads folder (or another folder that you designated for downloading files).

- **Downloading several files or all the files in a folder:** Select several files or, to download all the files in a folder, select the folder. Then click the Download button. Look for the files in the Downloads folder (or another folder you selected for holding downloaded files).

Managing Your Files on OneDrive

OneDrive is first and foremost a means of organizing and managing files. In your browser, select a file on OneDrive and use these techniques to move, copy, rename, or delete it:

- **Moving a file:** Click the Manage button and choose Move To on the drop-down list. You see a window that lists your OneDrive folders. Select a folder name and click the Move button.

- **Copying a file:** Click the Manage button and choose Copy To on the drop-down list. Then select a folder name and click the Copy button.

- **Renaming a file:** Click the Manage button and choose Rename on the drop-down list. Then enter a new name in the text box.

- **Deleting a file:** Click the Manage button and choose Delete on the drop-down list. (A message window with an Undo button appears for several seconds in case you regret deleting your files. Click the Undo button if you change your mind about deleting.)

To restore a file or folder that you deleted accidently, click Recycle Bin on the OneDrive Navigation bar. In the Recycle Bin window, select the file or folder that you want to resuscitate and click the Restore button.

Syncing Files between OneDrive and Your Machine

In computer terminology, *syncing* (the term comes from *synchronizing*) means to see to it that the data in two different places is the same. For example, you would sync data on a cellphone and a computer to make sure that the same telephone numbers are stored on both devices. Syncing is important for working on files on OneDrive because, unless your OneDrive files and the files on your iPad or Mac are in sync, you can end up with many different versions of the same file and not be sure which version is up-to-date.

These pages explore how to sync files between the iPad and OneDrive, and how to sync files between Office 2011 for the Mac and OneDrive.

Syncing files between the iPad and OneDrive

You will be glad to know that Office files on the iPad and Office files kept at OneDrive are synced automatically. In case you lose your Internet connection when you're working on a file stored on OneDrive, the iPad keeps a local copy of Office files you're working on. If you lose your Internet connection, you work on the local copy. This local copy is uploaded automatically to OneDrive when the Internet connection is restored.

You can tell when you're working on a local copy of a file from OneDrive by opening the File menu. If you see the words "Upload pending" under AutoSave, it means the edits you made to your file haven't been saved to OneDrive yet. The edits will be saved to OneDrive when the Internet connection is restored.

In case you're interested, Chapter 3 explores all the details of working without an Internet connection.

Syncing files between Office 2011 and OneDrive

To sync files between Office 2011 for Mac and OneDrive, you need an app called OneDrive. This app is available for free at the App Store.

After you download and install the OneDrive app to your Mac, you can tell the app which folders on OneDrive you want to sync on your Mac. The OneDrive app makes copies of folders on OneDrive and places these copies on your machine. Then, working in the background, the OneDrive app copies files back and forth between your Mac and OneDrive as necessary to make sure that the latest versions of all files are in both places and in sync with one another.

Open the Launchpad and click OneDrive to open the OneDrive app. After it opens, the OneDrive icon appears on the Mac toolbar, as shown in Figure 17-6. Clicking the OneDrive icon opens a drop-down menu with information about how much storage space you have on OneDrive and when files were synchronized. As far as syncing goes, these are the options worth knowing about on the menu:

- ✔ **Open OneDrive folder:** Opens the OneDrive folder so that you can see which folders are synced, as shown in Figure 17-6. You can open Office files from this folder. Click a folder to open it and then click the name of a file you want to open.

✔ **Preferences:** Opens the Preferences dialog box so that you can tell the OneDrive app how you want it to work, as shown in Figure 17-6:

- **General**: Place the OneDrive icon on the Dock and open the app at startup.

- **Choose Folders:** Tell the app which OneDrive folders you want to replicate and sync with on your machine.

- **About:** Unsync folders on your machine from OneDrive.

Click the OneDrive icon

OneDrive folder   Preferences

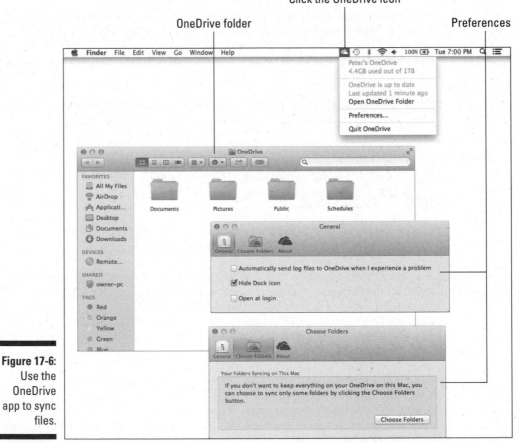

Figure 17-6:
Use the
OneDrive
app to sync
files.

Chapter 18

File Sharing and Collaborating

Starting in the OneDrive window, you can collaborate online by sharing Word documents, Excel worksheets, and PowerPoint presentations. This chapter explains how file sharing works. It shows you how, using OneDrive, you can share your folders and files with others, and how to change how files and folders are shared.

Sharing Files: The Big Picture

OneDrive generates a link for each file that is shared. This link is the means by which the people who share the file open it. Someone who has the link can click it and, in their web browser, open the file for viewing or editing in an Office program or Office Online application. (Chapter 17 explains what those are.)

The owner of a folder or file can share it using these methods:

✔ **Invite people by email:** Send the link by email on a person-by-person basis to the people with whom you will share the file. Figure 18-1 shows an example of sending links by email to share files. The recipient of this email message can click a link to open an Office file stored on OneDrive. In this case, the sender shared a folder with five files in it.

✔ **Get a link:** Generate a link and distribute it on your own or post it on a blog or web page.

✔ **Share with embedded HTML code:** Generate HTML code that you can embed in a blog or web page.

Click to open a file

Sharing Your Files and Folders with Others

Share files with others so that they can view or edit your work. Sharing is a way to collaborate with others on Office files. Starting in the OneDrive window, you can share a folder (that is, all the files in the folder) or an individual file.

Inviting people by email

Follow these steps to share a file (or all the files in a folder) by sending out an email message with links to the files (see Figure 18-1). All the recipient of your email message has to do to read or view the file is click a link.

1. **On OneDrive, select the file or folder you want to share.**

2. **Tap or click the Share (or Share Folder) button or link.**

   You can find the Share button or link:

   • On the OneDrive toolbar

   • In the Details pane

   As shown in Figure 18-2, you see the Share window. If you're sharing the file or folder already, the sharers' names appear on the left side of the window.

Choose Invite People   Enter addresses   Choose access privileges

3. Choose Invite People.

4. Enter the email addresses of the people with whom you will share the file or folder. Enter a message as well, if you want (see Figure 18-2).

If you want the recipients of your email invitation to be able to view without subscribing to Office 365, tap or click the Share button now; otherwise, keep reading.

5. Tap or click the Recipients Can Only View link.

As shown in Figure 18-2, drop-down menus appear.

6. Choose access privileges on the drop-down menu.

On the first menu, choose whether recipients can view the file(s) or view and edit the file(s).

On the second menu, choose whether recipients need an Office 365 subscription to view or view and edit the file(s).

7. Tap or click the Share button.

The Share window opens. It tells you who shares the file or folder with you. You can return to this window at any time to unshare files or folders as well as change how files and folders are shared. See "Investigating and Changing How Files and Folders Are Shared," later in this chapter, for details.

Generating a link to shared files

Follow these instructions to share a file (or all the files in a folder) by generating a hyperlink. After OneDrive generates the link, you can post it or send it to others.

1. **In the OneDrive window, select the file or folder you want to share.**

2. **Tap or click the Share (or Share Folder) button or link.**

   As shown in Figure 18-3, you see the Share window for generating a link to your file or folder.

3. **Choose Get a Link to generate the link to your file or folder.**

4. **Choose an access option on the drop-down menu.**

   Herewith are your choices:

   • **View Only:** Others can view the file (or all files in the folder if a folder is being shared), but not edit the file(s).

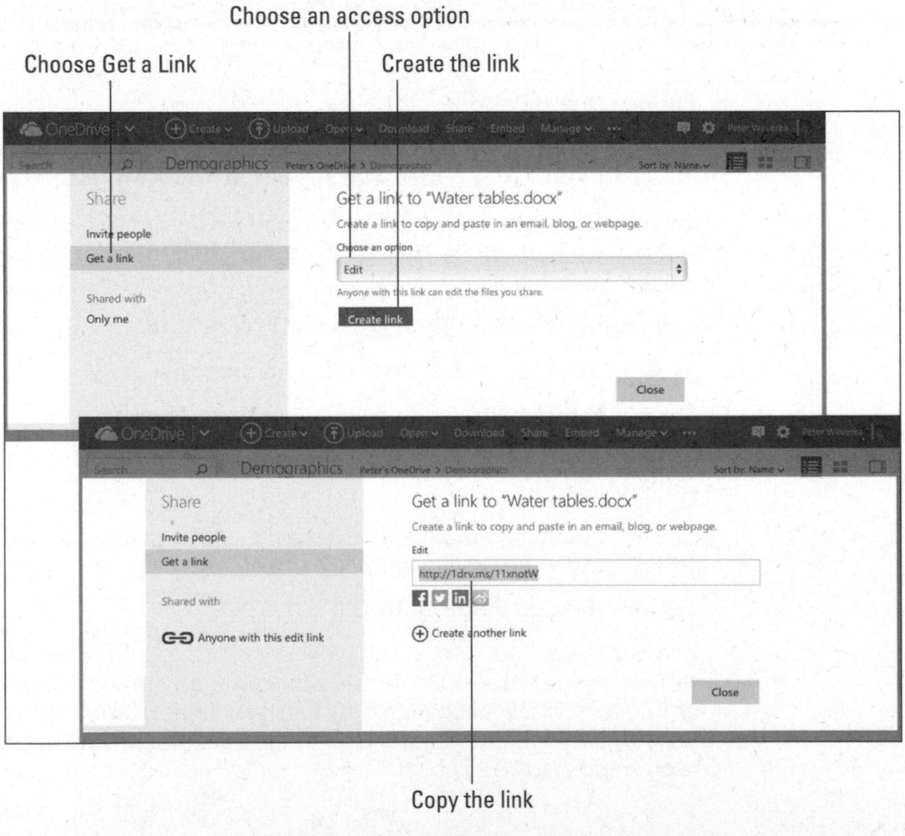

Choose an access option

Choose Get a Link   Create the link

Figure 18-3:
File sharing
by generat-
ing a link.

Copy the link

- **Edit:** Others can view *and* edit the file (or all files in the folder if a folder is being shared).

- **Public:** Absolutely anyone can view the file (or files in the folder if a folder is being shared), but not edit the file. The file is searchable by Google and other search engines. Anyone with an Internet connection can find the file and view it.

5. **Tap or click Create Link.**

   OneDrive generates the link. You can tap or click Shorten Link to generate a shorter and more manageable version of the link.

6. **Select the link (double-click it) and choose Copy.**

   You can now paste the link where you will — to a blog, web page, or email message. Later in this chapter, "Investigating and Changing How Files and Folders Are Shared" explains how to unshare files and change how they are shared.

Generating HTML code

Yet another way to share files is to generate HTML code for a link and embed the HTML code in a web page or blog. A visitor to the web page or blog can click the link and open the file you want to share. Follow these steps to generate HTML code for file-sharing purposes:

1. **In the OneDrive window, select the file you want to share.**

2. **Tap or click the Embed button on the OneDrive toolbar.**

   The Embed window opens.

3. **Tap or click the Generate button.**

   OneDrive generates the HTML code.

4. **Right-click the code and choose Copy.**

   Embed this code into a web page to create the link.

Seeing Files and Folders Others Shared with You

Go to the Shared window to see the names of folders and files that you shared with other and others shared with you. To go to the Shared window, tap or click Shared in the OneDrive Navigation pane (located on the left side of the window).

But how do you work on the files?

Now that you know how to share files, you may well ask, "But how do you work on a shared file?"

When you click the link to open a shared file, the file opens in a browser window. In this illustration, for example, an Excel file appears in the browser window. At this point, the person who has opened the file can edit it (if he or she has editing privileges) by tapping or clicking the Edit in Browser link. Tapping or clicking this link opens the file in an Office Online application — Word, Excel, or PowerPoint.

The Office Online applications all offer a button called "Open In." For example, if you peer closely at this illustration, you see an Open In Excel button (located on the right side of the Ribbon). Tapping or clicking this button opens Excel 2011, Excel 2014, or whichever version of the Excel software is installed on your computer. Now you can really go to town and work on the file using all the commands and features of the Office software.

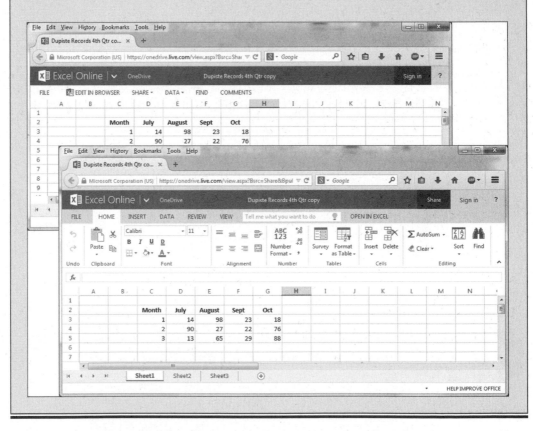

Open files and folders in the Shared Window the same way you open them in the Files or Recent Docs window — by tapping or clicking. You can also right-click and choose Open on the shortcut menu.

Investigating and Changing How Files and Folders Are Shared

The Details pane tells you everything you need to know about who shares a file or folder. To open the Details pane, select a shared file or folder and click the Show/Hide the Details Pane button.

Follow these steps to stop sharing a file or change how you share a file with someone:

1. **In the OneDrive window, select the file or folder in question.**

2. **Tap or click the Share button.**

   The Share window opens, as shown in Figure 18-4. This is the same window you use to share folders and files. The left side of the window tells you who shares the file with you.

3. **Select a name on the left side of the window.**

   The person's name appears in the center of the window.

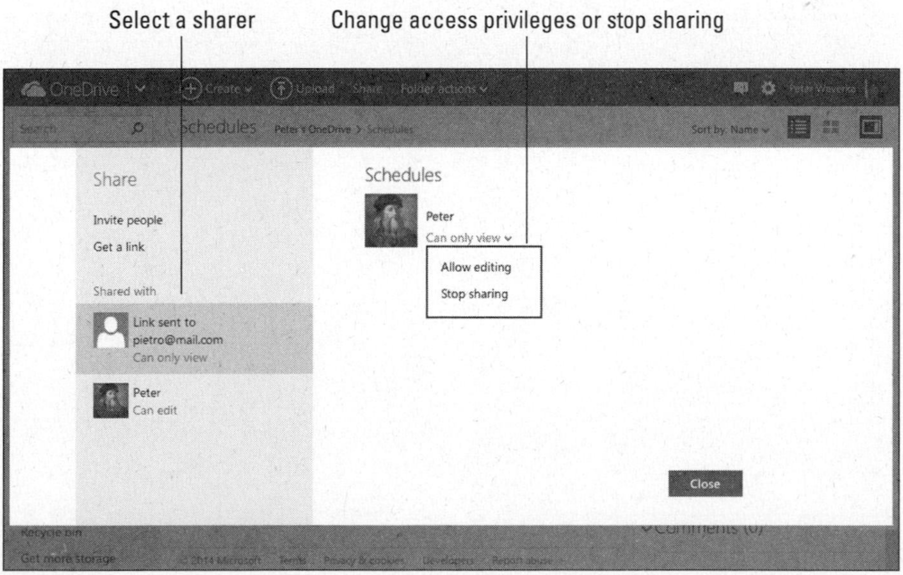

Select a sharer   Change access privileges or stop sharing

Figure 18-4:
Changing how a file is shared.

4. **On the drop-down menu, choose Allow Editing, Change to View Only, or Stop Sharing.**

   If you choose Stop Sharing, the person's name is removed from the Share window and the person is no longer permitted to view or edit the file.

   The Share window remains open in case you want to change how you share the file with others whose names are listed.

5. **Tap or click Close to close the Share window.**

Part VI

The Part of Tens

In this part . . .

- ✔ Discover ten (and more) especially useful Excel functions.

- ✔ Find out how to make your PowerPoint presentations more meaningful and forthcoming.

- ✔ Explore ten things that are really worth knowing about the iPad.

Chapter 19

Ten-Plus Functions for Crunching Numbers

*E*xcel offers more than four hundred different functions. I choose what I consider the most useful and most interesting functions for this chapter.

If you're not familiar with functions, check out Chapter 11. It explains how functions work, what function arguments are, how to enter arguments with functions, and how to include functions in formulas.

AVERAGE for Averaging Data

Might as well start with an easy one. The AVERAGE function averages the values in a cell range. In Figure 19-1, for example, AVERAGE is used to compute the average rainfall in a three-month period in three different counties.

Use AVERAGE as follows:

```
AVERAGE(cell range)
```

Excel ignores empty cells and logical values in the cell range; cells with 0 are computed.

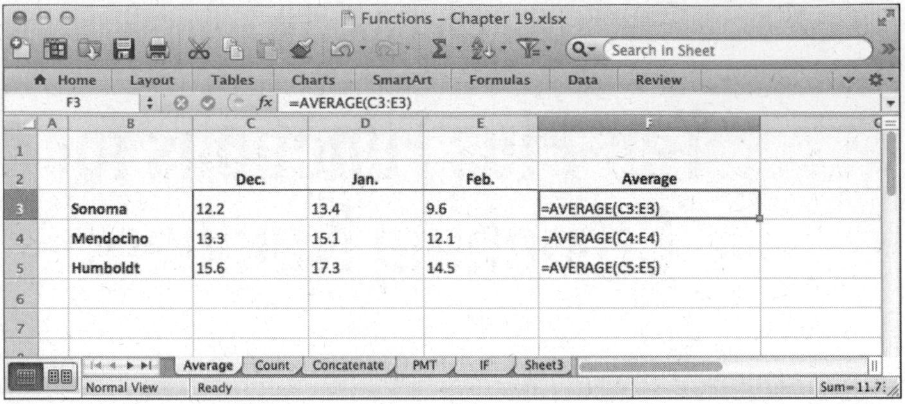

Figure 19-1:
Using
AVERAGE to
find average
rainfall data.

COUNT and COUNTIF for Tabulating Data Items

Use COUNT, a statistical function, to count how many cells have data in them. Numbers and dates, not text entries, are counted. The COUNT function is useful for tabulating how many data items are in a range. In the spreadsheet at the top of Figure 19-2, for example, COUNT is used to compute the number of mountains listed in the data:

```
COUNT(C5:C9)
```

Use COUNT as follows:

```
COUNT(cell range)
```

Similar to COUNT is the COUNTIF function. It counts how many cells in a cell range have a specific value. To use COUNTIF, enter the cell range and a criterion in the argument, as follows. If the criterion is a text value, enclose it in quotation marks.

```
COUNTIF(cell range, criterion)
```

At the bottom of Figure 19-2, the formula determines how many of the mountains in the data are in Nepal:

```
=COUNTIF(D5:D9,"Nepal")
```

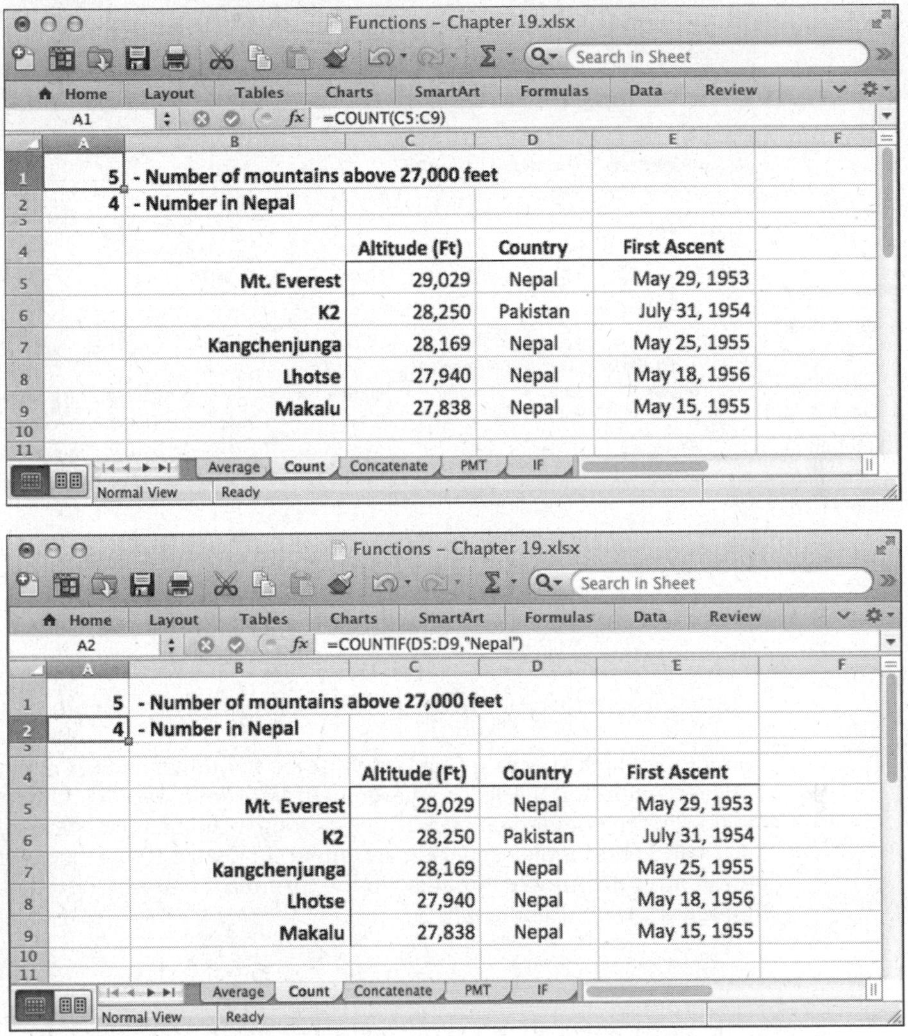

Figure 19-2: The COUNT (above) and COUNTIF (below) function at work.

CONCATENATE for Combining Values

CONCATENATE, a text function, is useful for combining values from different cells into a single cell. In the spreadsheet at the top of Figure 19-3, for example, values from three columns are combined in a fourth column to list peoples' names in their entirety.

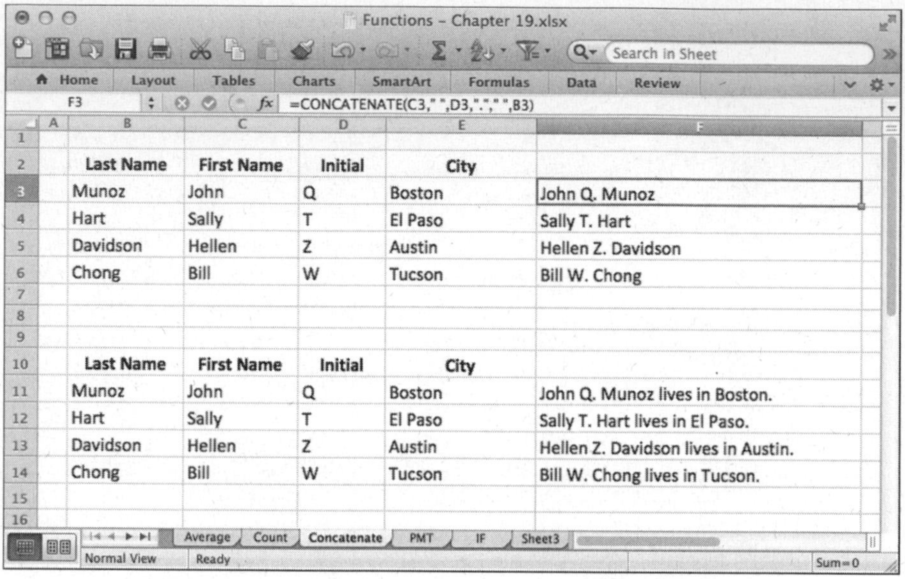

Figure 19-3:
Use the
CONCA-
TENATE
function to
combine
values from
cells.

Use CONCATENATE as follows:

```
CONCATENATE(text1, text2, text3. . .)
```

To include blank spaces in the text you're combining, enclose a blank space between quotation marks as an argument. Moreover, you can include original text in the concatenation formula as long as you enclose it in quotation marks and enter it as a separate argument. In Figure 19-3, I had to include a period after the middle initial, so in the formula, I entered a period in quotation marks as an argument:

```
=CONCATENATE(C3," ",D3,"."," ",B3)
```

In the spreadsheet shown at the bottom of Figure 19-3, I used the CONCATENATE function to write sentences ("John Q. Munoz lives in Boston."). I included the words "lives in" in the formula, as follows:

```
=CONCATENATE(C11," ",D11,"."," ",B11," ",
        "lives in"," ",E11,".")
```

PMT for Calculating How Much You Can Borrow

If you're looking to buy a house, a car, or another expensive item for which you have to borrow money, the question to ask yourself is: How much can I borrow and make the monthly payment on the loan without stressing my budget unnecessarily? Can you safely make a monthly payment of $1,000, $1,500, $2,000? How much you can afford to pay each month to service a loan determines how much you can realistically borrow.

Use the PMT (payment) function to explore how much you can borrow given different interest rates and different amounts. PMT determines how much you have to pay annually on different loans. After you determine how much you have to pay annually, you can divide this amount by 12 to see how much you have to pay monthly.

Use the PMT function as follows to determine how much you pay annually for a loan:

```
PMT(interest rate, number of payments, amount of loan)
```

As shown in Figure 19-4, set up a worksheet with five columns to explore loan scenarios:

- ✔ **Interest rate (column A):** Because the interest rate on loans is expressed as a percentage, format this column to accept numbers as percentages (tap or click the Percent Style button on the Home tab).

- ✔ **No. of payments (column B):** Typically, loan payments are made monthly. For a thirty-year home loan mortgage, enter 360 in this column (12 months × 30 years); for a 15-year mortgage, enter 180 (12 months × 15 years). Enter the total number of loan payments you will make during the life of the loan.

- ✔ **Amount of loan (column C):** Enter the amount of the loan.

- ✔ **Annual payment (column D):** Enter a formula with the PMT function in this column to determine how much you have to pay annually for the loan. In Figure 19-4, the formula is

```
=PMT(A3,B3,C3)
```

- ✔ **Monthly payment (column E):** Divide the annual payment in column D by 12 to determine the monthly payment:

```
=D3/12
```

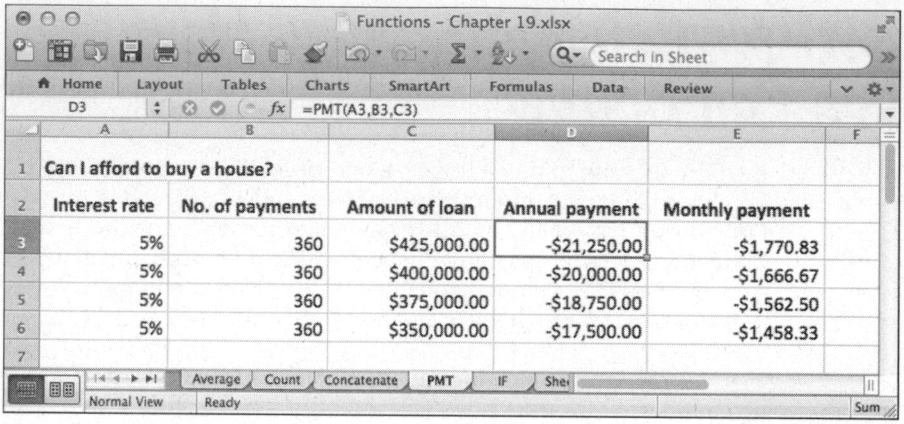

Figure 19-4:
Exploring
loan
scenarios
with the
PMT
function.

After you set up the worksheet, you can start playing with different loan scenarios — different interest rates and amounts — to find out how much you can comfortably borrow and comfortably pay each month to pay back the loan.

IF for Identifying Data

The IF function examines data and returns a value based on criteria you enter. Use the IF function to locate data that meets a certain threshold. In the worksheet shown in Figure 19-5, for example, the IF function is used to identify teams that are eligible for the playoffs. To be eligible, a team must have won more than six games. The IF function identifies whether a team has won more than six games and, in the Playoffs column, enters the word *Yes* or *No* accordingly.

Use the IF function as follows:

```
IF(logical true-false test, value if true, value if false)
```

Instructing Excel to enter a value if the logical true-false test comes up false is optional; you must supply a value to enter if the test is true. Enclose the value in quotation marks if it is a text value such as the word *Yes* or *No*.

In Figure 19-5, the formula for determining whether a team made the playoffs is as follows:

```
=IF(C3>6,"Yes","No")
```

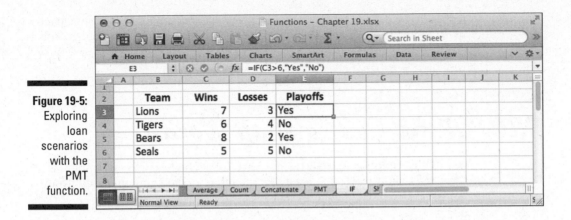

Figure 19-5: Exploring loan scenarios with the PMT function.

If the false "No" value was absent from the formula, teams that didn't make the playoffs would not show a value in the Playoffs column; these teams' Playoffs column would be empty.

LEFT, MID, and RIGHT for Cleaning Up Data

Sometimes when you import data from another software application, especially if it's a database application, the data arrives with unneeded characters. You can use the LEFT, MID, RIGHT, and TRIM functions to remove these characters:

✔ LEFT returns the leftmost characters in a cell to the number of characters you specify. For example, in a cell with CA_State, this formula returns CA, the two leftmost characters in the text:

```
=LEFT(A1,2)
```

✔ MID returns the middle characters in a cell starting at a position you specify to the number of characters you specify. For example, in a cell with http://www.dummies.com, this formula uses MID to remove the extraneous seven characters at the beginning of the URL and get www.dummies.com:

```
=MID(A1,7,50)
```

✔ RIGHT returns the rightmost characters in a cell to the number of characters you specify. For example, in a cell containing the words *Vitamin B1*, the following formula returns B1, the two rightmost characters in the name of the vitamin:

```
=RIGHT(A1,2)
```

✔ TRIM, except for single spaces between words, removes all blank spaces from inside a cell. Use TRIM to remove leading and trailing spaces. This formula removes unwanted spaces from the data in cell A1:

```
=TRIM(A1)
```

PROPER for Capitalizing Words

The PROPER function makes the first letter of each word in a cell uppercase. As are LEFT and RIGHT, it is useful for cleaning up data you imported from elsewhere. Use PROPER as follows:

```
PROPER(cell address)
```

LARGE and SMALL for Comparing Values

Use the LARGE and SMALL functions, as well as their cousins MIN, MAX, and RANK, to find out where a value stands in a list of values. For example, use LARGE to locate the ninth oldest man in a list, or MAX to find the oldest man. Use MIN to find the smallest city by population in a list, or SMALL to find the fourth smallest. The RANK function finds the rank of a value in a list of values.

Use these functions as follows:

✔ MIN returns the smallest value in a list of values. For the argument, enter a cell range or cell array. In the worksheet shown in Figure 19-6, the following formula finds the fewest number of fish caught at any lake on any day:

```
=MIN(C3:G7)
```

✔ SMALL returns the nth smallest value in a list of values. This function takes two arguments, first the cell range or cell array, and next the position, expressed as a number, from the smallest of all values in the range or array. In the worksheet shown in Figure 19-6, this formula finds the second smallest number of fish caught in any lake:

```
=SMALL(C3:G7,2)
```

✔ MAX returns the largest value in a list of values. Enter a cell range or cell array as the argument. In the worksheet shown in Figure 19-6, this formula finds the most number of fish caught in any lake:

```
=MAX(C3:G7)
```

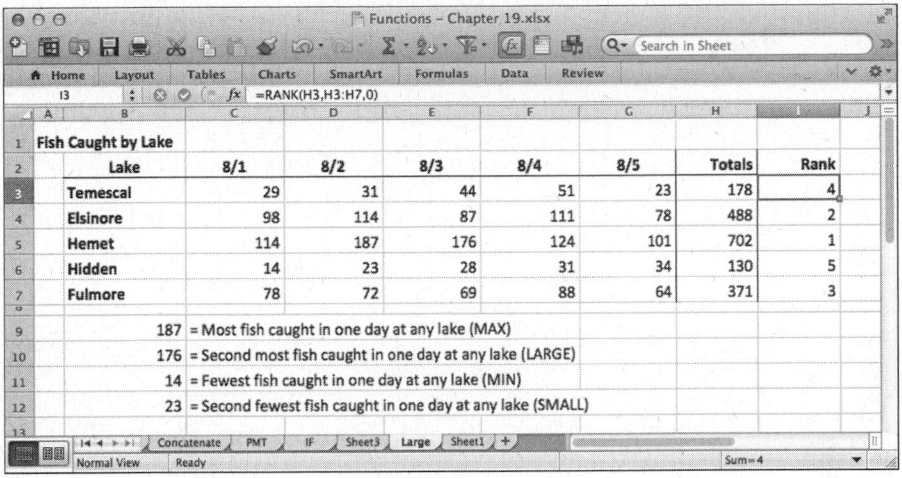

Figure 19-6:
Using
functions
to compare
values.

✔ LARGE returns the *n*th largest value in a list of values. This function takes two arguments, first the cell range or cell array, and next the position, expressed as a number, from the largest of all values in the range or array. In the worksheet shown in Figure 19-6, this formula finds the second largest number of fish caught in any lake:

```
=LARGE(C3:G7,2)
```

✔ RANK returns the rank of a value in a list of values. This function takes three arguments:

   • The cell with the value used for ranking

   • The cell range or cell array with the comparison values for determining rank

   • Whether to rank in order from top to bottom (enter 0 for descending) or bottom to top (enter 1 for ascending)

✔ In the worksheet shown in Figure 19-6, this formula ranks the total number of fish caught in Lake Temescal against the total number of fish caught in all five lakes:

```
=RANK(H3,H3:H7,0)
```

NETWORKDAY and TODAY for Measuring Time in Days

Excel offers a couple of date functions for scheduling, project planning, and measuring time periods in days.

NETWORKDAYS measures the number of workdays between two dates (the function excludes Saturdays and Sundays from its calculations). Use this function for scheduling purposes to determine the number of workdays needed to complete a project. Use NETWORKDAYS as follows:

```
NETWORKDAYS(start date, end date)
```

TODAY gives you today's date, whatever it happens to be. Use this function to compute today's date in a formula. The TODAY function takes no arguments and is entered like so, parentheses included:

```
TODAY()
```

To measure the number of days between two dates, use the minus operator and subtract the latest date from the earlier one. For example, this formula measures the number of days between 1/1/2015 and 6/1/2015:

```
="6/1/2015"-"1/1/2015"
```

The dates are enclosed in quotation marks to make Excel recognize them as dates. Make sure that the cell where the formula is located is formatted to show numbers, not dates.

LEN for Counting Characters in Cells

Use the LEN (length) function to obtain the number of characters in a cell. This function is useful for making sure that characters remain under a certain limit. The LEN function counts blank spaces as well as characters. Use the LEN function as follows:

```
LEN(cell address)
```

Chapter 20

Ten Tips for Making Glorious PowerPoint Presentations

In This Chapter

▶ Making the best use of PowerPoint

▶ Designing presentations with the right colors and fonts

▶ Engaging the audience

▶ Making your presentation stand out

This chapter picks up where Chapter 14 left off and describes a few things you can do to make your presentations stand out in a crowd. It offers design tips and a few tricks that you can use to connect better with the audience. I don't know how many hundreds of PowerPoint presentations I've sat through. I've seen the good and the bad. This chapter describes the most important things I observed in my long experience with watching PowerPoint presentations.

Don't Let PowerPoint Tell You What to Do

PowerPoint makes it easy to paint by numbers. Starting in the PowerPoint Presentation Gallery (in PowerPoint 2011) or the New window (in PowerPoint for the iPad), you can choose a readymade PowerPoint template and simply take it from there. These templates were designed by experts. They look very good. Choosing a ready-made template saves you the time and trouble of creating an original look for your presentation.

But choosing a ready-made template also makes your presentation look like other presentations. If you want your presentation to stand out in a crowd, consider creating a PowerPoint presentation from scratch. Or start with one of the templates and change it around to make it your own. Chapter 15 describes how to create slide backgrounds of your own and how to create a PowerPoint template. It also describes how to redesign a presentation.

Besides steering you to its ready-made templates, PowerPoint wants you to make bulleted lists. Many of the slide layouts have places for these lists, but how often do you really need them? Lists on PowerPoint slides have been known to cause people to yawn.

Figure 20-1 demonstrates how to get around using bulleted lists by employing tables, charts, and diagrams. Next time you consider writing a bulleted list, think how you can present information in ways apart from lists.

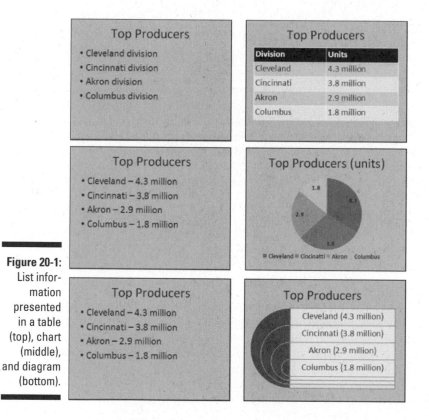

Figure 20-1: List information presented in a table (top), chart (middle), and diagram (bottom).

Make Your Company Colors Part of the Design

Most companies adopt two or three signature colors and employ them in packaging, stationery, advertisements, and company web pages, among other places. These colors help establish a company's "brand." For example, John Wiley & Sons, the company that published this book, employs black and yellow to help establish its *For Dummies* brand. *For Dummies* book covers, the Dummies.com website, and *For Dummies* book advertisements are mostly black and yellow. According to a rumor, Dummies.com employees wear black-and-yellow striped pajamas. If the company you work for employs its own set of colors to establish its brand, consider working those colors into your presentation design.

The trick, however, is to find out what your company's colors are. It isn't enough to say that a company's colors are red and green, for example, because there are many, many shades of red and green. You have to find out precisely which shade of red and green your company uses.

Finding out a color's RGB setting

Every color shade can be defined by its red-green-blue (RGB) color model setting. When you assign a color to a slide background, font, or shape in PowerPoint, you can assign the color according to its RGB setting, as shown in Figure 20-2. In order to employ your company's colors in a presentation design, you have to find out what each color's RGB setting is.

One way to find out is to ask a graphic designer who works for the company, "What's the RGB setting for each company color?" Graphic designers know these things. Another way is to use a Macintosh utility, DigitalColor Meter, to find a color's RGB setting.

Follow these steps on the Macintosh to use DigitalColor Meter to obtain the RGB setting of each company color you plan to use in a presentation design:

1. **Open a website or other item that displays the company colors.**

2. **Launch DigitalColor Meter.**

   This app is located in the Utilities folder. To open it, launch Finder and select Applications⇨Utilities⇨DigitalColor Meter.

3. **Return to the website or other item you opened in Step 1.**

4. **Switch to DigitalColor Meter.**

5. **Select Display in Generic RGB on the Settings menu, as shown in Figure 20-3.**

6. **Move the pointer over the item for which you need the RGB setting.**

As shown in Figure 20-3, DigitalColor Meter shows the color setting for the company color you're investigating.

7. **Write down the RGB setting for the color.**

Write it on a sticky note and paste it on your computer. Put the three RGB numbers where you can find them in a hurry. You can use these color settings to assign the company color to shapes, slide backgrounds, and fonts in PowerPoint, as I explain very shortly.

Repeat these steps to investigate each company color whose RGB setting you need for your presentation design. Be sure to write down the three RGB color setting numbers for each color.

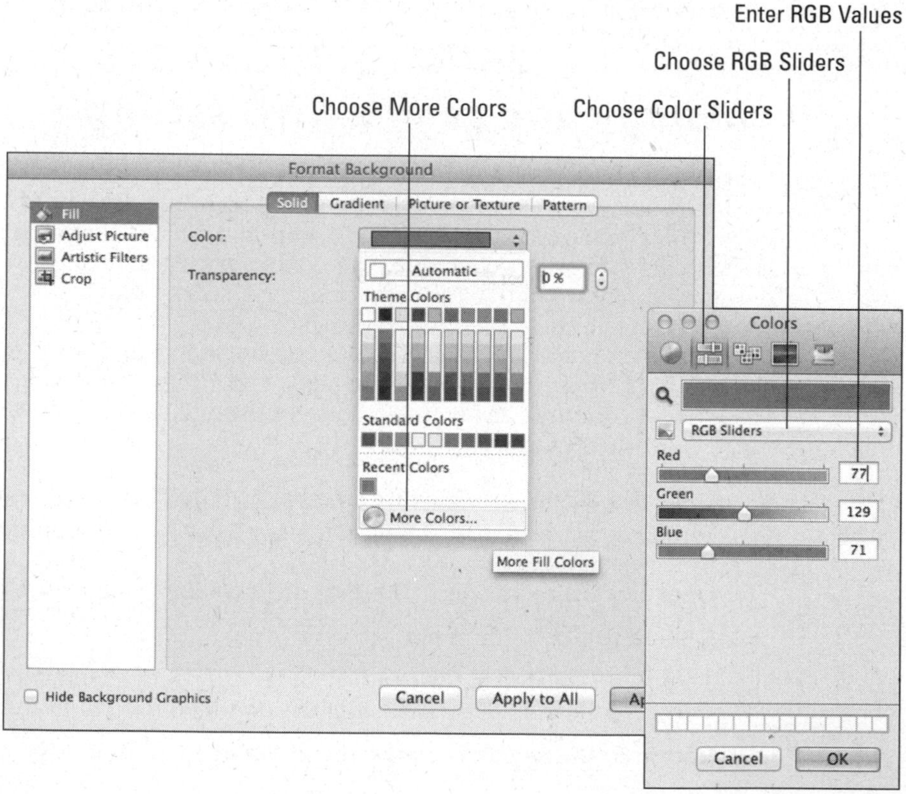

Figure 20-2:
Assigning a
color using
RGB values.

Move the pointer over the color   Choose Generic RGB

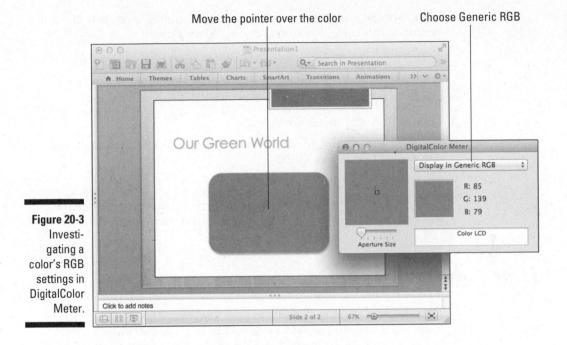

Figure 20-3
Investi-
gating a
color's RGB
settings in
DigitalColor
Meter.

Employing a company color in a PowerPoint design

After you know the RGB setting of each color you intend to use (see the previous topic in this chapter), you can follow these steps to assign the color to
slide backgrounds, fonts, and shapes in your presentation design:

1. **Select the shape, text, or slide that needs a color change.**

2. **Find your way to the appropriate Colors drop-down list.**

   Where you find this drop-down list depends on the item you're
   dealing with.

   - *Shapes:* Choose Format ⇨ Shape. The Format Shape dialog box
     opens.

   - *Fonts:* On the Home tab, open the drop-down menu on the Font
     Color button and choose More Colors. The Colors dialog box
     opens. Skip to Step 4.

   - *Slide backgrounds:* On the Themes tab, click the Background button
     and choose Format Background on the drop-down list. The Format
     Background dialog box opens.

3. **In the Format Shape or Format Background dialog box, go to the Solid tab, open the color menu, and choose More Colors.**

   More Colors is the last option on the menu (refer to Figure 20-2).

   The Colors dialog box shown in Figure 20-2 opens.

4. **Click the Color Sliders button.**

5. **Choose RGB Sliders on the menu.**

6. **Enter the three-number color setting you need to define your company color (see Figure 20-2).**

7. **Click OK.**

   Click OK again in the Format Shape or Format Background dialog box if you're assigning a color to a shape or slide background.

Use Large Fonts

Choosing the right size fonts in a PowerPoint presentation can be problematic because it's hard to tell which size font to use. On the printed page, 12-point font is considered a good size for reading, but PowerPoint slides don't appear on printed pages. They appear on large screens. What's more, how large the screens are varies from place to place. How do you know what constitutes readable type to an audience?

Here is the general rule for choosing font sizes:

- Title fonts should be between 36 and 44 points.
- Body fonts should between 24 and 32 points.

Use the Animation Feature in Bulleted Lists

If you read the start of this chapter, you know I'm not a fan of the bulleted list. From my experience, audiences don't focus on the presenter when a bulleted list appears on a slide. Instead, they read ahead of the presenter, scouring the list to see what's in store.

One way to keep the audience's attention when presenting bulleted lists is to "animate" the lists. You don't make the list appear all at one time; instead, you display each bulleted item one at a time so that the audience can direct its attention to each item. The bulleted items appear one by one when the presenter clicks the mouse.

Follow these steps in PowerPoint 2011 to "animate" a bulleted list so that items appear one at a time:

1. **Click in the bulleted list to select it.**

2. **Go to the Animations tab.**

3. **Open the Entrance Effects gallery and choose an effect.**

   For example, Appear makes bulleted items appear one by one when you click the mouse; Fade make the items fade onto the screen.

   After you make your choice, you see a preview of the animation you chose.

4. **Click the Play button on the Animations tab to see your animation again.**

5. **Go to the Slide Show tab and click the From Current Slide button to see your list as it will appear in slide shows.**

6. **Click the screen as many times as necessary to make all the bulleted items appear, and then press Esc to end the slide show.**

   How do you like your "animated" list? Use one of these techniques to remove the animations:

✔ Click the Undo button on the Standard toolbar and start all over.

✔ Click the Show or Hide the Toolbox button on the Quick Access toolbar to display the Custom Animation box (if it isn't already displayed). Then select animations you don't want in the box and click the X button at the bottom of the box.

Use Visuals, Not Just Words, to Make Your Point

Figure 20-4 shows an example of how a few words and a picture can convey a lot. This slide comes from the beginning of a presentation. It tells the audience which topics will be covered. Instead of being covered through long descriptions, each topic is encapsulated in a word or two, and the graphic in the middle shows plainly what the presentation is about. The slide in Figure 20-4 was constructed from text boxes and a graphic.

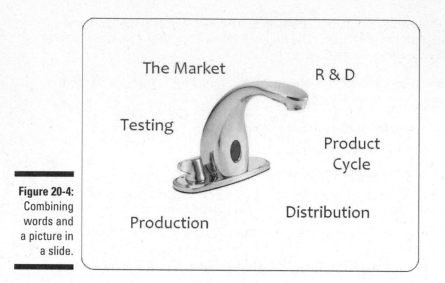

The Market

R & D

Testing

Product
Cycle

Distribution

Production

Figure 20-4:
Combining
words and
a picture in
a slide.

Navigate in a Nonlinear Fashion

A really good presentation is one in which the presenter brings slides onscreen as they are needed. Rather than bulldoze her way through the presentation, starting with the first slide and ending with the last, the presenter weaves around, taking a cue from the audience to decide which slide to show next.

It takes a confident presenter and somebody who knows her stuff to give a nonlinear presentation. Here are instructions for going to any slide — not just the next slide — in a presentation:

- **PowerPoint 2011:** Right-click the screen and choose Go to Slide. On the submenu that appears, choose a slide.

- **PowerPoint for the iPad:** Give the presentation in Presenter view. See Chapter 13 for details.

Another way to turn a presentation in a different direction is to use hidden slides. You can keep hidden slides in reserve and show them when necessary. Follow these instructions to hide a slide:

- **PowerPoint 2011:** Select the slide, and on the Slide Show tab, click the Hide Slide button. To show a hidden slide during a slide show, right-click the screen, choose Go to Slide, and select the slide on the submenu. You can tell which slides are hidden because their slide numbers are enclosed in parentheses.

✔ **PowerPoint for the iPad:** Select the slide, and on the Slide Show tab, tap Hide Slide. To show a hidden slide during a slide show, you must be in Presenter view (see Chapter 13). In Presenter view, hidden slides are blacked out on the screen.

Ask the Audience Questions

The purpose of any PowerPoint presentation is to engage the audience, and one of the easiest ways to do that is to ask the audience a question. It gets the audience's attention and introduces a topic that you want to tackle with your PowerPoint presentation.

Even better than asking a question is conducting a "raise your hands" survey, something along the lines of "raise your hand if you think dogs are better than cats." Getting the audience members to raise their hands rouses them a bit; at the very least, it prevents audience members from slouching in their chairs. If you can think of a "raise your hands" survey question that divides the audience equally between members who raise their hands and members who don't, so much the better. A question like that shows the audience members that other people in the room disagree with them. It stirs the blood. It gets people interested.

Pretend You're Speaking to Friends

I know how nerve-wracking public speaking can be. And I know how difficult it can be to pretend that a group of strangers are your friends. If you can make that leap, however, and pretend you're speaking to friends, it will make your voice sound that much better as you give your presentation. You'll be more convincing. The passion you have for your subject will show through.

Take Advantage of the Slide Show Gizmos

While giving a slide show, take advantage of the gizmos available in the lower-left corner of the screen for making the show a lot livelier. You can't fail to make your slide show different from the other guy's by doing these tricks:

✔ **Draw on the screen:** In PowerPoint 2011, click the Pen button and choose Pen (see Chapter 16 for details). In PowerPoint for the iPad, tap the Pen button on the Slide Show toolbar and drag onscreen (see Chapter 13 for details).

✔ **Blank out the screen:** In PowerPoint 2011, right-click and choose Screen⇨Black Screen or Screen⇨White Screen (see Chapter 16 for details). In PowerPoint for the iPad, tap the Black Out button on the Slide Show toolbar (see Chapter 13 for details).

Somebody drew on the slide shown in Figure 20-5.

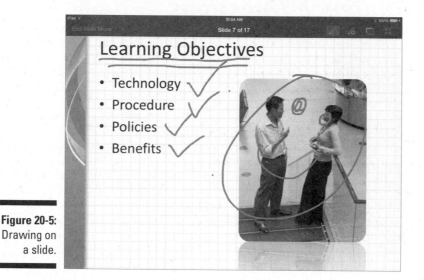

Figure 20-5:
Drawing on
a slide.

Spell Check Your Presentation

Be sure to spell check your presentation. The difference between a typo in 12-point text on the printed page with one person reading and a typo in 44-point text with a roomful of people looking on is striking. Spelling errors really stand out on large PowerPoint screens.

To run a spell check in PowerPoint 2011, choose Tools⇨Spelling.

In PowerPoint for the iPad, misspelled words are underlined in red. Double-tapping a red-lined word brings up the popover menu. Tap Suggest on this menu to see a list of suggested spellings and then tap a spelling if it is the correct one; otherwise, edit the word. (If misspellings aren't underlined in red, open the Settings app on the iPad Home screen, choose General, choose Keyboard, and turn on the Check Spelling option.)

Chapter 21

Ten Things All iPad Users Should Know

This chapter describes ten things every proud owner of an iPad should know. It suggests how to make the device easier to use, the battery last longer, and the screen easier to see. You also find out how to fix a screen that won't rotate, browse the Internet in private, and take a picture of what's on the screen.

Fix an iPad Screen That Won't Rotate

The iPad screen is designed to rotate when you physically turn the iPad, but sometimes the screen doesn't do that.

To fix an iPad screen that won't rotate, start by seeing whether you told the iPad *not* to rotate the screen in the Control Center. Swipe upward from the bottom of the screen to see the Control Center, as shown in Figure 21-1, and tap the Orientation Lock setting. This setting should say "Orientation Lock: Off" if you want to be able to rotate the iPad screen.

Figure 21-1:
The
Orientation
Lock
setting in
the Control
Center.

Orientation Lock setting

If your iPad screen still doesn't rotate, it could be because the Side switch is in the lock position. The Side switch is the little thingy above the volume control on the right side of the iPad (the right side if you're holding the machine with the Home button on the bottom). Try sliding the Slide switch up. Does your screen rotate now?

You can use the Side switch either to mute the sound or lock the screen. Follow these steps to tell the iPad how you want to use the Side switch:

1. **On the Home screen, tap Settings.**

2. **On the Settings screen, tap General.**

3. **Under Use Side Switch To, select Lock Rotation or Mute.**

Not all apps permit you to rotate the screen. Some apps are made to be permanently in landscape mode or portrait mode. It could be you can't rotate your iPad screen because the app you're looking at doesn't permit it.

Turn Down the Brightness to Save Battery Strength

Displaying items on the screen runs down the iPad's battery more than any other factor. To save battery power and run the iPad longer without having to recharge as often, consider turning down the brightness on the screen.

Follow these steps to control the brightness display:

1. **On the Home screen, tap Settings.**
2. **Tap Display & Brightness.**
3. **Drag the Brightness slider to the left as far as is comfortable.**

Place Apps on the Dock

The Dock is the little bit of real estate along the bottom of the Home screen. By placing icons for the apps you use most often on the Dock, you can get to the icons easier and thereby open the apps faster. Apps that you use most often are candidates for placement on the Dock.

Follow these steps to place an app icon on the Dock:

1. **Place and leave your finger on an icon on the Home screen.**

   The icon starts wiggling.
2. **Drag the icon onto the Dock.**
3. **Press the Home button once.**

You can place up to six icons onto the Dock. To remove an icon from the Dock, make the icon wiggle and drag it off.

Browse the Internet in Private

In Safari, the official browser of the Apple Corporation and the iPad, you can browse the Internet in private. Browsing in private means to travel the Internet without leaving a record on your browser of where you've been.

Telling Safari to browse in private

Follow these steps to browse in private with Safari:

1. **Tap the Privacy icon (the overlapping squares) in the upper-right corner of the Safari screen.**

   Figure 21-2 shows where the Privacy icon is located. After you tap the Privacy icon, the Private and Done buttons appear in the upper-right corner of the screen.

2. **Tap the Private button.**

   After you tap it, the Private button is highlighted to show that you're in Privacy mode. What's more, you see thumbnail versions of the web page or pages that were open previously when you were in Privacy mode.

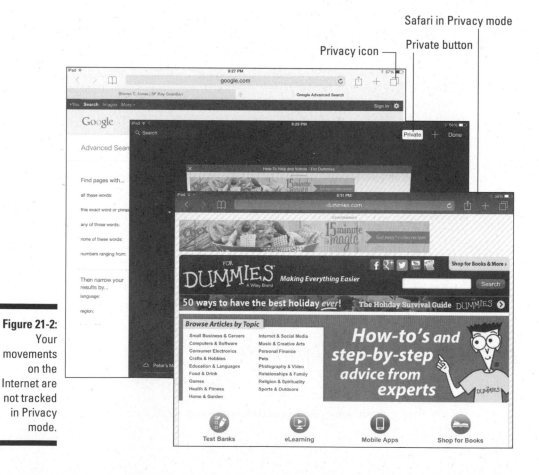

Figure 21-2: Your movements on the Internet are not tracked in Privacy mode.

3. Tap the Done button.

The web page you were visiting the last time you were in Privacy mode appears on the Safari screen.

You can tell when you're browsing privately because

- The border of the Safari screen is dark instead of gray or white.
- When you tap the Privacy icon (see Figure 21-2), the Private button is highlighted.

When you switch to Privacy mode, you see the web page or pages that were open last time you were in Privacy mode. This can be a problem if you share your iPad with others and you don't want them to know where you were browsing. If you share your iPad and you're concerned about others seeing where you've been on the Internet, close as many open windows as you can before switching out of Privacy mode. Moreover, since you can't close all open windows in Safari (one must always be open), open a window that you don't mind others seeing before you switch out of Privacy mode.

Switching Out of Privacy mode

Follow these steps to stop browsing in private:

1. Tap the Privacy icon (the overlapping squares) in the upper-right corner of the Safari screen.

The Private button is highlighted if you're currently browsing privately.

2. Tap the Private button.

The Private button is no longer highlighted, and you see a thumbnail screen of the web pages or pages that were open when you switched to private browsing.

3. Tap the Done button.

The border of the Safari screen turns dark gray or white instead of black to show that you are no longer in Privacy mode.

You can erase your browsing history from the iPad by following these steps:

1. On the Home screen, tap Settings.

2. Tap Safari.

3. Tap Clear History and Website Data.

Invert Colors to Work in the Dark

Need to work in the dark? Say you're in a movie theater and have to check your email without drawing attention to yourself. In that case, invert the colors on the iPad screen. Where you used to see dark text on a light background, you see light text on a dark background.

Follow these steps to invert the colors on the screen:

1. **On the Home screen, tap Settings.**
2. **Tap General.**
3. **Tap Accessibility.**
4. **Turn on the Invert Colors setting.**

   Retrace your steps when it's time to work in the light of day.

Take a Picture of the Screen

Take a picture of what's on the iPad screen when you need to share what's onscreen with other people. Screen captures you take with the iPad land in the Photos app. Starting in the Photos app, you can share screen captures with other people.

To capture what's on your iPad screen, hold down the Sleep/Wake button, and while holding down the button, press the Home button. The screen flashes and your hear the sound of a camera shutter.

To view your screen capture, open the Photos app and tap your capture.

To send a screen capture, select it in the Photos window and tap the Share button. You see a pop-up menu with options for sharing the screen capture by instant message and email, among other ways.

Split the Keyboard in Half

People who prefer to type with their thumbs rather than their fingers find it easier to enter text when the keyboard is split in half, as shown in Figure 21-3. Follow these steps if you're all thumbs and you want to split the keyboard:

1. **Display the keyboard by tapping in a text box on the screen.**

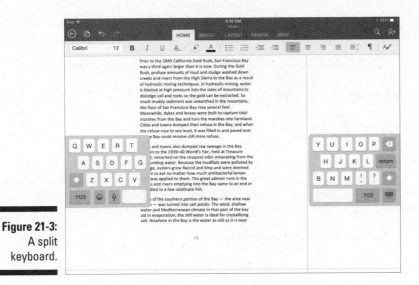

Figure 21-3:
A split
keyboard.

2. **Tap and hold down the Keyboard button.**

   This button is located in the lower-right corner of the keyboard. A popover menu appears.

3. **Drag your finger over the Split command on the popover menu to select Split.**

To "unsplit" the keyboard, tap and hold down the Keyboard button and then drag your finger over the Dock and Merge command.

Use Your iPad in Flight

You can use your iPad while traveling by air, except to visit the Internet. To use your iPad in flight, switch to Airplane Mode by following these steps:

1. **Open the Control Center.**

   To open the Control Center, swipe upward from the bottom of the iPad screen.

2. **Tap the Airplane Mode icon (a picture of an airplane).**

   Briefly, the top of the Control Center reads, "Airplane Mode: On."

Return to the Control Center and repeat these steps to turn off Airplane Mode. Chapter 1 goes into more detail about Airplane Mode. Chapter 3 explains how to save Office files to the iPad so that you can work on them while you are in-flight and don't have an Internet connection.

Make Folders for Storing Apps on the Home Screen

On a Home screen crowded with numerous app icons, finding the app you want to open can be difficult. To make the task easier, you can organize icon apps into folders. Then all you have to do to open an app is find the folder where its icon is located, tap to open the folder, and tap the app icon.

Follow these steps to create a folder for storing icons:

1. **Place and leave your finger on any icon on the Home screen.**

   The icons start wiggling.

2. **Drag an icon that you want to place in a folder over another icon you want to place in the same folder.**

   The iPad automatically creates a new folder for the two icons.

To give your new folder a name, tap it, and on the keyboard, enter a name.

Chapter 2 explains folders in detail, including how to move icons into them, rename them, and delete them.

Turn on Multitasking Gestures

To take advantage of all the gestures available to iPad users, you must activate a feature called Multitasking Gestures. Unless you activate this feature, you can't use the four-finger side-swipe, the four-finger pinch, or the four-finger upward swipe.

Follow these steps to turn on Multitasking Gestures:

1. **On the Home screen, tap Settings.**
2. **On the Settings screen, tap General.**
3. **Turn on Multitasking Gestures.**

Chapter 1 describes all the gestures you can use to manipulate items on the iPad screen.

Index

• G •

About the Author

Peter Weverka is the bestselling author of many *For Dummies* books, including *Office 2013 All-in-One for Dummies,* as well as three dozen other computer books about various topics.

Dedication

For Susan Christophersen, who also edited this book

Acknowledgments

This book owes a lot to many hard-working people at the offices of Wiley Publishing in Indianapolis, and I want to express my gratitude to all of them. I would especially like to thank Katie Mohr for giving me the opportunity to write it, Susan Christophersen for editing it, Broccoli Information Management for indexing it, and Michelle Krasniak for making sure all instructions are correct. The idea to publish this book came out of a dinner I had with Aaron Black, and I want to thank him, too.

Publisher's Acknowledgments

Senior Acquisitions Editor: Katie Mohr

Project and Copy Editor: Susan Christophersen

Technical Editor: Michelle Krasniak

Editorial Assistant: Claire Brock

Sr. Editorial Assistant: Cherie Case

Project Coordinator: Patrick Redmond

Cover Image: © iStock.com/RyanKing999

Apple & Mac

iPad For Dummies,
6th Edition
978-1-118-72306-7

iPhone For Dummies,
7th Edition
978-1-118-69083-3

Macs All-in-One
For Dummies, 4th Edition
978-1-118-82210-4

OS X Mavericks
For Dummies
978-1-118-69188-5

Blogging & Social Media

Facebook For Dummies,
5th Edition
978-1-118-63312-0

Social Media Engagement
For Dummies
978-1-118-53019-1

WordPress For Dummies,
6th Edition
978-1-118-79161-5

Business

Stock Investing
For Dummies, 4th Edition
978-1-118-37678-2

Investing For Dummies,
6th Edition
978-0-470-90545-6

Personal Finance

Personal Finance
For Dummies, 7th Edition
978-1-118-11785-9

QuickBooks 2014
For Dummies
978-1-118-72005-9

Small Business Marketing
Kit For Dummies,
3rd Edition
978-1-118-31183-7

Careers

Job Interviews
For Dummies, 4th Edition
978-1-118-11290-8

Job Searching with Social
Media For Dummies,
2nd Edition
978-1-118-67856-5

Personal Branding
For Dummies
978-1-118-11792-7

Resumes For Dummies,
6th Edition
978-0-470-87361-8

Starting an Etsy Business
For Dummies, 2nd Edition
978-1-118-59024-9

Diet & Nutrition

Belly Fat Diet For Dummies
978-1-118-34585-6

Mediterranean Diet
For Dummies
978-1-118-71525-3

Nutrition For Dummies,
5th Edition
978-0-470-93231-5

Digital Photography

Digital SLR Photography
All-in-One For Dummies,
2nd Edition
978-1-118-59082-9

Digital SLR Video &
Filmmaking For Dummies
978-1-118-36598-4

Photoshop Elements 12
For Dummies
978-1-118-72714-0

Gardening

Herb Gardening
For Dummies, 2nd Edition
978-0-470-61778-6

Gardening with Free-Range
Chickens For Dummies
978-1-118-54754-0

Health

Boosting Your Immunity
For Dummies
978-1-118-40200-9

Diabetes For Dummies,
4th Edition
978-1-118-29447-5

Living Paleo For Dummies
978-1-118-29405-5

Big Data

Big Data For Dummies
978-1-118-50422-2

Data Visualization
For Dummies
978-1-118-50289-1

Hadoop For Dummies
978-1-118-60755-8

Language &
Foreign Language

500 Spanish Verbs
For Dummies
978-1-118-02382-2

English Grammar
For Dummies, 2nd Edition
978-0-470-54664-2

French All-in-One
For Dummies
978-1-118-22815-9

German Essentials
For Dummies
978-1-118-18422-6

Italian For Dummies,
2nd Edition
978-1-118-00465-4

e Available in print and e-book formats.

Available wherever books are sold. **For more information or to order direct visit www.dummies.com**

Math & Science

Algebra I For Dummies,
2nd Edition
978-0-470-55964-2

Anatomy and Physiology
For Dummies, 2nd Edition
978-0-470-92326-9

Astronomy For Dummies,
3rd Edition
978-1-118-37697-3

Biology For Dummies,
2nd Edition
978-0-470-59875-7

Chemistry For Dummies,
2nd Edition
978-1-118-00730-3

1001 Algebra II Practice
Problems For Dummies
978-1-118-44662-1

Microsoft Office

Excel 2013 For Dummies
978-1-118-51012-4

Office 2013 All-in-One
For Dummies
978-1-118-51636-2

PowerPoint 2013
For Dummies
978-1-118-50253-2

Word 2013 For Dummies
978-1-118-49123-2

Music

Blues Harmonica
For Dummies
978-1-118-25269-7

Guitar For Dummies,
3rd Edition
978-1-118-11554-1

iPod & iTunes
For Dummies, 10th Edition
978-1-118-50864-0

Programming

Beginning Programming
with C For Dummies
978-1-118-73763-7

Excel VBA Programming
For Dummies, 3rd Edition
978-1-118-49037-2

Java For Dummies,
6th Edition
978-1-118-40780-6

Religion & Inspiration

The Bible For Dummies
978-0-7645-5296-0

Buddhism For Dummies,
2nd Edition
978-1-118-02379-2

Catholicism For Dummies,
2nd Edition
978-1-118-07778-8

Self-Help & Relationships

Beating Sugar Addiction
For Dummies
978-1-118-54645-1

Meditation For Dummies,
3rd Edition
978-1-118-29144-3

Seniors

Laptops For Seniors
For Dummies, 3rd Edition
978-1-118-71105-7

Computers For Seniors
For Dummies, 3rd Edition
978-1-118-11553-4

iPad For Seniors
For Dummies, 6th Edition
978-1-118-72826-0

Social Security
For Dummies
978-1-118-20573-0

Smartphones & Tablets

Android Phones
For Dummies, 2nd Edition
978-1-118-72030-1

Nexus Tablets
For Dummies
978-1-118-77243-0

Samsung Galaxy S 4
For Dummies
978-1-118-64222-1

Samsung Galaxy Tabs
For Dummies
978-1-118-77294-2

Test Prep

ACT For Dummies,
5th Edition
978-1-118-01259-8

ASVAB For Dummies,
3rd Edition
978-0-470-63760-9

GRE For Dummies,
7th Edition
978-0-470-88921-3

Officer Candidate Tests
For Dummies
978-0-470-59876-4

Physician's Assistant Exam
For Dummies
978-1-118-11556-5

Series 7 Exam For Dummies
978-0-470-09932-2

Windows 8

Windows 8.1 All-in-One
For Dummies
978-1-118-82087-2

Windows 8.1 For Dummies
978-1-118-82121-3

Windows 8.1 For Dummies
Book + DVD Bundle
978-1-118-82107-7

🄴 Available in print and e-book formats.

Take Dummies with you everywhere you go!

Whether you are excited about e-books, want more from the web, must have your mobile apps, or are swept up in social media, Dummies makes everything easier.

Leverage the Power

For Dummies is the global leader in the reference category and one of the most trusted and highly regarded brands in the world. No longer just focused on books, customers now have access to the For Dummies content they need in the format they want. Let us help you develop a solution that will fit your brand and help you connect with your customers.

Advertising & Sponsorships

Connect with an engaged audience on a powerful multimedia site, and position your message alongside expert how-to content.

Targeted ads • Video • Email marketing • Microsites • Sweepstakes sponsorship

21 Million Monthly Page Views & 13 Million Unique Visitors